10.95

TERRY EAGLETON was born in Salford in 1943. He was educated at local schools and at Cambridge University where he became a Fellow in English. In 1969 he became Fellow and Tutor at Wadham College, Oxford. His publications include: *Shakespeare and Society* (1967), *Exiles and Emigrés* (1970), *Myths of Power: A Marxist Study of the Brontës* (1976), *Criticism and Ideology* (Verso 1976), *Walter Benjamin* (Verso 1981) and *The Function of Criticism* (Verso 1984).

Terry Eagleton

Against the Grain

Essays 1975–1985

VERSO
Verso is the imprint of New Left Books

WITHDRAWN
HIEBERT LIBRARY
FRESNO PACIFIC UNIV.-M. B. SEMINARY
FRESNO, CA 93702

**British Library
Cataloguing in Publication Data**

Eagleton, Terry
  Against the grain.
  1. English literature——History and criticism
  I. Title
  820.9   PR83

First published 1986
© Terry Eagleton 1986

Verso
15 Greek Street, London w1v 5lf

Typeset in Baskerville by
Cover to Cover, Cambridge

Printed by The Thetford Press
Thetford, Norfolk

ISBN 0–86091–134–9
ISBN 0–86091–841–6 Pbk

Contents

Preface   1

1. Macherey and Marxist Literary Theory   9
2. Form, Ideology and *The Secret Agent*   23
3. Liberality and Order: The Criticism of   33
   John Bayley
4. The Idealism of American Criticism   49
5. Fredric Jameson: The Politics of Style   65
6. Frère Jacques: The Politics of Deconstruction   79
7. Marxism, Structuralism and   89
   Post-structuralism
8. Wittgenstein's Friends   99
9. Capitalism, Modernism and Postmodernism   131
10. The Critic as Clown   149
11. Brecht and Rhetoric   167
12. Poetry, Pleasure and Politics   173
13. The Revolt of the Reader   181
14. The Ballad of English Literature   185

Notes   187
Index   197

For
Robin Gable
and
Ken Hirschkop

There is no document of civilization which is not at the same time a document of barbarism. And just as such a document is not free of barbarism, barbarism taints also the manner in which it was transmitted from one owner to another. A historical materialist therefore dissociates himself from it as far as possible. He regards it as his task to brush history against the grain.

(Walter Benjamin,
'Theses on the Philosophy of History')

Preface

The essays collected together in this volume were all written over the last decade. Though they are not reprinted here in exact chronological order, some comments on their general lines of development, and the relation of such developments to my work as a whole, will perhaps be useful.

The first half of the 1970s witnessed a remarkable resurgence of Marxist cultural theory in Britain, largely under the impact of a major revival of radical political activity in Western society as a whole. The Vietnam, civil rights and student movements of the late 1960s and early 1970s; the growth of the women's movement in Britain in the early 1970s; anti-imperialist struggle in the north of Ireland, and some major offensives by the labour movement: all of these events created a general political climate peculiarly conducive to theoretical debate on the left. Central to that renewed preoccupation with theory was the work of Louis Althusser and his associates, which was then becoming available in English translation. The appeal of Althusser's work, generally speaking, was that while it seemed on the one hand in its concerns with ideology and the 'relative autonomy' of super-structures to offer key theoretical concepts to those engaged in the socialist analysis of culture, it presented itself simultaneously, in its rehabilitation of the 'scientific' Marx, Leninism and in its vigorous anti-humanism, as in some sense politically revolutionary. This proved a compelling conjunction for those British Marxists for whom cultural theory, in a world of quickening political struggle, was somewhat disreputably associated with a political left reformism – that of the early New Left and its subsequent survivals – which no longer appeared adequate to the exigencies of the historical moment. Althusserianism, in short, offered a way of cutting the link between cultural politics and theoretical labour on the one hand, and left reformism on the other; its theoretical richness and intricacy, and its trenchant defence of the centrality of theoretical enquiry as such, were coupled with a political abrasiveness and apparent rupture with idealism (summarizable in its steady anti-Hegelianism) which was not, in the British context at least, the customary concomitant of a discourse of culture and theory. In this dual structure lay much of the secret of Althusserian Marxism's appeal to radical intellectuals of that period. It at once made general room for their particular intellectual preoccupations, while enabling them in its anti-humanism vehemently to distance what lay closest to themselves. It confirmed such intellectuals in their professional status, while setting them violently – and so sometimes consolingly – at odds with the governing humanistic ideologies of their institutions.

My own *Criticism and Ideology* (1976), along with its more popularizing pedagogical co-text *Marxism and Literary Criticism* (1976), had their roots in this theoretical milieu, though neither work was in my view as uncritically indebted to Althusserian Marxism as has sometimes been suggested. The opening essay of the present volume, on the 'first Althusserian critic' Pierre Macherey, belongs then to this historical moment, though I have revised its critical conclusion; and the accompanying examination of a Conrad novel, originally intended for *Criticism and Ideology* but finally omitted from that book, is included as a working example of a critical method influenced by the Althusserian school. The essay which follows, on the work of the liberal humanist critic John Bayley, is intended to refresh the reader's memory of the conventional bourgeois criticism with which the work of Macherey is at odds.

One decade after the essay on Macherey was written, it should be possible to attempt in brief outline a more balanced appraisal of Althusserian Marxism, enumerating alongside its achievements those limitations which I either culpably overlooked at the time, or which have only become fully visible in the tranquillity of historical retrospect. The position which I would now wish to adopt in relation to the work of Althusser, sketched with extreme schematism, is the following. The benefit of each of Althusser's major theoretical concepts was that it sought to correct what could often be convincingly exposed as flawed or false conceptions in other traditions of Marxist thought; but, in almost every case, the alternative formulations offered turned out to be gravely and sometimes equally at fault. Thus, a blatantly incoherent and indefensible empiricism was countered by an epistemology which valuably reinstated the constructive, specific character of conceptual thought only at the cost of lapsing into a species of neo-Kantianism, which risked pressing the 'real' to a vanishing point beyond discourse, expunging the role of evidence in theoretical debate and producing an untenably 'immanentist' account of the procedures of theoretical validation. A proper dismissal of the premature historicist conflation of theory and practice, in which the former became no more than the self-consciousness of the latter, led to an effective transcendentalism of Theory, just as a much-needed deconstruction of vulgarly teleological notions of history capsized into a bleak conception of social formations as self-reproducing 'eternalities'. An essentialistic, homogenizing historicism was rightly opposed by a differentiated theory of temporality and of the structure of social formations, but with the ultimate effect of collapsing all general historical configurations to the level of localized 'conjunctures'. A politically timely anti-humanism, seeking to dislodge the fetishized subject of existentialist, phenomenological and Christianized brands of Marxism by a recovery of the structural character of Marx's thought, fell almost instant prey to a 'structuralist' ideology which marginalized both subjects and class struggles. A fertile, suggestive theory of ideology, which broke decisively with older mechanistic models, threatened to expand the concept of ideology to the point where it was emptied of political efficacy.

All of these theoretical gains and losses had their correlative political ambiguities. Althusser's insistence on the relative autonomy of the superstructures, for example, belonged with an indispensable left critique of Stalinism and other economisms, with its quasi-Maoist reminder that infrastructural change alone can never be sufficient for full socialism; but it also belonged with a Eurocommunist left reformism, in its relative neglect of class struggle at the point of production for the importance of struggle within the (relatively autonomous) state. The doctrine of relative autonomy also helped to separate the economic and political instances within the Soviet Union, thus shielding the 'socialist' nature of the former from the undemocratic character of the latter. Althusser's opposition to 'historicism' was at once a rejection of the 'rightist' variants of that creed (Stalinism, economism), *and* of the revolutionary left historicism of Korsch, Gramsci and the early Lukács. The assault on historicist and empiricist epistemologies was similarly ambivalent: if it usefully defended the status and material reality of revolutionary theory against any pragmatic or euphoric move to dissolve it into historical consciousness, it also, in the rightist inflection, sequestrated that revolutionary theory from the historical practice of class struggle. Theoretical anti-humanism represented at one and the same time a productive break with a theoretically eclectic, politically compromised 'Marxist humanism', and an effective abandonment of the collective subject of proletarian revolution. The theory of ideology addressed the reality of bourgeois hegemony with fresh urgency and resourcefulness, at the same time as the 'universalizing' of ideology involved a 'right' pessimism and elitism in respect of working-class consciousness.

As the 1970s ran their course, and a global crisis of capitalism generated a shift in political power in Britain and elsewhere to the far right, the intellectual climate on the left within which these questions had been debated was markedly transformed. Two diverse political directions appeared to be indicated by the deadlocks beyond which Althusserian Marxism was unable to move. On the one hand, in a more pragmatic, politically dispirited milieu, it was possible to distil from that body of theory its more 'rightist' elements, and press these through to a point which led beyond Marxism altogether, into the burgeoning sub-cultures of post-Marxist and post-structuralist thought. In France, this path was to lead finally into the most wretched political reaction: the defence of NATO and the 'free world' by Althusser's former pupil Michel Foucault, the befuddled mysticism of the erstwhile Maoists of *Tel Quel*, the political despair of a cultic hedonism and formalist fetishizing of 'plurality'. The alternative direction, one adopted in these essays, lay in a defence of Marxism as the only ultimately adequate response in an epoch of capitalist crisis, growing social devastation and intensified anti-imperialist struggle. Just as Althusser had sought to defend Marxism against its humanist and reformist interpreters, so it now proved necessary to defend Marxism against aspects of Althusser's own work, and *a fortiori* against his post-Marxist progeny. Yet such a project could never in my opinion entail a retreat to some pure, primordial Marxism, sublimely uncontaminated by these various evolutions – a position which could only prove imaginary. On the contrary, it would need to think Marxism through once again in the light of the most suggestive, potentially progressive aspects of contemporary non-Marxist developments.

Some of the essays reprinted here, then – 'Wittgenstein's Friends', 'The Idealism of American Criticism', the responses to the work of Michael Ryan and Perry Anderson – represent among other things an attempt at a dialectical assessment, from a Marxist standpoint, of the losses and gains implicit in these trends. There is, of course, no question of some triumphant theoretical synthesis, which could only be premature and intellectualist. Such a synthesis would be untrue to what is in my view the essentially transitional nature, theoretically speaking, of the situation in which we now find ourselves, strung out as we are, for example, between certain essentialistic notions of social totality which are plainly discreditable, and an equally ineffectual politics of the fragment or conjuncture. The fact that such matters, which are of the most pressing strategic importance to present-day socialists, are not at the moment susceptible of satisfying theoretical resolution is a sign that they are indeed much more than theoretical – that these dilemmas are the mark at the level of theory of certain real deadlocks and difficulties at the level of political history, and in part await for their successful resolution upon developments in that latter realm. This is no excuse, naturally, for omitting to think them through now.

My own work since *Criticism and Ideology* – in particular my study of Walter Benjamin, *The Rape of Clarissa, Literary Theory: An Introduction* and *The Function of Criticism* – is stamped by the altered political conditions of the late 1970s and early 1980s. At the end of the 1970s, it was possible to look back and feel that what had happened over that decade was, so to speak, an intensive laying-in of theoretical capital. But what had also occurred over that period was a rapid constriction of immediate political possibilities in the face of intensifying capitalist attack. The accumulation of theoretical resources throughout the 1970s meant that the left was better equipped in principle to analyse and challenge the mechanisms of bourgeois hegemony; but at the same time that theoretical labour had, in part inevitably, served as a compensatory substitution for dwindling political opportunities of a fully radical kind. In the latter part of the 1970s, then, the left was confronted with a severe crisis of relationship between theory and practice. In a political environment where conjunctural issues of tactics and strategy were increasingly urgent, it became possible to view the 'high' theory of the earlier part of the decade, in scornful or elegaic retrospect, as privileged intellectualist irrelevance. My own *Walter Benjamin, or Towards a Revolutionary Criticism* (1981) took, as the title suggests, a rather different view. Drawing upon the example of Walter Benjamin, it sought to diversify Marxist theory with its openings towards feminism and some aspects of post-structuralism; to deconstruct – both in its form and content – objectionably monolithic versions of such theory; to broach questions of cultural politics, and to recover in both style and theme a pleasure and playfulness which could not be grimly deferred until theory had done its work, but which, as for Brecht and Bakhtin, were part of the here and now. In these ways, then, the Benjamin study could be seen as participating in the new political ethos, and stood at a considerable distance from *Criticism and Ideology*: it was more preoccupied with questions of experience and the subject, with that difference or heterogeneity which escapes formalization, with humour, the body and the 'carnivalesque', with cultural politics rather than textual science. Yet what governed (in part unconsciously) the choice of Benjamin as a topic was not only that his work could be read as strikingly prefiguring many of these contemporary concerns, but the fact that it did so in a resolutely revolutionary context. Like his friend Theodor Adorno, Benjamin felt the need for what Francis Mulhern has called a 'modernist Marxism', one which had thought its way beyond impoverished Enlightenment categories; but this did not, for Benjamin at least, entail any relinquishing of the traditional imperatives of class politics. If Benjamin was much concerned with 'conjunctures' he also remained faithful to what he termed 'tradition'. At a time when political predilections appeared to be polarizing out between deconstruction and revolution, personal fulfilment and political orthodoxy, play and theory, difference and history, my turn to Benjamin was among other things an attempt to resist such premature dualities, with all the risks of falling between two stools.

The Rape of Clarissa (1982) continued the dialogue between Marxism and other discourses (feminism, deconstruction and psychoanalysis), finding in the texts of Samuel Richardson a paradigmatic site where these currents were relevant in the eighteenth century, and attempting to reproduce such a conjuncture for our own time. *Literary Theory: An Introduction* (1983) reflected at a more popular level a shift from the 'theoretical' to the 'political', insisting as it did that methodological questions in cultural analysis must be subordinated to political goals. It also began an inquiry into the historical institutions of criticism which was to be expanded in *The Function of Criticism* (1984), a work which invites the critical enterprise – mine as much as anyone else's – to turn reflexively upon itself, ponder its institutional history and consider its future political possibilities.

The later essays in this volume reflect some of these changed concerns. 'Capitalism, Modernism and Postmodernism' broadens its focus of inquiry from the literary text to the shape of contemporary culture as a whole and continues the dialogue with post-structuralism. 'The Critic as Clown' seeks to extract a certain radical populist iconoclasm from the criticism of William Empson, and is another sign of the influence of Mikhail Bakhtin on my work. It is intended among other things as a contrast to the study of John Bayley, showing that Marxist cultural theory can learn from the writing of some non-Marxist critics even as it necessarily polemicizes against the work of certain others. Since Brecht is a name which condenses many of the motifs of my later work, a place where comedy, deconstruction and the carnivalesque co-exist with the most resolute of revolutionary impulses, it is logical that there should be an essay here on him too. 'Poetry, Pleasure and Politics' represents a crude sketch for a materialist and psychoanalytical theory of aesthetic value, while my essay on reception theory, 'The Revolt of the Reader', is intended as a brief exercise in iconoclastic criticism, towards which I see the latter part of the book as sinking by slow stages. The nadir of this gradual abandonment of theoretical seriousness and intellectual responsibility arrives with the book's final offering, a stray fragment from my other life, as an occasional writer and performer of political songs. It is printed here partly as a reminder that there is a life after theory, and partly to round off the volume into a closed organic totality, since otherwise its number of items would stand at a sinister, unsettling thirteen.

I am particularly grateful to Francis Mulhern, who read through these essays with typical scrupulousness and insight, and contributed several valuable suggestions.

Acknowledgements are gratefully made to the editors of the following books and journals, where these essays first appeared: *New Left Review* for 'Liberality and Order: The Criticism of John Bayley' (*New Left Review* 110, July–August 1978), 'The Idealism of American Criticism' (*New Left Review* 127, May–June 1981), 'Wittgenstein's Friends' (*New Left Review* 135, September–October 1982), and 'Capitalism, Modernism and Post-modernism' (*New Left Review* 152, July–August 1985); *The Minnesota Review* for 'Macherey and Marxist Literary Theory' (Fall 1975), reprinted in G. H. R. Parkinson, ed., *Marx and Marxisms*, Royal Institute of Philosophy Lecture Series, 14, Cambridge 1982; Johns Hopkins University Press for 'Fredric Jameson: the Politics of Style' from *Diacritics* (Fall 1982) and for 'Brecht and Rhetoric' and 'The Revolt of the Reader' from *New Literary History* (Spring 1982); Mouton Publishers for 'Frère Jacques: The Politics of Deconstruction' from *Semiotica* (1984); Routledge and Kegan Paul Ltd. for 'Poetry, Pleasure and Politics' from *Formations* (1983) and for 'Marxism, Structuralism and Post-Structuralism' from *Economy and Society* (1984); *Literature and History* for 'Power and Knowledge in *The Lifted Veil*'; *The Sociological Review* for 'Form, Ideology and *The Secret Agent*' (first published in Diana Laurenson, ed., *The Sociology of Literature: Applied Studies*, University of Keele 1978).

T.E.

1.

Macherey and Marxist Literary Theory

A resurgence of interest in the materialist aesthetics of Walter Benjamin and Bertolt Brecht has helped to free Marxist criticism from the neo-Hegelian forms within which it has long been imprisoned. Yet the central category of those materialist aesthetics – the 'author as producer' – remains a *transitional* concept, potently demystificatory but politically indeterminate. And crucial though the analysis of the relations between 'base' and 'superstructure' *within* art itself clearly is, its historical explanatory power is not yet fully evident. Defoe and Fielding practise the same mode of literary production, but it is their ideological antagonism which claims our attention. *Henry Esmond* was the only novel of Thackeray to be published complete, rather than in monthly serialized parts; but though this difference of productive mode undoubtedly impresses itself on the novel's form, it leaves the 'Thackerayan ideology' essentially intact. No one expects modes of literary production and literary 'superstructures' to form a symmetrical relationship, dancing a harmonious minuet hand in hand throughout history; yet even if we allow for disjunction and uneven development, it seems true that the 'author as producer' concept is one which must, as it were, lie dormant over certain spans of literary history. The aesthetic redefinition of fiction as 'organic form' which develops in late nineteenth-century England, to discover its major ideologue in Henry James, is doubtless related to those shifts in literary production (from serialization and the 'three-decker' novel to the single volume) determined by general economic demands; yet it is not clear how such material mutations become an *active* element in the reconstruction of fictional ideologies.

This is not the kind of question which the work of Pierre Macherey proposes to answer, despite the title of his major work.[1] Like Lukács and unlike Benjamin, Macherey moves almost wholly within the terrain of a work's 'superstructures'. 'Production' refers not to the material apparatus, technological infrastructures and social relations of an artefact, but to its *self*-production as a chain of significations. Yet if Macherey's work resembles that of the neo-Hegelians in its dissolution of the text's materiality to a set of mental significances, it resembles it in little else. Indeed the thrust of Macherey's project is nothing less than the liberation of Marxist criticism from every taint of Hegelianism and empiricism; and to say that amounts to saying that he is, effectively, the first Althusserian critic. His intention is to inaugurate a radical 'epistemological break' with what has come before, to construct an entirely distinct problematic; and since he is therefore, in my view, one of the most challenging, genuinely innovatory of contemporary Marxist critics, the rest of this essay will be mainly given over to an exposition of his positions.

Macherey begins with a bold application of Althusserian epistemology to critical inquiry. Criticism and its object – the literary text – are to be radically distinguished: science is not the reduplication of an object but a form of knowledge of it which displaces it outside of itself, knows it as it cannot know itself. Criticism is not merely the elaboration of the text's self-knowledge; it establishes a decisive rupture between itself and the object, distancing itself from that object in order to produce a new knowledge of it. To know the text is not to listen to, and translate, a pre-existent discourse: it is to produce a *new* discourse which 'makes speak' the text's silences. Such an operation, however, is not to be misconceived as the hermeneutical recovery of a sense or structure hidden in the work, a sense which it possesses but conceals; it is rather to establish a new knowledge discontinuous with the work itself, disjunct from it as science is disjunct from ideology. Scientific criticism is in this sense the antagonist of empiricist critical 'knowledge', which ends effectively by abolishing itself, allowing itself to be reabsorbed into a literary object which it has left essentially unchanged. Criticism is not an 'instrument' or 'passage' to the truth of a text, but a transformative labour which makes its object appear other than it is.

Scientific criticism, then, produces a new object, refusing the empiricist illusion of the text as a 'given' which offers itself spontaneously to the inspecting glance. Such empiricism merely *redoubles* the artefact: it succeeds in saying less in saying more. But this empiricist illusion is coupled with what might seem its opposite: the 'normative' illusion, which measures the text against a ghostly model of what it might be. The normative illusion constitutes a refusal of the object as it is: it 'corrects' it against an independent, pre-existent model of which the empirical text is an imperfect copy, an inessential appearance. Grasping the text as the mere fictive rehearsal of an ideal object which precedes it, an ideal present within the text as the abiding truth or essence from which it may lapse and deviate, the typical gesture of normative criticism is to inscribe a 'Could do better' in the text's margin. The determinateness of the work is radically denied: normative criticism assumes that it could have been different from what it is. As such, the normative illusion is merely a displacement of the empiricist fallacy: it treats and modifies the object so that it can be better consumed. To attribute the text's empirical characteristics to an ultimate, always pre-given model which is the truth of the text's phenomenality is merely an epistemological variant of the naive empiricism which 'receives' the work as a spontaneous consumable given.

For Macherey, the literary object is determinate, and so can be the object of rational study. It is the effect of a specific labour, the product of a writer who does not fabricate the materials with which he works. (This is why it is mere mystification to speak of the author as a 'creator'.) Those materials are not neutral, and so spontaneously assimilable to a unity imposed upon them by the writer; they preserve, rather, a specific weight and autonomy of their own. The 'necessity' of the text is not the reflection of the author's sustaining, unifying intention; the writer's 'choice' of how to construct his narrative is the mere illusion of a choice, since his 'decisions' are already determined by the exigencies of the narrative itself. (The hero, in a given fictional genre, cannot disappear in the first few pages.) The writer 'discovers' rather than 'invents' his narrative, 'encounters' rather than 'creates' his solutions; he is the first reader of his own work. The true necessity of the text manifests itself in the fact that not a word of it can be changed and nothing can be added, even though it appears at each moment as though a new topic could be chosen, an alternative narrative selected. But it is precisely this ceaseless shadowy presence of other possible phrases which could be pronounced, this ineradicable sense that things could have been other than they are, which enforces the constraining necessity of the text we actually have before us. There is, after all, only one text; each of its moments is 'free', surprising, but each is definitive too. The work is at once achieved and changing, presenting itself as a contradictory combination of arbitrariness and necessity; and the task of criticism is to theorize the *necessity of this diversity*. The work's 'necessity' is not an initial 'given' but a product – a product which presents itself as the meeting-place of several diverse 'lines of necessity', several distinct and conflictual chains of meaning. The determinateness of the artefact, then, inheres not in its achieved 'unity', but in the necessity of its internal ruptures and contradictions – although it is important not to reduce contradiction itself, in Hegelian fashion, to a mere moment of an underlying unity, the self-divided appearance of a single abiding sense. The question which literature poses to criticism is that of the 'organization of a multiple', the laws of a form of necessity which preserves the real diversity by which the work is constructed. Such diversity characterizes every text, and the 'adventure story' is its image: for every work is constituted by an interior 'rupture' or 'decentrement' worked upon its initial situation, as the adventure story operates by surprise and reversal. The work, then, is neither improvised nor *pre*-determined; it works, instead, by a sort of 'free necessity', in which we continually discover the ineluctable beneath the form of the unforeseen, and vice versa.

The form of that 'free necessity' is nothing less than literary language itself. Literature institutes a new relationship between word and object which cancels the distinction between 'true' and 'false'; rather than conforming to an independent order of things, it confers its own truth on itself, suggests itself the order of truth on which it is founded. It is the source of its own sense, having nothing, it seems, either before or behind it, apparently free from the hauntings of any alien presence. It is autonomous to the degree that it lacks depth: everything is unrolled on the surface, a surface which is, however, multiple and diverse. Literary language confronts nothing exterior to itself: its units signify only in their internal interrelations. It is, in effect, a kind of tautology, endlessly repeating, prolonging and reproducing itself. It is language 'reduced to its thinness', reflecting nothing, apparently doubling nothing, sustained merely by the mechanisms of its own complex, irregular unfolding. Liberated in this sense from quotidian determinants, literary language acquires an unusual freedom and improvisatory force; but such improvisation is merely one of appearance. For the fact that literary language carries within itself the principles of its own veridicity produces a certain form of necessity: because such language is radically *irreducible* it is thereby fixed unalterably in itself, 'necessary' in so far as it is incapable of modification. (It is, indeed, *inferior* literature which, unable to produce the principles of its own veridicity, slips constantly towards an external order – tradition, morality, ideology – for verification.)

The necessity of the text, then, is not the index of a cohering authorial will; nor do we escape from that idealist problematic if we merely transpose it and posit, *à la* Goldmann, a 'collective unconscious' as producer. The necessity of the text – which is precisely what renders it *readable*, yields us a determinate object of analysis – inheres rather in the fact that the text *produces itself* – unfolds and activates its multiple lines of meaning without conformity to 'intention', pre-given normative model or external reality. The task of criticism is to discover in each text the laws of that self-production, or (what amounts to the same thing) the conditions of a work's possibility – 'conditions' understood not as the point of departure, the primordial germ to which the process of production can be reduced back, but the real process of the work's self-constitution, the specific composition of the concrete diversity of its elements.

Macherey's insistence on the text's determinateness might seem at first glance in contradiction with his theory of criticism as transformative of its object. For if nothing in the text can be changed or added, how does this differ from the empiricist 'reception' of the work as spontaneous fact? The answer lies in properly discriminating the concepts of the work's *autonomy* and its *independence*. The work's autonomy consists in its establishing a *difference*, a separation, with the languages, ideologies, and histories which surround it – a measurable, determinate distance which may be the object of scientific knowledge. The work is constituted precisely by its relations with what it is not; if this were not so it would be wholly 'independent' of what surrounds it and thus unreadable and even invisible. The work is the production of a difference from what surrounds it; in being sundered from those surroundings, snatched into its own space, it ceaselessly alludes to them. No text can be 'independent': it subsists in its complex relations to other uses of language, and so to ideologies and social formations. But for Macherey these realities are inscribed within the letter of the text primarily by virtue of their *absence*. Every discourse presupposes the absence of that of which it speaks, installing itself in the empty space created by its distancing of the object. The 'truth' of a literary work, then, is not secreted within it like a nut in a fruit, awaiting extraction at the hands of 'interpretative' criticism. The work's significance lies in its relation to what it is not, and so, paradoxically, is at once interior and absent simultaneously.

It is for this reason that the work must be at once *treated*, transformed, for it to become a theoretical fact, and yet must also be left as it is, recognized in its determinateness. It is important to recognize first of all that the necessity of the text is founded on the conflictual multiplicity of its meanings, and that to explain the work is therefore to distinguish the principle of its diversity. The postulate of the work's *unity*, which has always more or less haunted bourgeois criticism, must be unequivocally denounced; it is not unity, but the distance which separates the work's several meanings, which is at issue. The mutual confrontation of those divergent meanings in the text signals a certain *incompleteness*: the work is not closed on itself, a 'totality' turning around a concealed centre, but radically decentred and irregular, unachieved and insufficient. Yet this incompleteness or 'hollowness' of the artefact is not one which criticism can correct by adding something to it; it is, rather, a *determinate* incompleteness which cannot be altered. The text is, as it were, complete in its incompleteness, unachieved by virtue of the very reality it is. *What is lacking to it – its absence – is precisely what constitutes it as an object.* It is necessary to determine what a text lacks – lacks without which it would not exist, would have nothing to say. To explain the work, then, is to demonstrate that it does not exist in itself as some ideal plenitude of meaning, but bears inscribed in its very letter the marks of certain determinate absences which are the very principle of its identity. 'Hollowed' by the elusive presence of other works against which it constructs itself, turning around the absence of certain words to which it incessantly returns, the literary work consists not in the elaboration of a single meaning, but in the conflict and incompatibility of several meanings. That conflict, moreover, is precisely what binds the work to reality: ideology is present in the text in the form of its eloquent silences, its significant gaps and fissures. The distance which separates the work from its ideological matrix embodics itself in a certain 'internal distance' which separates the work from itself.

How is this to be understood? In launching his literary project, Macherey would claim, a writer discovers that what he 'wanted' to say is blocked, contorted, and deformed by ideology; in trying to articulate one meaning, the work finds itself ideologically constrained to articulate another. Thus, Jules Verne's fiction 'wants' to represent bourgeois progress as a march forward to the future, yet finds itself (on account of certain contradictions inherent in that ideology[2]) enforced to represent this march in images bound to the past. The effect of this ideological torsion is a set of hiatuses within the work itself – a *découpage* which appears in Verne as a discrepancy between levels of 'representation' and 'figuration'. We may thus read a text, as it were, 'in reverse', constructing what it attempts to say athwart what it actually finds itself saying.

Criticism, then, does not site itself in the same space as the text itself, allowing it to speak or completing what it leaves unsaid. On the contrary, it installs itself in the text's very incompleteness in order to *theorize* that lack of plenitude – to explain the ideological necessity of its 'not-said', its constitutive silences, that which it can show but not say. It is these silences which the critic must make speak; it is the 'unconsciousness' of the work which he interrogates, an unconsciousness which is nothing less than the play of history itself on the work's margins. In saying one thing, a text must at the same time say another, which is not necessarily the same; it is by its very nature unable to say simply one thing at a time. What the work 'says' as a whole, then, is not just this or that chain of meaning, but their conflict and difference; it articulates the hollow space which divides and binds together its multiple senses.

The relation between fiction and ideology is, for Macherey, one of considerable complexity. It is clear that the work does not 'reproduce' ideology, in a way which would make its own contradictions reflective of historical contradictions. On the contrary: the contradictions within the text are the product of the ideologically determined *absence* of such a reflection of real contradictions. It is the work's problematical *relationship* to ideology which produces its internal dissonances. Rather than 'reproducing' ideology, the text *produces* it, setting it in motion and endowing it with a form; and in doing so it reveals in its own internal dislocations the gaps and limits which signify that ideology's contradictory relation to real history. In the text, that is to say, the ideology begins to speak of its absences and manifest its limits – not in the Lukácsian sense that the work's aesthetic potency allows it to overreach ideological mediations into a more direct encounter with historical truth (a position Macherey rejects as naively empiricist), but because, in transforming rather than merely reproducing ideology, the text necessarily illuminates the 'not-said' which is the significant structure of the 'said'.

The literary work, then, does have a significant relation to historical reality, although one of a highly mediated and refracted kind. For Macherey, literary language occupies a kind of intermediate space between science and ideology: it resembles scientific discourse in the rigour of its internal organizations and in bearing within itself the criteria of its own veridicity; but it also mimes quotidian discourse, which is the language of ideology. It is at once the analogue of a true theoretical knowledge and the caricature of ideology. Rather than imitating reality, it deforms it; it is capable of becoming an 'image' of reality only by virtue of the distance which separates it from what it imitates, since the image which conforms wholly to its object confounds itself with it and loses its imaging character. Baroque art, founded on the principle that the more one distances the more one imitates, is for Macherey a fundamental model of all literary production. Yet though literary discourse deforms and distances reality, it is not thereby the mere play of an illusion, an objectless message (as Barthes would have it) whose substance is reducible to the codes which formulate and communicate it. Fiction, by endowing the ideological illusion with a form, fixing it within determinate limits, 'interrupts', 'arrests', 'realizes', and completely transforms it, to the point where it ceases to be merely illusory. The literary work, in thus transforming the ideological illusion, implicitly yields a critique of its own ideological status, becoming the substitute for, if not the equivalent of, a theoretical knowledge. Fiction is not *truer* than illusion; but by establishing a transformative relation to ideology, its own deceptions begin to betray and uncover the more radical deceptions of ideology itself, and in so doing contribute to our deliverance from them. For Macherey, ideology is in its 'natural' state diffuse, amorphous and decentred, the invisible colour of everyday life, less an articulated structure than a boundless medium. In entering literature, however, ideology finds itself subjected to a *formalization* which, strictly speaking, it cannot tolerate. This formalization exposes those limits, slips and incoherences of ideology normally concealed in everyday life; and it is for this reason that, once worked upon by the literary text, ideology begins to come apart at the seams. It is the very *coherence* of the textual forms which produces the *incoherence* of the ideological content.

Macherey's theory of literary production entails a concept of *structure* radically distinct from that of the structuralist ideology. The structuralist critical enterprise revolves on the decipherment of the text's enigma, the disengagement from it of a cryptic but coherent sense. The literary artefact is constructed as a message, and the critic's function is to isolate the transmitted information. The work, accordingly, has no autonomous value in itself: it is an intermediary, the simulacrum of a concealed structure. Structuralist analysis, which elaborates a 'copy' of the work itself, is thus the simulacrum of a simulacrum. It is, in that precise sense, Platonic: the writer's production is merely the appearance of a production, since its true object lies behind it. To criticize is thus to reduce the 'externality' of the text to the structure secreted in its 'interior' – to *extract* the truth of the object from its inner space. Such extraction, for Macherey as for Althusser, is merely another form of empiricist epistemology – an adequation and conformity of 'knowledge' to its privileged object. But the work has, in fact, neither exterior nor interior; it is not to be conceived in the metaphysical terms of depths and surfaces. If the work has an interior in any sense at all, it is one exhibited as an exterior: the work hides nothing, keeps no secret, is entirely 'readable' and offered to view. Structuralism, like 'normative' criticism, refuses the text's autonomous reality; it seeks for the laws immanent in a work, as one might seek for the laws of gravity within a falling body. But just as the laws of gravity are in fact *elsewhere*, situated on the quite distinct terrain of scientific knowledge, so scientific criticism gives the work a new dimension rather than discovers a deep meaning buried within it. It does not rest in its object, repeating its discourse in other terms; it is a matter not of an 'otherwise-said' but of a 'never-said'. An analogy can be drawn with Freud, who rather than searching for a hidden meaning in the depths of conscious discourse, situates this meaning elsewhere, in the structure he names the unconscious.[3] The 'structure' of the literary work, similarly, is not to be discovered *in* the work itself; it is a

structure to which the work *belongs*, without copying or containing it. To speak of the work in terms of structure, then, can be to
fall easy victim to the organicist fallacy of the work as harmonious totality; it is to forget that structure is the principle of
difference rather than unity, and so must necessarily be absent
from the relations it serves to explain. (Contradiction, for example, can be thought only as absence, not as positive presence.)
It is in its very conflictual diversity that the work can be said to
belong to an ideological structure, which disrupts its manifold
meanings. The text's significance is to be found not 'in' but
'beside' it, on its margins, where it relates to what it is not, in the
conditions of its very possibility.

This exposition of Macherey's critical theory has been extremely partial and schematic: I have said nothing, for example,
about his analysis of Lenin's critique of Tolstoy, and little of his
lengthy dissection of the work of Verne. The critical comments
which follow must be equally truncated and selective.

In ascribing the power he does to literary form, Macherey
runs the risk of a peculiarly Marxist variety of formalism. For
though his contention that form distantiates the ideological is
suggestive, why should this distantiation automatically be *subversive*? Why is 'form', in some new essentialism, ascribed a
single, eternal effect? For such distantiation is surely also
capable of powerfully *underwriting* the ideology of the text. Is not
form in any case always itself 'ideological'? And whether it
subverts or underwrites depends not merely upon the particular
transaction between form and ideology in question, but upon
the concrete historical and ideological situation in which the test
is situated and received. Macherey's early work, committed as it
is to an 'intrinsicist' literary science which treats the text solely in
terms of its production rather than also in terms of its consumption, completely suppresses the reality of the literary text as an
historically mutable practice which 'lives' only in the process of
its transaction with particular readers. It thus damagingly reproduces the 'scientism' of Althusser's work, presupposing some
quite unproblematized, transcendental reader/critic.

Macherey's formalism is in part a result of his Althusserian
notion of ideology. For if ideology is conceived of as an essentially *non-contradictory* region, then it would indeed take something like art to press it up against its own limits and force it into
handing over its guilty secrets. Ideology, however, has no such
homogeneity: it is certainly *homogenizing* in tendency, but it

nowhere, fortunately, has the success which Macherey assigns to it. Althusser's own work has grievously underplayed the degree to which ideology, as a terrain of *class struggle*, is itself labile, internally contradictory, non-monolithic: his essay on ideology in *Lenin and Philosophy* images it, in effect, as an omnipotent superego which inexorably submits the individual subject to its needs, and links this undialectical view with an equally undialectical functionalism and economism, whereby ideology exists merely to reproduce the conditions whereby the subject is inserted into its economic place. Behind this theory lurks a particular politics, one shared by Macherey himself: the politics of the French Communist Party, whose political collaborationism finds itself reflected in a view of ideology divorced from class struggle. For Althusser and Macherey, ideology is effectively coterminous with the 'lived'; but it is difficult to see what cutting edge such an 'expansionist' definition of ideology can have. Since Macherey (although not Althusser) is prepared to term ideology 'illusion', fiction really alludes to another fiction (ideology), which in turn alludes to historical reality. Now it is certainly true that fiction is, in this sense, constituted by what one might term a 'double deformation', whereby ideological materials which are already a 'misrecognition' of the real are raised to the second power, 'produced' in their turn by certain fictional devices. Fiction, by 'fixing' the ideological in this process, establishes what Althusser terms an 'internal self-distantiation' from the ideology in which it bathes, breaks it up and reassembles it into a peculiar visibility; so the 'double deformation', we might say, partially cancels itself out, inverting itself back into an analogue of theoretical knowledge. But ideology does not have to have recourse to fiction to become the analogue of a knowledge, since it is more than just the bad dream of the infrastructure: it is not, in a word, just 'false consciousness', the very truth to which Althusser and Macherey wish to attest, but which Macherey seems at times to end up denying. (And if Macherey seems to this extent to fall back into the Hegelian–Marxist tradition he rejects, so do both Macherey and Althusser in their implicit desire to salvage a certain *privileged status* for art, to rescue it from the 'shame' of the 'merely ideological', and elevate it almost – but not quite – to the rank of theory.)

Since *Pour une théorie de la production littéraire*, Macherey's work has undergone radical new development. In two seminal articles,

'On Literature as an Ideological Form: Some Marxist Propositions', and 'The Problem of Reflection',[4] he appears to have broken decisively with his earlier intrinsicism and formalism – that is to say, with the residues of bourgeois aesthetics still lurking in his book. Abandoning the bourgeois-idealist category of 'literature' which still dominates *Pour une théorie*, he is now prepared to see what counts as an artefact as historically and conjuncturally determined; and he has shifted his attention away from the 'text-in-itself' to its material determinants, to the process whereby 'Literature' signifies those pieces of writing ephemerally and variously *constituted* as such by being inserted into the ideological apparatuses in such a way as to produce specific 'literary effects' – effects which, in so far as they have definite ideological functions, intervene into the class struggle. His model for this work has been the suggestive inquiries of Renée Balibar into the fostering, within the French pedagogical system, of a linguistic division (between *français ordinaire* and *français littéraire*) which plays its role in the enforcement, within the post-revolutionary creation of a 'national language', of certain class divisions which that common language threatens.

If Macherey's earlier work could be convicted of a certain Marxist formalism, however, this later writing is not entirely free of a certain sociologistic functionalism and reductionism. 'Literature' becomes no more than the functional support of a particular ideological apparatus, in an argument which is considerably too narrow, homogenizing and specific to the history of France. It is surely the case that 'literature' is contradictorily constituted in a whole range of social institutions, and is by no means confined for its definitions to the educational system. Moreover, though the phenomenon of literature has now been thoroughly historicized, the theory which analyses it has not. Science or theory is not, in Macherey or in Althusser, itself viewed as an historical product, but rather intervenes into history from some apparently transcendental vantage point. It is useful to characterize scientific theory as a 'symptomatic' reading of ideologies, capable of rendering some account of the mechanisms by which such ideologies maintain certain silences, *why* such silences must be maintained, and *how* an ideology does not speak of certain things. But there is no reason to suppose that such a discourse is launched from anywhere but an historical position, and is thus itself always in principle vulnerable to a 'symptomatic' reading by another discourse.

A final problem may be briefly touched upon, concerning the vexed question of 'reflection'. Macherey's comments on Lenin's treatment of Tolstoy (the 'mirror of the Russian Revolution') brilliantly succeed in retrieving Lenin's critique from a crude reductionism; if Tolstoy's work is indeed a mirror, then it is, as Lenin recognizes, an angled, selective one thronged by fragmented images, as notable for what it does not, as for what it does, reflect. But such a drastically modified mirror might hardly be said to be a mirror at all; and indeed by the time of his later essays Macherey has effectively transposed the epistemological question of the 'text–reality' relation to an ontological one: that of the *material reality* of 'art' itself, which figures as an active force in the reproduction of social reality rather than as a mere reflex of it. This is a timely reminder; but the epistemological issue is thereby displaced rather than resolved. It is no answer to the question of how 'art' relates to 'reality' to reply that art is indubitably real. Macherey himself would now seem to have abandoned these inquiries: he is a philosopher rather than a literary critic, and his latest work is a study of Hegel and Spinoza. They remain, however, problems which Macherey's work has enabled us to take up in a fresh way, and for this we must be enduringly in his debt.

2.

Form, Ideology and
The Secret Agent

There is a sense in which Conrad's *The Secret Agent* is altogether too convenient a text to select for discussion in this kind of book. For it is, self-evidently, a 'political' novel, and a materialist criticism should not give itself an easy ride by choosing as its object texts which 'spontaneously' conform to its method. Better, surely, to select an 'innocent' work – a Beddoes verse-tragedy or medieval love-lyric – than to risk the perils of methodological circularity, a mirror-image reciprocity between 'approach' and object. *The Secret Agent* may well seem too ideologically 'guilty' a fiction to strain the assumptions of an ideologically oriented criticism; one may be merely repeating the evasion of the theological critic who works on nothing but Dante and Hopkins, or the semiotician for whom Joyce is the only true literature there is. Yet I am not in fact particularly concerned here with the explicitly 'political' dimension of the novel, and certainly not with what might be termed a 'sociological' reading of it. Not that a 'sociology' of the novel can yield us nothing: it is *textually* relevant that a single historical incident is all the evidence there ever was to back up that vision of an anarchist-haunted London which *The Secret Agent* projects. The sociology of anarchism can tell us much about the novel's perceptions – can lead us, for example, to ask why Michaelis should be categorized as an anarchist when he is clearly close to a Marxist, or how it comes about that the nihilist Professor and time-serving Ossipon can be subsumed under the same political heading. There is nothing in the least empiricist about such questions, but this essay will not be concerned with them. For I have chosen *The Secret Agent* because it seems to me a peculiarly paradigmatic example of the complex relations within fiction between forms and ideologies, formal elements and ideological sub-ensembles, aesthetic devices and codified perceptions. That this is so because of the unusual 'fore-grounding' of the ideological which the novel effects is doubtless true; but I would claim that what can be observed with peculiar visibility in this self-consciously tendentious text is merely a convenient index of what occurs in the self-structuration of every literary work. We need, then, to beware of the ease with which an 'ideological' text yields us insights for materialist criticism, at the same time as we need to insist that such a text can indeed provide a provisional model for such a materialist method.

The specific form of *The Secret Agent* is composed of a complex amalgam of genres – a compound of spy-thriller, Dickensian 'imaginative realism', 'metaphysical' meditation and (in a loose sense of the term) naturalism. Each of these constituent genres contributes to an ideological contradiction between the 'exotic' and 'domestic' – a contradiction united in the novel's central character Verloc, the seedy domesticated double-agent. The spy-thriller inserts the fascination of the foreign into the sordidly routine world of *Realpolitik*; 'Dickensian' realism involves an imaginative caricature of the familiar. The naturalist form produces, and is the product of, the bourgeois illusion of 'normality', of the solid indestructibility of the quotidian world. Yet the laboriously self-parodic quality of that naturalism in *The Secret Agent* intimates its self-contradictory character. For naturalism, in fetishizing the material world, dislocates subjectivity from it, banishing it into its own autono-mous zone where it inevitably presents itself as mysterious, unmotivated and opaque. The very form selected to produce the 'naturalness' of the world, when pressed to a caricaturing extreme, highlights the 'mystery' of subjectivity and so puts itself into question. This contradiction is vital for the 'ideology of the text' (hence the calculatedly self-parodic nature of its naturalist modes), for while *The Secret Agent* is constrained to defend the 'naturalness' of the quotidian world against the revolutionary dreams of anarchism, it is equally constrained not to do so at the cost of denying the value of subjectivity itself. But here the text encounters further contradiction. The more it confirms the 'naturalness' of the given by raising it to a *metaphysical* level, producing a 'metaphysical materialism' (the 'indestructibility of matter' and so forth), the more it is forced to conspire, as it were, with the 'metaphysical' dreams of the anarchists themselves, inhabiting that world of discourse in its very drive to undermine it. Moreover, the *repellent* vision of the world as a desert of brute matter which such self-parodic naturalism produces is bound to render the views of the anarchists more palatable – to make the grotesque, nihilist Professor something more than a madman. The forms of the text, then, produce and are produced by an ideological contradiction embedded within it – a contradiction between its unswerving commitment to bourgeois 'normality' and its dissentient 'metaphysical' impulse to reject such 'false consciousness' for a 'deeper' insight into the 'human condition'.

This contradiction, in fact, arises from the internal conflicts of the Conradian ideology – a form of 'metaphysical' conservatism equally hostile to petty-bourgeois myopia and revolutionary astigmatism. The form of the work is an attempt to 'resolve' this contradiction by operating a naturalist mode which neverthe-less, in its self-parodic quality, detaches itself ironically from its own vision. It is, as it were, naturalism to the second power – an Olympian, dispassionate view of reality which then views itself in precisely the same light in order to distance itself sceptically from its own presuppositions. It is for this reason that the familiar Conradian device of 'point of view' cannot be used, since its effect would be both to 'humanize' the action and allow an access to the workings of subjectivity which must be blocked. Yet the Conradian formal device habitually coupled with nar-rational viewpoint – the dislocation of chronological narrative – *is* used, since the text can preserve its resolute 'objectivity' only by literally *not seeing* events which lie beyond its scope. The killing of Stevie is unpresented – happens, so to speak, in the reader's absence; and the murder of Verloc is presented with extreme obliquity, squinted at sideways rather than frontally encountered. Both events reveal sinister forces capable of destroying the quotidian forces which must be 'shown' at the same time as the novel proclaims the impossibility of attesting textually to their authentic existence. Yet the device is also calculated to draw our attention to the threatening *reality* of these subterranean forces: the fact that they cannot be shown directly underscores their 'untypicality' at the same time as it shockingly intensifies their effect. The text, indeed, operates here a triple irony on the reader. Its contemptuous caricaturing of the anarchists as conformist parasites or febrile freaks, coupled with its resolute fetishizing of social reality, reassures the reader of the anarchists' despicable impotence. But it conspires with that assumption only the more brutally to subvert it: for the anarchists emerge, after all, as repugnant killers, responsible for dismembering a mentally defective child. In a third twist, however, such destructiveness is 'metaphysically' illusory: the dream of negating material reality and reconstructing the world from nothing is itself negated by the stubborn indestructibility of matter, symbolized by the tell-tale surviving pieces of Stevie's flesh.

Yet this 'resolution' of contradiction merely produces another. For that very survival of matter suggests the sickening vision of a universe endlessly, mechanically permutating its various materials – the ideology, in short, of crass bourgeois scientism and positivism which the anarchists set out to explode. The novel's 'metaphysical' symbolism is thus in partial contradiction with its naturalist forms: the former, in raising the ideology of the latter to an unchallengeable cosmic vision, at the same time protests in mute horror at its devastating implications. Yet the text confronts a severe problem in selecting the terms in which such a protest is to be couched. For 'humanitarian' protest is ruled out on two opposed grounds: as incompatible with the book's clinical naturalism, and, contradictorily, as a merely feeble reflex of the bourgeois ideology of which that naturalism is the product. On the one hand, the novel exploits naturalist devices to dramatize a bourgeois society from which humane feeling is expelled, and in parodying that society implies a satirical protest against it. But in discerning a 'metaphysical' basis to such behaviour in the neutral, dispassionate cosmos, it enforces its own sense of the pathetic inefficacy of the humane, as part of a 'degenerate' sentimental cult of the human subject. It is, moreover, a cult of which the utopian brotherhood of anarchism is an even more degenerate extension. This contradiction is incarnated in the idiot Stevie, whose human tenderness is at once a function of his muddled, mentally regressive naivety, and a 'mystical' intimation of values critical of bourgeois society – values which are in him, however, literally inarticulable, mere broken murmurs of dissent. The silence of Stevie is ideologically determinate: the text is unable to endorse the callous inhumanity of the social world, but unable to articulate any alternative value because *value itself* is 'metaphysically' trivial, an illusion of false consciousness or (in the case of Winnie's claustral love for Stevie) a mere biological reflex. The text's satire of humanitarianism, then, springs from a 'metaphysical' ideology deeply sceptical of such banal petty-bourgeois pieties – an ideology which, despite its Olympian omniscience, is no more than a 'higher' expression of bourgeois inhumanity itself and a rejection of that utopian humanitarian-ism which threatens it. The silence of Stevie is the product of the mutual cancellation of the text's ideological contradictions: the text can 'speak' only by *activating* such contradictions, not by surmounting them into a determinate 'solution'. It is for this reason that *irony* is its dominant mode of discourse.

The silence of Stevie, symbolized in his scribbled, spiralling circles of infinity, is 'mystical' because it gestures towards that which can be shown but not stated, a condition of which art itself is for Conrad the prototype. It is in this sense that Stevie, the 'mad artist', defines the status of the text of *The Secret Agent* as a whole. The novel is unable to speak *of* its contradictions; it is, rather, precisely its contradictions which speak. Stevie's silence is 'mystical' in a sense of the term appropriate to Ludwig Wittgenstein's *Tractatus Logico-Philosophicus*. Language, for the *Tractatus*, can do no more than 'show' the structure of the world in the structure of its own world-picturing propositions; it cannot *speak* of reality directly, but can only intimate obliquely, by allowing itself to be cancelled out, the reality which tran-scends it. There is a figurative analogy here, inexact but instruc-tive, with the relations between text, ideology and history. For it is as though the text, also, cannot speak directly of historical reality, but 'shows' something of its structure in the conflictual ideological structure of its own propositions. Just as for the *Tractatus* language is coterminous with the world, so for the text ideology is coterminous with history, permeating its own sign-systems; and it is for this reason that the text cannot cast a direct glance 'behind' that ideology to the history it signifies. What it can do instead is indicate the presence of that reality by the very sign of contradiction it produces within it. The text, to adapt Marx's comment on Adam Smith, thus does not 'really' resolve problems, but reveals them by contradicting itself – reveals them not merely by failing to resolve them but by its very efforts to do so. *The Secret Agent* may be seen in this sense as a paradigm of a particular case of the text–ideology relationship. As the *Tractatus* must end by lapsing into mystical silence, intimating the real only by inducing its own self-negation, so *The Secret Agent* is constituted by the 'mystical' absence figured above all in Stevie – an absence ideologically defined by the text as metaphysical, but in fact the 'hollow' scooped out by the clash of its contradictions. Constrained at once to consecrate 'normative' reality as a material process on which the subjective is slavishly contingent, and to reject such dreary positivism in the name of those privileged, cataclysmic moments in which the subjective is assertively alive, the novel subsists in a series of 'gaps' – between what can be known and what can be shown, between the discourse of 'experience' and of description, between the styles of metaphysics and social documentation. These gaps, the product of ideological conflict, are then themselves ideologically rendered so as to be accommodated. The text cannot, of course, know them for what they are, for if it did it would cease to exist; it therefore images them as those crevices in ordinary discourse through which the abyss of an infinite silence is to be glimpsed.

It is an abyss on the edge of which the nihilist Professor is continually poised – the Professor who, wired up for instant self-consignment to eternity, is thus a graphic image of the text itself. For the text, too, images itself ideologically as moving at the still point of the turning world, pivoted like Stevie between time and eternity at the prime meridian of Greenwich Observatory, able to reveal the truth of itself only by that ceaseless process of 'self-detonation' which is irony. Only by the 'revolutionary' act of negating its every proposition and reconstructing itself *ex nihilo* could the text articulate reality; yet this, it knows, is impossible, for it is doomed to work with discourses ridden with ideological contradiction, or – as the text itself would say – condemned to the eternal 'inauthenticity' of language itself, which can never crystallize 'pure' truth. Irony is thus both a sign of self-contradiction and a protection against it, a sardonic mode of survival; the final contradiction is that the Professor's nihilism is both metaphysically intelligible and politically impermissible. Whereas the *Tractatus* can ignore the ideological effects of its retreat to the mystical which is the other face of language (for such a retreat leaves everything just as it was), *The Secret Agent* cannot do so – cannot, as a text, allow itself to disappear down the abyss of the unspeakable, permitting its propositions to be retrospectively cancelled, leaving itself with absolutely nothing to say. Its commitment to *discourse* is unavoidably a commitment to the largely 'inauthentic' social practices which such discourse articulates – a commitment, as it were, to the later Wittgenstein world of the *Philosophical Investigations*, with its appeal to ordinary language-games as the criteria of the real. Such games appear in this text too – indeed 'game' is a central metaphor of *The Secret Agent*; and they appear because language and society must be protected against the minatory invasions of the absolute. More exactly, the arbitrary game of bourgeois legality, in which police and criminals are reversible counters, must itself be absolutized, raised to the status of that greater self-validating game of fixed pieces and endlessly shifting positions which is the universe itself. Since the social game is arbitrary, there is no reason why this, rather than some other piece of gratuitous practice, should not be absolutized; that the rules of any game are both arbitrary and absolute is the novel's metaphorical assurance for this. The novel's own 'game' is then the operation of this ideological effect. In a series of mutually cancelling moves, it satirizes Winnie Verloc's blinkered petty-bourgeois viewpoint from the standpoint of the anarchist activity she ignores, while simultaneously satirizing the anarchists as petty-bourgeois hypocrites from the standpoint of the 'fanatical' Professor. Conversely, it condemns the Professor's metaphysical 'extremism' by an appeal to the humanity of Winnie and Stevie, while at the same time questioning such sentiments from a 'metaphysical' vantage point which is at least 'on terms' with that of the Professor himself. This stalemated game is then at once the product, and possible resolution, of the novel's contradictions. For if stalemate suggests non-resolution, it equally suggests a kind of finality which can pass as a solution. Stalemate is both ending and non-ending, completion and unachievement. In one sense, the novel ends on the latter note, bereft of a Victorian 'settlement': the Professor walks away through the London streets, the interdependent forces of legality and criminality continue their reversible cat-and-mouse encounters. But that, precisely, is the point – that the game will *go on*, even though neither side wins. In this sense, incompletion is itself a solution – it is the perpetuity of the social game which matters, to which the only threat is the deathly spectatorial Professor. *His* sense of the game's absurdity must be acknowledged if the text is 'clinically' to transcend its own materials, but it is an insight which can be accommodated within a vision of indestructibility which belongs to the same Godlike view. The novel thus 'gets somewhere' even though it appears not to – just as *walking*, one of its dominant images, seems a mere static marching on the spot, but (notably in the case of Verloc's surreal walk to the embassy) *mysteriously* lands you at your destination. Progress,

narrative, diachrony are radically questioned by textual forms
and images, but not in the end abolished: although they cannot
exactly be accounted for within a reified world drained of
dynamism, they none the less cryptically persist. This internally
contradictory image, of motion held within stasis or stasis accommodating motion, is an effect of the formal and ideological
contradictions of the text, whereby events are seen at once
durationally and *sub specie aeternitatis*. That narrative is possible
and chronology viable – in short, that something *happens* – is a
mark of the novel's relation to the ideology of bourgeois realism,
of its endorsement of the 'normative' assumptions of the bourgeois world. But the naturalist form which puts such narration
to work has the effect of 'freezing' and spatializing it, becoming
in this sense the reflection, 'on earth' as it were, of that vision of
time from eternity which belongs to the novel's 'metaphysical'
dimension. That dimension is the ideological product of a radical scepticism about progress, change, causality and temporality
which belongs to the 'radical conservative' sub-ensemble which
Conrad inhabits, hostile to 'orthodox' bourgeois liberal doctrines
yet dependent on the social order they help to sustain. Naturalism manages to 'solve' this contradiction by appearing at once
'temporal' and 'spatial', accommodating 'realist' duration while
framing and fashioning it into immobility. In doing so, it fulfils
two contradictory functions: it intensifies the stolid 'normality'
of the world, but also 'naturalizes' the metaphysical viewpoint of
it, and so allows that viewpoint to be upheld while rescuing it
from the 'unworldly' extremism of the Professor (and to some
extent of Stevie). 'Nothing can really be changed' is the message
of the book's metaphysical materialism, a message both negative
and affirmative in its implications. As against revolutionary
metaphysics, it is affirmative; in so far as it necessarily banishes
along with such revolutionism any 'spiritual' vision beyond the
crassly materialist, it is profoundly pessimistic. This contradiction, and its 'solution', embed themselves in the work in ways we
have examined: for violent change (Winnie), motion (Verloc),
spiritual vision (Stevie), *do* insist on thrusting themselves into the
text, although in ways which can only be enigmatically alluded
to. Some ideology of the 'humane' must be obliquely recognized,
if a source of value is to be provided from which both the
Professor and bourgeois society can be criticized; yet such values
are too close to bourgeois sentimentalism and anarchist Romanticism to be countenanced. In other works, Conrad is able to

lend such values a concrete location – the 'organic' society of the ship's crew, inimical alike to bourgeois individualism and subversive egalitarianism. But no such court of moral appeal is available in the wholly urbanized society of *The Secret Agent*; and value is thus, as in the *Tractatus*, forced beyond the frontiers of the world, exiled beyond what can be articulated. Yet because it is thus forced beyond the world, everything seems to be left exactly as it was; and this provides the text with a kind of resolution, or, better, with the illusion of one. The world of *The Secret Agent*, as of the *Tractatus*, just is 'everything that is the case'; and in this sense there is no need of a resolution because *there is nothing, it seems, to resolve*. The world goes on: and this is at once the question, and the answer, of the text.

I have tried in this excessively terse and abstract account of Conrad's novel to demonstrate a certain complexity in the text–ideology relation. The Conradian ideology is itself internally complex, compounded of elements of various ideological subensembles (of the 'emigré', Merchant Code, Romantic artist and so on) as well as of major elements of the dominant ideology (imperialism). *The Secret Agent* is also an internally complex formation; but the one formation does not merely 'reflect' the other. The complexity of the text is the product of certain contradictions between its component elements – contradictions which are in turn produced by the mutually conflictual relations of those elements to mutually conflictual aspects of the Conradian ideology *as that ideology is produced by the novel*. If, for example, there are certain contradictions between the aesthetic elements of form and symbolism, this is because the novel so produces ideology as to place them in relation to different ideological 'levels', or indeed to different ideologies. If there are internal contradictions within a single aesthetic element (say, between 'spatial' and 'durational' devices in narrative), this comes about because the text so produces ideology as to place the same aesthetic element in simultaneous relation to different ideologies or ideological 'levels'. If there is contradiction in characterization, so that, for example, Stevie is a type both of the anarchists themselves and of their innocent victims, this occurs because ideology is so produced as to relate Stevie and the anarchists at once to the same and to different ideologies. And so on: there is no need to list the possible permutations of such a method, or to emphasize how in the textual process any one such permutation overdetermines another, so that the effect of isolating them for purposes of demonstration is inevitably one of a certain crudity. But to give a relatively simple example, with reference to *The Secret Agent*: one aesthetic element (naturalism) may so produce one aspect of ideology (bourgeois 'normality') as to throw it into contradiction with another ideology or level of ideology ('metaphysical nihilism') and thus put itself into contradiction with aspects of another aesthetic element (symbolism). This process, whereby aesthetic elements constantly *displace* and *recast* ideological elements as they are displaced and recast by them, is the very process of the text's 'self-determination', in which each proposition, each 'problem' provisionally 'solved', produces a fresh problem, and that another. It is this *necessity* of the textual process which is the object of scientific literary study.

3.

Liberality and Order:
The Criticism of John Bayley

Few English literary critics command more respect than John
Bayley, Warton Professor of English Literature in the University
of Oxford. The author of six full-length critical studies,[1] as well
as of numerous articles and reviews, Bayley has not only become
established as a revered figure within the literary academic
world; he has also become an influential force within 'metropolitan' literary culture, controlled as that apparatus largely is by
Oxford English graduates. That Bayley should be honoured as
an authoritative, almost patriarchal figure within literary circles
is in one sense unsurprising. In a university faculty undis-
tinguished for its critical vigour, stubbornly pre-Leavisian in
ideology, timorously enclosed in traditional literary scholarship,
Bayley's work stands out for its imaginative idiosyncrasy. In an
English critical milieu still strikingly parochial in its interests –
the residue of that militant patriotism which helped to give birth
to 'English' as an academic discipline – his close familiarity
with Russian, French, German and American literature is
particularly impressive. Relatively untainted by Oxford
academicism, and apparently unidentified with any critical
'school', Bayley's work seems to offer a paradigm of independence and authenticity.

It is, moreover, work which at its best can be quite remarkably
perceptive. Working with the flimsiest theoretical scaffolding,
Bayley nevertheless succeeds in producing critical insights which
are rarely less than interesting and on occasions brilliantly pro-
vocative. His 'feel' for the quality of a literary text, for its
distinctive flavour and nuance, is difficult to match within contemporary criticism; himself the author of an early novel,[2] he

displays a novelist's sensitivity to the 'intentions' of the writers with whom he deals. Disowning any facile schematism or reductive 'content analysis', Bayley can show himself superbly aware of the constraints and potentialities of literary form; and within the limits of his own critical 'theory', he is perhaps more intriguingly unpredictable in the accounts he will produce of a writer than almost any other English critic of comparable eminence. Much of his criticism of Shakespeare, Keats, Kipling, Lawrence, Hardy and others contains local insights of considerable acuity, worked through with an almost painful honesty and clear-sightedness; his generosity of spirit combines with a bracing alertness to the intransigencies of a text, so that his best work seems at once tolerantly open and discriminatingly shrewd. He is, perhaps, one of the most *inimitable* critics in England today, nobody's fool and nobody's camp-follower, free at once of slick professionalism and gauche amateurism in his resolute devotion to the business of criticism. The whole body of his work is caught within a spurious belief that the truth of a text resides in the consciousness of its author: it is this relationship, between work and authorial intent, which he has explored again and again, in an enviably wide acquaintance with literature. Yet it is remarkable to what illuminating uses this discredited theoretical doctrine is turned, in his accounts of, say, Yeats, Auden, Tolstoy and Hardy; few better examples could be found within contemporary criticism of the uneven relations between theory and practice.

Bayley's work, moreover, has the virtues of consistency. It is characteristic of university English schools that their more publicly known members lead a double life. The racy iconoclasm of their journalistic output contrasts tellingly with the bland caution of their scholarly productions. All that unites the two is a shared absence of personal conviction. Intellectual seriousness is reserved for the editing of texts; criticism functions as a little light relief from such sober enterprises, an occasional display of colour supplement cleverness. It is symptomatic in this respect that the present Merton Professor of English Literature at Oxford devoted much of his inaugural lecture to demonstrating the futile subjectivism of his own discipline. Bayley, however, makes no such adjustments: his literary style, which (true to his own critical premises) seems consciously to sacrifice any facile *brio* of form to a felt sincerity of content, survives unruffled from critical study to newspaper review.

Doggedly courted though he is by almost all of the major metropolitan literary periodicals, he writes for them only on his own admirably uncompromising terms. In this sense, he emerges as a distinctively 'old-fashioned' critic, estranged in tone and sensibility from the brittle modishness of his younger epigones. Part of that estrangement is a matter of social background. What distinguishes Bayley from most prominent English critics is the impeccable ruling-class orthodoxy of his social upbringing and career. Born in 1925, he was educated at Eton and New College, Oxford, became an officer in the Grenadier Guards and served in Special Intelligence during the war; he was then elected a Fellow of three Oxford colleges in succession, and has remained at Oxford ever since as the occupant of a university chair. He is married to the novelist Iris Murdoch, herself of *haute-bourgeois* Anglo-Irish provenance, who became an Oxford academic after a high-ranking career in the Civil Service. It is, then, particularly intriguing that Bayley continues to exercise such ideological power, in a literary world where others of his sensibility and 'social tone' are undoubtedly marginal.

Something of the secret of that power can be discovered in Bayley's first published book, *The Romantic Survival*, a study of Yeats, Auden and Dylan Thomas. In praising Romanticism for its 'power of investing ordinary objects with wonder and strangeness', he none the less enters a *caveat* about the 'Romantic imagination' as such. It is likely to be overburdened with the abstracting, integrative drive of a singular, self-conscious vision; in its obsession with a 'conscious unifying aim', it lacks the relaxed, half-random 'naturalness' of a Shakespeare. Such a case implies a definite hostility to the 'modernism' of a Hulme, Pound or Eliot, whose 'rather prim and devitalized concepts' contrast tellingly with the 'enormous, if disorderly' nineteenth-century cult of the 'creative imagination'. There is a correlative suspicion of the 'analytical' criticism with which such modernism is habitually coupled. Bayley professes himself disconcerted by the proposal that the task of criticism should be the analysis of meaning rather than the description of enjoyment, and protests that the poem, 'like a human being, [has] a life of its own which is ultimately mysterious and irreducible' (p. 69). The Romantic critic, furnished with his 'experience and flair', can just *see* whether a poem is 'good', 'whereas the analyst will not admit that it is good until he has seen exactly what is in it, what it may mean'

(p. 70). This brutal insistence on knowing exactly what it is you are appreciating must be rejected for 'a whole-hearted submission to a poetic experience before we begin to analyse it' (p. 72).

Love Against Ideology

A rather more programmatic rendering of this irrationalism may be found in Bayley's second, most influential study, *the Characters of Love*, which offers studies of *Troilus and Criseyde, Othello* and *The Golden Bowl*.[3] 'Love', in this work, figures as a metaphor of the desirable relationship between an author and his or her characters. 'What I understand by an author's love for his characters is a delight in their independent existence *as other people*, an attitude towards them which is analogous to our feelings towards those we love in life' (pp. 7–8). This, Bayley complains, is a dying habit: 'Characters, it seems, are no longer objects of affection. The literary personality has gone down in the world' (p. 8). Proust, indeed 'Gallic logic' in general, may be blamed for this rash of emotionally deprived literary characters, this tendential fall-off in personality-value. The 'hopelessly competitive plurality of our experience', lovingly endorsed by a Shakespeare, Balzac or Tolstoy, has become subject to formalizing rules, narrowing abstractions, assertive authorial egoisms. Tolerance, personality, contingency are destructively banished from literary texts; into their place flood opinions, monomaniacal absolutisms, tendentious purposes and 'insights'. The grubby hands of ideology have gripped the genial world of nineteenth-century realism – a world whose gratifying lack of ideology is well enough signalled by the fact that it was a world concerned with 'Nature'. 'Nature' is not an ideological concept: it suggests, instead, an involuntary fidelity to what is constant in human affairs, to the universal humours and foibles of men and women, to birth and death, joy and sorrow. It also suggests a certain hierarchy – not, of course, one of social class, although that, Bayley thinks, might 'come into it' – but rather one of human feelings; and Bayley presses home its pre-ideological character by noting its preference for the family rather than for sex, average tranquillity rather than exceptional violence.

Once there was Shakespeare, who 'caught Nature as effortlessly as one might catch a train'; now there is modern fiction, anguished, bullying and self-brooding, uncertain about the

'natural' relationships between 'parents, wives and children'.
The English are on the whole good at Nature, whereas the
Americans are not. Henry James got better at it as he went
along: 'he had to learn, from prolonged sojourn in England, to
take human nature as it came' (p. 273). Sustained by Nature,
which does much of their work for them, the greatest writers can
avoid the shabby 'ideological seriousness of Sartre and the
moderns', manifesting a magnificent refusal to take their art too
seriously. *Joy* is a reliable sign of this: it is lacking in *Ulysses*, which
is 'leaden with its own art, sunk in its richness like a great plum-
cake' (p. 285), but appears as a 'Shakespearian buoyancy', a
'lightheartedness in the exercise of the muscles', in that irresis-
tible child of Nature P. G. Wodehouse. Since 'psychological and
sociological theory' are all the time tediously insistent on erec-
ting barriers between men, joy is a handy way of breaking them
down. But Nature has now deserted the novel: instead of dealing with matters of real moment, the novel now 'importunes us
with awareness of how suburban families live, or negroes, or
intellectuals, or men in camps and prisons, or the young, or the
very old' (p. 290). A little lightheartedness might dispel these
unnatural preoccupations, and one symptom of it will be a
tolerance of disunity and division in fictional form. The authoritarian visions of modernism refuse to embrace the world as it is,
as a muddled, mixed, up-and-down sort of place, callowly concerned as they are to make some coherent sense of things.

Bayley's *penchant* for formal disunity has become more evident
in his subsequent work. It accounts in part for his admiration for
Tolstoy, whose characters, he tells us in *Tolstoy and the Novel*, feel
threatened by their environment when it 'becomes unified and
makes sense' (p. 44). Tolstoy is another child of Nature: his
works reveal that fine, cavalier absent-mindedness in the creation of 'character' which Bayley most admires, as opposed to
despicably knowing what one is about. Such creation in him is
'an involuntary process, a recognition, like stubbing a toe or
shaking a hand' (p. 59). Significantly, then, the title of Bayley's
next work is *The Uses of Division* which, dealing primarily with
Shakespeare, Keats, Dickens, Kipling and Lawrence, opposes
the fetishism of organic unity in the name of 'the felicities of a
genius inherently baffled and divided', and once more appeals
to traditional realism as the custodian of these values. Modernism's abandonment of conventional restraints – continuity,
progress, character, even the 'happy ending' – threatens to

deprive the reader of 'freedom' and 'privacy' by imprisoning him or her more securely within a tyrannical authorial consciousness. There are, however, safeguards against such deprivation: elsewhere in his work, Bayley comments that the main purpose of the class system is to protect the privacy of the individual.

The vigilant reader may by now have begun to detect the presence of certain ideological pressures within Bayley's critical case; but this would be to mistake the character of his work. He is not, he insists in *The Characters of Love*, constructing anything as explicit as a *theory*: 'For any purposes except my present argument my categories and distinctions are probably as unreal as most of the abstract paraphernalia of literary criticism' (p. 33). Like most English literary critics, he is happy to maintain a modestly agnostic, humbly sceptical attitude towards the value of his own pronouncements. By the time of *Tolstoy and the Novel*, indeed, his refusal to be explicit has become considerably more explicit: 'All novelists with an implied or stated theory about the Novel's relation to life are certainly alienated' (p. 58). It is not, naturally, from the standpoint of any 'theory' that Bayley is able to launch this remarkably Olympian judgement; even though he has been arguing since 1957, in book after book, for 'realism' against 'formalism', 'character' against self-consciousness, pluralistic contingency against diagrammatic 'typicality', he is surely not to be convicted of having engaged in anything as cumbrously indelicate as 'theorizing'. Such a charge would understandably come as a surprise to Bayley, since throughout the length of his work he shows little or no interest in what are commonly called 'ideas'. (This does not, however, prevent him from studding his texts with self-consciously placed generalizations, which sometimes read as though they were intended as detachable *bons mots*.) The blankness of his criticism in this respect is matched only by his unflinching suppression of the fact that literary texts are produced from particular historical conditions. His ability to move from Balzac to Dickens, Shakespeare to Pushkin, is facilitated by the fact that he remains for the most part serenely unhampered by the demands of historical specificity. There are references to historical conditions in such works as his book on Tolstoy; but they remain for the most part largely gestural. For all his emphasis upon the routinely 'real' as opposed to the inhumanly formal, his 'reality' remains in this respect an utterly abstract affair.

Bayley's Romantic irrationalism is naturally what motivates his alarm at 'analytical' criticism, with its brusque violation of humanist pieties. For him, the literary text is essentially a *subject*, with a subject's rights to privacy, freedom and interiority. It is not quite that he opens 'literature' up to 'life'; it is rather that he suffuses literature with all the delightful unpredictability of persons, so that excessive analysis of a text becomes equivalent to grievous bodily harm. And just as criticism 'appreciates' rather than dissects the text, so other critics have 'appreciated' Bayley's critical texts, in a graceful spiral of mutual confirmation. 'Love', 'charm', 'sweet-temper': these are among the terms which criticism has seen fit to use of Bayley's work, transforming those texts into 'subjects' in their turn. In the end, his books are made to sound like 'characters' one would think more of marrying than of examining.

'Character', indeed, provides the lynch-pin of Bayley's critical ideology: the metaphysic which he finds in that particular organization of textual significations has survived, in English criticism at least, a half-century or more of philosophical and psychoanalytical reflection. (The powerful, if partial, critique of the notion launched by *Scrutiny* and its associates is thus particularly impressive.) 'Character' provides an assuring centre of unity, yet is essentially unpredictable; it thus offers a parallel to 'Nature', which is at once settled, hierarchical *Lebenswelt* and delightfully disordered. In both cases, it is clear enough that liberal disorder is dependent upon conservative order – upon that customary world of the carelessly taken-for-granted, refuge from the vulgarity of rational argument, within which the gentleman may wear his art and opinions lightly. That the historical supports of such an attitude are, increasingly, available only in Oxbridge is not evident to Bayley, any more than he is aware that his passion for the wonderfully pointless, his shy distaste for the high roads of history, his elevation of the contingent over the central, reflect by and large a view of life from the Oxford senior common room window. The areas of society which make such an existence possible in the first place are not remarkable for the 'joyous equanimity' with which stray details may be tenderly savoured.

The Problem with Hardy

It seems peculiarly appropriate, then, that Bayley's latest work

should be a study of Thomas Hardy. For Hardy is a writer of
'Nature', a major realist, and one who seems notably uncon-
cerned, in his mixed, disparate literary forms, with that pursuit
of organic unity which obsessed a James. Not that Bayley's
interest in such formal dissonances has anything in the least in
common with recent Marxist and semiotic demystifications of
the 'unity' of the literary text. For Pierre Macherey, such texts
suffer internal displacement and disruption by virtue of the
symptomatic absences enforced upon them by the ideological
matrices from which they emerge; it is around these eloquent
silences that the text's various chains of signification begin to
fissure and unravel.[4] Bayley's concept of textual diffusion, by
contrast, is purely empiricist: it is precisely because the text is
'free' of ideological intrusions that it is able to mime all the
lovable muddle of life itself. But Hardy is a less easy writer to
appropriate than he thinks. Indeed Hardy has always proved a
peculiarly *recalcitrant* author for bourgeois criticism; such critics
have been hard put to know quite what to do with him. From the
first full-length *belle-lettristic* study by Lionel Johnson in 1894, to
this latest contribution by Bayley, Hardy has proved a constant
source of embarrassment and unease to the custodians of
'English Literature'. It is not surprising that the title of an
influential essay on Hardy published a decade ago read: 'What
Kind of Fiction Did Hardy Write?';[5] *how to read* Hardy has been
a constant cause for anxiety.

The name 'Thomas Hardy', like that of any other literary
producer, signifies a particular ideological and biographical
formation; but it also signifies the process whereby a certain
set of texts are grouped, constructed, and endowed with the
'coherency' of a 'readable' *oeuvre*. 'Thomas Hardy' denotes that
set of ideological practices through which certain texts, by virtue
of their changing, contradictory modes of insertion into the
dominant 'cultural' and pedagogical apparatuses, are processed,
'corrected' and reconstituted so that a home may be found for
them within a literary 'tradition' which is always the 'imaginary'
unity of the present. But this, in Hardy's case, has been a process
of struggle, outrage and exasperation. He is a major realist, the
creator of 'memorable' scenes and characters; yet he can be
scandalously nonchalant about the 'purity' of orthodox verisimilitude, risking 'coincidence' and 'improbability'. With blunt
disregard for formal consistency, he is ready to articulate form
upon form – to mingle realist narration, classical tragedy, folk-

fable, melodrama, 'philosophical' discourse, social commentary, and by doing so to betray the laborious constructedness of literary production. He is, acceptably enough for a Victorian, something of a 'sage'; yet his fictional meditations assume the offensively palpable form of 'ideas', obtrusive notions too little 'naturalized' by fictional device. He seems, gratifyingly enough, a novelist of the 'human condition'; yet the supposedly dour, fatalistic bent of his art, its refusal to repress the tragic, has had a profoundly unnerving effect upon the dominant critical ideologies, and must be rationalized as 'temperamental gloom' or a home-spun *fin-de-siècle* pessimism. His 'clumsy' provincialism and 'bucolic' quaintness are tolerable features of a 'peasant' novelist; but these elements are too subtly intertwined with a more sophisticated artistry and lack of rustic 'geniality' to permit a confident placing of him as literary Hodge.

A predominant critical strategy has therefore been simply to write him out. Henry James's elegant patronage ('the good little Thomas Hardy') finds its echo in F. R. Leavis and *Scrutiny*, who expel Hardy from the 'great tradition' of nineteenth-century realism. More generally, Hardy criticism may be seen to have developed through four distinct stages, all of which may be permutated in the work of any particular critic. Hegemonic in Hardy's own lifetime was the image of him as anthropologist of Wessex – the charming supplier of rural idylls who sometimes grew a little too big for his literary boots. After the publication of *The Dynasts*, a new critical phase is initiated: Hardy is now, in G. K. Chesterton's notorious comment, 'the village atheist brooding and blaspheming over the village idiot', the melancholic purveyor of late nineteenth-century nihilism. It is this view, conveniently distancing as it is, which on the whole dominates the earlier decades of the century;[6] but throughout the 1940s and 1950s, Hardy's reputation is more or less in decline. An Anglo-Saxon criticism increasingly controlled by formalist, organicist and anti-theoretical assumptions ('New Criticism' in the United States, *Scrutiny* in England) can make no accommodation for Hardy's texts; R. P. Blackmur insisted in 1940 that Hardy's sensibility was irreparably violated by ideas.[7] From the late 1940s onwards, however, there is a notable shift towards a more 'sociological' reading of Hardy. In 1954, an influential study by Douglas Brown focused sentimentally upon the conflict between rural 'warmth' and urban invasion;[8] and four years later John Holloway was reflecting upon Hardy's 'vision of the passing of the old rhythmic order of rural England'.[9] Safely defused by such mythologies, Hardy could now for the first time merit the attention of critics more preoccupied with colour imagery than with the Corn Laws or the Immanent Will; and the 1960s and 1970s have witnessed a stealthy recuperation of his texts by formalist criticism.[10] In the year of the anniversary of his death, then, the critical floodgates stand wide open: he has been phenomenologized,[11] Freudianized,[12] biographized,[13] claimed as the true guardian of 'English' liberal-democratic decencies against the primitivist extremism of emigré modernists.[14]

The Scandal of Hardy's Language

From the beginning, however, the true scandal of Hardy has been his language. If there is one point on which bourgeois criticism has been virtually unanimous, it is that Hardy, regrettably, was really unable to *write*. Since this is rather a major disadvantage for a novelist, it is not surprising that criticism has found such difficulties with his work. Confronted with the 'unrealistic' utterances of his 'rustics' and his irritating 'oddities of style', criticism has been able to do little more than inscribe a 'Could do better' in the margins of Hardy's texts. The *Athenaeum* of 1874, reviewing *Far from the Madding Crowd*, complained that Hardy inserted into the mouths of his labourers 'expressions which we simply cannot believe possible from the illiterate clods whom he describes'. A reviewer of *The Return of the Native*, who protested *en passant* about the 'low social position of the characters', found that Hardy's characters talked as no people had ever talked before: 'The language of his peasants may be Elizabethan, but it can hardly be Victorian.' If the language of the 'peasants' was odd, that of their author was even odder. Again and again, Hardy is berated for his maladroit, 'pretentious' use of Latinisms, neologisms, 'clumsy and inelegant metaphors', technical 'jargon' and philosophical terms. On the one hand, criticism is exasperated by Hardy's apparent inability to write *properly*; on the other hand, it sneers at such attempts as the bumptiousness of a low-bred literary upstart. *Scrutiny* in 1934 bemoaned his 'clumsy aiming at impressiveness'; a doughty defender like Douglas Brown none the less finds his prose 'unserviceable, even shoddy'; and David Lodge informs us that 'we are, while reading him, tantalized by a sense of greatness not quite achieved'.

The ideological secret of these irritabilities is clear. Early Hardy criticism passionately desires that he should be a categorizable chronicler of bumpkins, and protests when such 'rustic realism' is vitiated; later criticism desires to take Hardy seriously as a major novelist, but is forced to acknowledge that, as an 'autodidact', he was never quite up to it. What is repressed in both cases is the fact that the significance of Hardy's writing lies precisely in the *contradictory* constitution of his linguistic practice. The ideological effectivity of his fiction inheres neither in 'rustic' nor 'educated' writing, but in the ceaseless play and tension between the two modes. In this sense, he is a peculiarly interesting illustration of that literary-ideological process which has been analysed in the work of Renée Balibar.[15] 'Literature', Balibar argues, is a crucial part of that process whereby, within the 'cultural' and pedagogical apparatuses, ideologically potent contradictions within a common language (in the case of post-revolutionary France, *'français ordinaire'* and *'français littéraire'*) are constituted and reproduced. The 'literary' is an ensemble of linguistic practices, inscribed in certain institutions, which produce appropriate 'fictional' and ideological effects, and in doing so contribute to the maintenance of linguistic class divisions. Limited though such an analysis is by its residual 'sociologism', and fragile though it may be when exported from the specific pedagogical conditions of bourgeois France, it nevertheless has a marked applicability to Hardy. It is not a question of whether Hardy wrote 'well' or 'badly'; it is rather a question of the ideological disarray which his fictions, consciously or not, are bound to produce within a criticism implacably committed to the 'literary' as yardstick of maturely civilized consciousness. This is not to suggest that the question of the aesthetic effects of Hardy's texts can be reduced to the question of their ideological impact; that a text may embarrass a dominant ideology is by no means the criterion of its aesthetic effectivity, though it may be a component of it. But in Hardy's case, these two issues are imbricated with a peculiar closeness.

The only critic who has understood this fact is, characteristically, Raymond Williams, who finds in the very letter of Hardy's texts the social and ideological crisis which those texts are constructed to negotiate.[16] Williams, indeed, has been one of the most powerfully demystifying of Hardy critics, brilliantly demolishing the banal mythology of a 'timeless peasantry' dislocated by 'external' social change. But his text, symptomatically, has had little general influence; and the same may be said of Roy Morrell's masterly study,[17] which tackled and defeated several decades of belief that Hardy was a 'fatalist'. Despite these interventions, criticism remains worried by the precise status of Hardy's 'realism'; and it is not difficult to see why. For the contradictory nature of his textual practice cannot but throw into embarrassing relief those ideologically diverse constituents of fiction which it is precisely fiction's task to conceal; it is by 'not writing properly' that he lays bare the device.

John Bayley, however, is typically undisturbed by Hardy's 'disunity'; indeed it is precisely this, among other things, which attracts Bayley to him. In his introduction to the New Wessex edition of *Far from the Madding Crowd*, Bayley writes perceptively of that peculiarly Hardyesque diversity 'in which the separate ingredients seem quite unconscious of each other's presence', and recognizes the necessary recalcitrance of such fiction for the remorselessly 'organizing' intelligence of a Leavis or Trilling.[18] Pierre Macherey, however, has pointed out that the familiar bedfellow of 'normative' criticism is empiricism: the one seeks to 'correct' the text against a ghostly model of what it 'might have been', the other sinks itself tolerantly into the text 'as it is'. Neither method is thereby able to displace the work into its material determinants – to accomplish the difficult dialectical feat of 'refusing' the text's phenomenal presence while acknowledging that such a presence is *necessary* and *determinate*.

Bayley's Sublimation

Bayley, accordingly, offers us in his latest book not a corrective criticism, but a placid, middle-brow endorsement of Hardyesque 'diversity' and 'incongruity' as a valid reflection of the ups and downs of 'life', with its co-existence of 'absurdity, felicity and sublimity'. Hardy's characters can be 'wonderfully ridiculous' as well as deeply moving; his fictions are comfortably traditional, but at the same time not too distressingly 'literary' or *voulu*. We should not, in short, be too harsh on him: his very 'failures' can be savoured, given enough critical charity. His 'lukewarmness' can become addictive; he does not particularly mind 'falling flat', but then that is pretty much how life is; his very 'weakness' is 'deep down, reassuring'. The utter tedium of Hardy's novels is precisely the source of their unique charm: this is my caricature, rather than a quotation from Bayley, but it perhaps suggests just how Bayley's essay represents the ultimate, logical 'processing' of the 'text-functions' we know as 'Thomas Hardy'. Aesthetic 'weaknesses' are still identified by the traditional criteria of bourgeois criticism, but then, in that very act, complacently forgiven; 'disunity' is tolerated, not as an index of the ideological-linguistic torsions within which those texts struggle, but as a consoling mimetic image of 'life'. The final emasculation of Thomas Hardy is modestly, courteously carried through.

It cannot be achieved, however, without a drastic rewriting of the received Hardy canon. For Bayley, Hardy starts to go wrong somewhere midway through *The Mayor of Casterbridge*. The earlier work manifests a 'naturalness, a current of vitality and seeming joy in creation' which palls as we approach those later, intransigently 'ideological' novels, *Tess* and *Jude*. Hardy's 'rich equanimity', his genial Shakespearian expansiveness, then begins to fall prey to the 'deliberated' and 'doctrinaire'.[19] *Far from the Madding Crowd* displays an accepting 'joy' which 'as Matthew Arnold said can calm and satisfy us as no other [power] can';[20] but there is clearly neither 'joy' nor ideological sedative in Hardy's later fictions, and they must consequently be unobtrusively relegated, with reservations, to the realm of the 'artificial' and 'theoretical'. Any such rewriting of Hardy is, naturally, an ideological gesture of the most flagrantly significant kind. What it does, in effect, is exactly to repeat the gestures of Hardy's contemporary critics, who wished he would confine himself to the woods rather than blunder into drawing-rooms. It is quite clear that *Jude the Obscure*, for Bayley as much as for the outraged Mrs Oliphant (if for rather different reasons), is still an unacceptable text. Naturally so: for not only does it see, and see through, the dominant ideological apparatuses of Victorian England (religion, education, the family), but it also threatens to see through a related ideological formation: literary realism. No 'realist' account of that novel – a novel itself obsessed with writing, production, literacy, representation – is able to take its pressure; no stretching of 'verisimilitude' can domesticate such calculated 'improbabilities' as Sue leaping out of the bedroom window to escape Phillotson, or Jude drunkenly reciting the Nicene Creed in an Oxford pub. With *Jude the Obscure*, the 'realist' Hardy turns and rounds on his readership; and we have the historical record of how they, in turn, rounded upon and

savaged him. John Bayley, committed as he is to a naive mimeticism, does not examine these aspects of the novel; instead, he
tells us that Sue Bridehead has an 'irresolution . . . distorted out
of its natural form by the ideas and tendencies of the time that
Hardy seeks to impose'.[21] It is entirely logical that an apparently
'innocent' aesthetic ideology, which values fiction for showing us
life 'as it is', should be coupled with this callous anti-feminism.

The period of Bayley's early critical production is the time in
which, by and large, 'New Criticism' held sway in the United
States and *Scrutiny* in England. It is not difficult to read Bayley's
work as an implicit riposte to this phenomenon – as the rearguard action of a partially by-passed Oxford humanism, com-
pounding both liberal and reactionary elements. Leavis is
certainly the critic whom Bayley refers to most frequently; and
the appearance of a lengthy apologia for Shakespeare's *Othello* in
The Characters of Love, following on Leavis's trenchant interro-
gation of the play's status in *Scrutiny*, is surely not fortuitous.
Indeed that book can be read as a deliberate attempt to mount a
counter-attack on Leavis's criticism – besides the case of Shakespeare, there is the effort to salvage James's *The Golden Bowl* from
Leavis's rejection of it as decadent formalism. Bayley and Leavis
share a similar empiricism, a penchant for 'realism' as a paradigm case of literary production, and a hostility to 'theory'. But
Leavis's devotion to close critical analysis, aspects of modernism
and 'significant organization' are precisely, for Bayley, the ideological enemy. Leavis's aesthetic represents a curious cross-breed
of formalism and mimeticism, as his ideological position com-
pounds organicist collectivism and liberal individualism. Bayley
seeks a parallel fusion in his coupling of 'character' and 'Nature'
(Shakespeare's characters exist 'both in themselves and as parts
of a natural structure'); but since his 'Nature' is essentially an
empiricist concept (in contrast to Leavis's quasi-metaphysical
notion of 'Life'), he pleads for mimetic rather than formalist
modes in its literary embodiment. Leavis's organicist nostalgia is
one kind of idealist response to industrial capitalism; Bayley's
anti-organicism is another, identifying all 'totalities' either as
'ideological' and authoritarian, or as the imposed, monomaniacal visions of an errant modernistic individualism. In place
of this 'existential' individualism, Bayley offers the more traditional liberal individualism associated with the concept of
'character' – a concept which, as I have indicated, depends upon
essentially *un*liberal notions of order, hierarchy, convention and

custom – in a word, upon a Burkeian trust in 'Nature'. This combination of liberal-individualist and reactionary components is undoubtedly one source of Bayley's ideological power: he seems to satisfy at once the demands of a patrician conservatism and of an exploratory, agnostic individualism. The cult of 'character' re-surfaces in the late 1950s and 1960s to challenge, in the name of both traditionalist 'appreciation' aesthetics and what John Goode has termed 'neo-liberalism',[22] a criticism which seems intent on deconstructing the unitary self into 'themes' and 'image-patterns'. The 'technocracy' of the 'New Criticism', itself an effect of the 'end-of-ideologies' era, is seen by 'neo-liberalism' as the latest ideological threat to humanist values.

Rearguard action though it was, the force of this critical ideology should not be underestimated. While Europe was passing through its major critical systems – classical philology, phenomenology, hermeneutics, psychoanalysis, structuralism – English criticism managed to survive essentially unscathed, so deep were its roots in a commonplace philistine empiricism.[23] It was such philistine empiricism which powered the 'neo-liberal' enterprise, and continues to do so today. For what is literature if not the very home of the contingent, of the uniquely experienced, the last, gloriously untidy refuge from an increasingly 'uniform' and 'ideological' world? English criticism is already coyly flirting with various forms of more elaborate aesthetic theory; but it is unable to effect a break with the still extremely powerful ideology which Bayley's work signifies. The ideological significance of Bayley's criticism might in the end come down to this – that his position is almost painful in its theoretical paucity, but that it is legitimated by the sheer force of his personal sensitivity and perceptiveness as a standpoint to be respected and adopted. In this sense, part of Bayley's task is to ratify English criticism's inability to confront its own intellectual nullity. That this is so was well demonstrated by his generous obituary notice on F. R. Leavis, in which he remarked on the fact that Leavis had 'marvellous taste'.[24] One might as well congratulate Gramsci on his common sense.

4.

The Idealism of American Criticism

From the mid-1930s to the late 1940s, American literary theory fell under the sway of a curious hybrid of critical technocracy and Southern religious-aesthetic conservatism known as the 'New Criticism'.[1] Offspring of the failed agrarian politics of the 1930s, and aided by the collapse of a Stalinized Marxist criticism, New Criticism yoked the 'practical critical' techniques of I. A. Richards and F. R. Leavis to the re-invention of the 'aesthetic life' of the old South in the delicate textures of the poem. Ravaged by scientific rationalism, the 'world's body'[2] had been shamefully denuded; it was now the task of criticism to restore that sensuous particularity, resisting the remorseless abstraction of experience with its cognitions of poetic ambiguity. But since a mere Romanticism was no longer ideologically plausible, New Criticism couched its nostalgic anti-scientism in toughly 'objectivist' terms: the poem had the gemlike hardness of an 'urn' or 'icon', a structure of complex tensions cut loose from the flux of history and authorial intention, autotelic and unparaphrasable. Critical analysis, then, mimed the reifying habits of industrial capitalism even as it resisted them; 'disinterested' aesthetic contemplation parodied the very scientism it was out to challenge. If the *texture* of the poem eluded rationalist enquiry, its functionalist *structure* held contradictions in harmonious balance. As a provisional unification of responses, an eirenic interplay of opposing beliefs, poetry promised to scoop out a contemplative space within the Cold War. In response to the reification of society, New Criticism triumphantly reified the poem.

Northrop Frye as Proto-structuralist

For perhaps a decade after the demise of New Critical theory, New Critical practice lingered on. Indeed as Richard Ohmann has shrewdly suggested, it was a practice eminently suited to the pedagogical conditions of post-war America, where the probing of an isolated literary fragment offered a convenient way of coping with a rising university population.[3] But New Criticism proved in the end too particularist, too modest and unmethodical to provide the kind of apology for poetry which a monopoly capitalist age demanded. What was needed was a critical method which, while vigorously preserving the formalist, anti-rationalist bent of New Criticism, fashioned it into a global theory of rigorously 'scientific' proportions. The answer, in a word, was the Canadian Northrop Frye's mighty totalization of literary genres, *Anatomy of Criticism*, published in 1957 but gestating since the New Critical decline of the late 1940s.

It is here that Frank Lentricchia takes up the narrative, in his invaluable survey of that rich gamut of idealisms, all the way from Frye to Harold Bloom, which has served as modern American criticism.[4] Frye's perverse achievement was to press the two contradictory thrusts of New Criticism to a parodic extreme. New Critical objectivism became an aggressive literary positivism, eschewing evaluation for a cumbersome system of mythological categories into which any individual work could be briskly slotted. Ransom's aestheticist nostalgia mushroomed to a full-blooded formalism, a neo-Kantian disdain for literary cognition and referentiality in a world where myth alone could transcend the torture chamber of history. If Frye is in some sense a proto-structuralist in his pathological monism, he is perhaps in another sense a proto-post-structuralist: for at the centre of his system wells a transcendental lack or desire, source and impulse of all structuration, which will be staunched only in the kingdom of heaven. It is true that this conception in Frye is strictly speaking more Sartrean than post-structuralist, since desire is for him an originary centre, untrammelled by the discourses to which it gives rise. But the curious unity in his work of a structuralist scientism and debased 'post-structuralist' Romanticism is nevertheless striking. It is a savage irony that he first encountered both 'system' and 'desire' in his early study of William Blake, *Fearful Symmetry* (1947).

Lentricchia, in an otherwise excellent account, does not quite pursue these parallels. Nor does he attend to Frye's work since the *Anatomy*, in which the ideological motivations of that earlier text become flagrantly clear. In *The Stubborn Structure* (1970) and elsewhere, Frye explicitly advances literature, in the manner of Matthew Arnold, I. A. Richards, F. R. Leavis and the New Critics, as both surrogate for and complement to science, an essential palliative for the displacement of religious ideology. (Like several of the New Critical luminaries, Frye is a professing Christian – indeed a clergyman.) Yet the totalizing drive of a utopian mythology, necessary to loosen the tightening grip of Cold War ideologies, is at odds with liberal pluralism – is, indeed, in some danger of formally reproducing the very ideologies it is supposed to spurn. In *The Critical Path* (1971), Frye will consequently strike a cerebral balance between conservative 'myths of concern' and liberal 'myths of freedom', correcting authoritarian tendencies with the latter and political irresponsibility with the former. The only mistake – that of the revolutionary – is to misinterpret myths of freedom as historically realizable goals. The New Critical dilemma – textual pluralism, structural integration – is reproduced rather than resolved.

In so far as Frye's myths are ontologically grounded, they contrast with existentialist 'fictions' – those mental products ironically aware of their own arbitrariness. Lentricchia accordingly passes from Fryc to Sartre (a significant influence on the American critics Murray Krieger and Paul de Man), relating the bland neo-Kantianism of the one to the tragic epistemology of the other. If Frye's fastidious aestheticism can posit the external world only as horrifying facticity, Sartre's existentialism is in pursuit of an elusive real which is nevertheless paradoxically granted determinacy over consciousness. So it is that Sartre's *The Psychology of the Imagination* scornfully devalues the 'image' as mere congealed unreality, at the same stroke as it celebrates the imagination as a negating – and so emancipatory – surge of consciousness. It is clear at any rate that by the time we arrive at Sartre and Wallace Stevens that glib counterposing of coherent fiction to chaotic reality, which is, as Lentricchia remarks, 'one of modernism's characterizing shibboleths', has become entrenched as the purest critical cliché.

The Misadventures of American Criticism

It was fortunate for American criticism, then, that Georges

Poulet of the phenomenological 'Geneva School' had just stepped off the boat, arriving at Johns Hopkins University in 1952.
If Frye's 'structuralist' decentring of both author and reader
threatened a traditional humanism, phenomenology was always
at hand to reinstate the subject. Poulet, as Lentricchia points out,
was never really a phenomenologist – his epistemology is more
Cartesian than Husserlian – and the subject he reinstated was of
a peculiarly submissive kind, bowed in humble Heideggerian
fashion to the ineffable *quiditas* of its literary object. Yet his
criticism pulled off the improbable trick of at once retrieving the
contemplative subject from a contaminating world, and allowing
it to be 'opened', 'filled' and 'invaded', in latently sexual fashion,
by the irresistibly seductive text. The subject submits to discourse, but without dispersal; unshackled by history, 'withdrawn
from any power which might determine it from the outside',[5] it
elicits the eidetic essence of the literary work through an imaginary identification with it. Criticism becomes an enormous
Lacanian ego, an ensemble of imaginary identifications unscathed by the symbolic order. Whereas New Criticism offered
the poetic artefact as touchstone of authentic value, Poulet
offers the epistemology of reading itself, that erotic coupling of
subject and object everywhere absent in 'exterior' reality. Enthused by this monogamous vision, the young J. Hillis Miller,
now *doyen* of the Yale Derrideans, became self-appointed
American propagandist of the Geneva School. Criticism was to
spurn the squalidly historical, reject evaluation, and sink within
the phenomenological essence of the literary text. After his
Derridean baptism, Miller continued to defend Poulet by sug-
gesting, remarkably, that this self-confessed Cartesian was an
unwitting member of the one true church, a deconstructionist
malgré lui-même.

In 1975, the American importation of European literary
theory boomed with the appearance of Jonathan Culler's
Structuralist Poetics, a text designed to render Parisian radicalism
safe for the Free World. Frank Lentricchia is particularly alert to
the tactics whereby Culler's sweetly reasonable survey, with its
violent depoliticization and silent elisions, delivered a defused
time-bomb to the American academy. The embarrassing self-
abasement of a Poulet gives way in Culler's work to a thrusting
will to textual 'mastery', a technocratic obsession with readerly
'competence'. Notwithstanding its ambiguous appeal to the
reader's codified constructions of the text, Culler's structuralism

is largely compatible with New Criticism. It served chiefly to lend that anaemic formalism a new lease of life, reducing the philosophical scandal of structuralism to a technical armoury in the service of the enduring object Literature. Yet as Jacques Derrida would no doubt argue, no method can be deformed without being always already deformable; the fault lay as much in the text of structuralism as in Culler's reading of it. In a rapid, penetrating critique of structuralism from Saussure to Barthes, Lentricchia shows that the latter's *Le plaisir du texte*, with its anarchistic opposition of *'jouissance'* and 'ideology', naively consummates a crippling repression of history born with Saussure's suspension of the referent and Husserl's bracketing of the empirical object.

The most fundamental issues in modern literary theory are on the whole epistemological ones. It is to this root – recently extirpated by some English theorists, but curiously weedlike in its tenacity – that many questions of meaning and value, intention and effect may be unravelled. Paramount among these issues today is the question of the determinacy of the literary text, its power to organize, constrain and disseminate meanings. The history of modern American criticism is among other things a rhythm of restless oscillation between a Heideggerian servility to the literary object, and an anarchic assertion of readers' power over this dominative discourse. Perhaps both positions answer to enduring motifs of American ideology: the first to a 'frontier' consciousness that Nature was there before we were; the second to a euphoric individualism which sucks all Nature into its maw. But the two cases are secretly complicit. There are times when the work's historicity may best be refused by fetishism: invested with all the dense material force of history itself, literature plugs the intolerable gap where history should be, flaunting itself as an erotic alternative to social practice. There are other times when the repression of the work's historicity means dematerializing the work itself, reducing it to a mirror in which the critic may find obediently reflected back his or her own interpretative strategies. Such is the position of the leading American reception theorist Stanley Fish, a literary interpreter who, as Lentricchia poker-facedly points out, appears to deny that there is anything to be interpreted. But it is also the increasingly fashionable case of the Yale post-structuralists (Paul de Man, Geoffrey Hartman, J. Hillis Miller and to some extent Harold Bloom), whose recycling of the work of Jacques

Derrida for Ivy League consumption may be seen as the latest instance of US cultural imperialism. Despite their Nietzschean iconoclasm, the Yale Derrideans, are, as Lentricchia suggests, 'traditionalism's last formalist buttress'. Their celebration of the 'groundlessness' and self-destruction of discourse, its ambiguous eluding of historical constraint, depends on the bare-faced device of transforming history itself to 'text', sheer amorphous stuff awaiting the latest yarn-spinner. In this they are apostates to their master, who has publicly acknowledged, perhaps a little late in the day, the determinate forces of author, intention, productive matrix and historical conditions in the construction of meaning, and has vigorously denied that he is a pluralist.[6]

In a coruscating analysis of the work of Paul de Man – whose uncle Henri, incidentally, crops up in Gramsci's *Prison Notebooks* – Lentricchia shows how it is no accident that the Yale Derrideans set out, by and large, as Romanticists. De Man's rhetorical indeterminacies, at once vertiginous and complacent, belong to a linguistic free play whose dark shadow is the Romantic despair of ever capturing the thing within the word. Discourse and being are mutually exclusive; and de Man, caught like the rest of us in a Hobson's choice between them, is forced with strained euphoria to abandon the latter and cling to the former. If there is something a little laboured about his hedonism, there is also something rather suspect about his pluralism, through which a suppressed authoritarianism occasionally peeps. An 'end-of-ideologies' thinker, de Man has launched one of the most aggressive, dogmatic ideological movements which American literary theory has witnessed for some time.

De Man's Nietzschean epistemology, as Lentricchia points out, lands him in unavoidable contradiction. There cannot be a universal object named literature, yet rhetorical 'undecidability' is the essence of all literature. Although no discourse is decidable, criticism can apparently decide that some texts are undecidable. No critical interpretation is truer than any other, yet some interpretations 'come closer' to the literary work. Tricked by the ruses of tropology, the mind does not even 'know whether it is doing or not doing something',[7] but de Man, writing in an ineradicably tropological discourse, appears to know that it does not know this. Since there is no real difference between critical and literary discourse – both are mere self-cancelling rhetorics – criticism is inevitably forced to disown the knowledge it inevitably claims, in a gesture banally reminiscent of traditional liberalism. For Harold Bloom, de Man's *confrère*, criticism is in competition with its literary object, a creative misreading of a literary text which is itself a creative misreading of another text. Bloom's particular brand of 'intertextuality' – poems are born out of anxious Oedipal rivalry with a castrating, precursor poem, which they disarm by a systematic distortion – retains a Romantic humanism distasteful to de Man: literature as a dynastic battle of lonely heroes, aspiring to topple their ancestors. Its Freudianism is the dark shadow cast by such humanism in a post-Romantic epoch, and as a modern theory it would hardly be palatable without it; yet for all its bristling array of psycho-analytic devices, it is, as Lentricchia suggests, eminently suited to American 'Great Books' courses. With Bloom, author of a major work on Blake, we recircle to the mythopoeic vision and enclosed literary universe of Northrop Frye – only now through the passage of a post-structuralism which has rendered such consolations troublesome and ambiguous. The myths of the autonomous imagination have become, in Bloom, the myth of the autonomous imagination.

In a chapter on the traditionalist critic E. D. Hirsch, Lentricchia rebuffs Hirsch's attempt to stop the relativist rot through a return to fixed authorial meaning by exposing the flaws of the Husserlian epistemology on which it is based.[8] Traditionalists like Hirsch, he argues, 'are not wrong to insist that a power of determinacy may play within discourse, but merely mistaken in locating such a power in a freely individual authorial intention which seeks to impose itself upon language from "outside"'.[9] Here, indeed, is the core of Lentricchia's own case. New Critical autonomy and post-structuralist free play both thrive on an ignorance of discourse as *power* – as a semantic field organized, bounded and articulated by the historical forces with which it is furrowed. The hero of *After the New Criticism* is accordingly our contemporary ideologist of pan-powerism, Michel Foucault. The book is by no means blind to the defects of Foucault, whose political pronouncements have rarely been less than ambiguous and, on occasions, fatuous. It refuses the 'fashionable and casual historical despair of contemporary criticism', insisting that an abandonment of the transcendental subject need not entail the abandonment of historical knowledge. Yet Lentricchia's use of Foucault remains somewhat decisionist: disturbed by his more blatant epistemological excesses, he none the less 'choose(s) to set aside' these features for more felicitous ones. Whether or not

Foucault's work will really admit of such *découpage* perhaps remains to be seen. The American intellectual left have found in Foucault a convenient instrument for belabouring Derrida; but such recourse is in part necessitated by the weakness of a native Marxism. It is itself a symptom of political crisis that, in a work which could certainly be described as Marxian, Marx himself receives a mere three glancing references and Marxism none whatsoever. Vigilantly aware of ideological determinations, Lentricchia leans heavily upon Foucault, who has no time for the concept of ideology.

The Contrast with English Criticism

The narrative which this book has to deliver is undoubtedly grim. From Cleanth Brooks to Harold Bloom,[10] American literary criticism develops by way of inventing new idealist devices for the repression of history. Yet this very resourcefulness is in its perverse way impressive. Taken together, Ransom, Frye, Poulet, Krieger, Hirsch, de Man and Bloom (to give a mere handful of salient names) constitute a formidably rich and intricate corpus of literary theory. If they are often wrong, they are for the most part subtly and productively so. No greater contrast could be provided with the condition of literary theory in Britain. Since the demise of *Scrutiny*, almost nothing of major importance has appeared in the field. The leading British cultural theorist of the century – Raymond Williams – was only in his very early writing a 'literary critic', and would now consciously refuse the appellation. The most familiar critical names – Donoghue, Ricks, Bayley, Lodge, Bradbury, Bergonzi – are known less for their criticism than for their literary journalism or comic novels. No one ˊof their critical studies can match those of their American counterparts in either substance or flair. The sole exception to this stricture, in terms of critical acumen and theoretical insight, is Frank Kermode. The departure of George Steiner from Cambridge to Geneva was an ominous symptom of English parochialism. English criticism is littered with pathbreaking works by critics who never really fulfilled their promise: L. C. Knight's *Drama and Society in the Age of Jonson*, Ian Watt's *The Rise of the Novel*, Arnold Kettle's *Introduction to the English Novel*, Richard Hoggart's *The Uses of Literacy*, are signal instances. This may be partly a matter of material conditions: the American academic is expected to produce, in a way in which those who win English chairs of literature on the strength of a single major work are not. The productivity of Raymond Williams – some twenty works in a period of thirty years, many of stunning originality – threatens to eclipse that of his English colleagues taken together. But it is equally a question of ambience: inertly traditionalist though the main reaches of the American literary academy still are, it remains true that the dynamism and intensity of American theoretical debate, its intellectual generosity, conceptual ambitiousness and openness to European influence, provide a durable context for significant work. Frank Lentricchia's study is not merely a record of that context; it is a remarkable product of it.

Epoch and Genre

The American absorption of Sartre and structuralism conspired with the presence of the emigré Frankfurt school to produce in the early 1970s what is now a lively resurgence of Marxist criticism. The ur-text of that renaissance was the publication in 1971 of the elegant, authoritative *Marxism and Form*, by Fredric Jameson – himself, significantly, the earlier author of what remains one of the most rewarding studies of Sartre.[11] With the publication of his latest book, *The Political Unconscious: Narrative as a Socially Symbolic Act*,[12] Jameson completes a triptych of works (the forerunners were *Marxism and Form* and *The Prison-House of Language* (1972)) which establishes him as without question the foremost American Marxist critic, and one of the leading literary theorists of the Anglophone world. *The Political Unconscious* has all of Jameson's now familiar strengths: his global range of literary and theoretical allusion, his combination of an insistently 'structural' habit of mind with a rich responsiveness to textual detail, his prestidigitatory ability to produce striking, original insights of his own out of received notions. Jameson composes rather than writes his texts, and his prose, here as in previous works, carries an intense libidinal charge, a burnished elegance and unruffled poise, which allows him to sustain a rhetorical lucidity through the most tortuous, intractable materials.

The Political Unconscious, despite its dazzling range of allusion to contemporary thinkers (Habermas, Baudrillard, Deleuze,

Hjelmslev, Greimas, Genovese, Foucault and others), is far from a fashionable book. Its informing philosophical principle is that 'the human adventure is one': that history has 'the unity of a single great collective story', whose names are the succession of modes of production and forms of class struggle. Its cognate critical assumption is that there exists one privileged, perdurable habit of consciousness – 'the central function or *instance* of the human mind' – whose name is narrative. These are not doctrines likely to delight the various sub-cultures of Anglo-phone post-Marxism. In this work, Jameson boldly emerges as what indeed he was plainly enough all along: a shamelessly unreconstructed Hegelian Marxist, for whom after all the Derridean dust has settled and schizoid babble subsided, *History and Class Consciousness* remains the definitive text. He was never divided between that and the structuralist interests of *The Prison-House of Language*: the sympathies of that work were those of a 'totalizing' Lukácsian for whom structural thought is inherently congenial. Its inwardness with structuralism was as much a matter of style as of belief: the effect of a hermeneutical criticism which, while never relinquishing its own rolling rhetorical inflections, merges with its object to the point where it is sometimes difficult to decide whether what we are witnessing is exegesis or critique.

The first third of Jameson's book is devoted to a lengthy meditation entitled 'On Interpretation'. Political criticism, he claims, far from offering an optional auxiliary to other methods, is the absolute horizon of all interpretation, within which these partial alternative modes assume their subordinate place. Marxism figures as the 'master-code' within which literary texts are to be rewritten by criticism: Hegelian 'mediation' may be redefined semiotically as a 'transcoding' operation whereby a single discourse can analyse and articulate two or more objects (text and history, for example) simultaneously. But this is not the spurious symmetry of Goldmannian 'homologies': the relations between text and 'social sub-text' are the dynamic ones of 'production, projection, compensation, repression, displacement and the like'. Literary works are to be grasped not primarily as objective structures but as symbolic practices, strategies for providing formal or imaginary 'solutions' to unresolvable social contradictions. Criticism shows up such strategies by reinscribing the text in order to show that up, in turn, as a rewriting of a prior historical or ideological sub-text – a sub-text which is by no means identical with some common-sense external reality, but which must always be (re)constructed after the fact. The paradox of the sub-text, indeed, is that it is at once object and projection of the text: the literary work produces its own sub-text, drawing the real into its linguistic texture, at the very moment that it stands operationally over against it. The peculiarity of fiction is that 'it brings into being that very situation to which it is also, at one and the same time, a reaction'.[13] It is thus always open to criticism to relinquish either end of this difficult dialectic: to veer, in short, into either formalism or reflectionism.

So far, however, we have remained within the text. The next operation is to grasp the text as belonging to a particular 'ideologeme', as a *parole* of the vaster *langue* of class discourse, a symbolic move in a strategic ideological confrontation between the classes. In a third and final operation, these discourses will themselves be situated within the organizing unity of a mode of production. Jameson's originality, however, is that he does not leave this latter term as an inert extra-textual object, to be relegated to the economists; for the succession and synchrony of modes of production is also a sequence and composite of dominant codes or sign-systems (magic and mythic narrative, kinship, religion, 'politics' in its narrower sense, relations of personal domination, commodity fetishism) which will fix the outer boundaries of historical genre. At this level, then, we are speaking of the individual text grasped as a complex field of force in which 'messages' emitted by sign-systems peculiar to distinct modes of production may enter into determinate contradiction with one another. Such 'messages' are nothing less than the ideology of form itself; for form, as Jameson sees, is immanently an ideology in its own right. The imprint of a mode of production on the literary work, then, can be traced in the host of conflicting generic messages (some cultural survivals, some contemporary, others anticipatory) of which the work is composed.

What Jameson has done, in fact, is to rescue the academicist category of genre for a materialist criticism. Genre, he persuades us, is an indispensable mediation between immanent textual analysis, the history of cultural forms and the evolution of social life. Yet it is, of course, an historically stubborn affair, persistent across different modes of production, and the question then becomes how the ideological messages immanent to the form itself are refashioned in its various historical realizations.

In a chapter entitled 'Magical Narratives', we are given a brief history of romance, from Chrétien de Troyes to Hugo von Hofmannsthal, which suggests how this issue might be tackled. And in so far as romance involves wish fulfilment, it rejoins that other spinal theme of the study, the psychical mechanisms (displacement, projection, condensation and the like) whereby literary texts strive to negotiate the unruly materials they call up. Whereas conventional psychoanalytic criticism sees fantasy as primal and the ideological as mere secondary revision or rationalization, Jameson concludes an absorbing chapter on realism and desire in Balzac by boldly inverting this priority: Balzac's textual ideology is neither repression nor expression of his works' unconscious dynamics, but their very enabling possibility – 'those conceptual conditions of possibility or narrative presuppositions which one must "believe" . . . in order for the subject successfully to tell itself this particular day-dream'.[14] It is for this reason that, as Lukács recognizes but falsely explains, the ideology of Balzac's texts is so askew to their author's historical beliefs: the emergent fantasy of the novels, aspiring to subvert the political reality-principle, must posit the most elaborate ideological obstacles to its own gratification.

Critical Pluralism and Its Limits

I have suggested that Jameson is essentially an Hegelian Marxist; but it would be equally plausible to see him as an unashamed Marxist pluralist. His typical intellectual habit is to ponder two or more apparently incompatible theses, show how each is symptomatic of a real historical condition, and thus accommodate or even dissolve the contradictions between them. So it is that, in a discussion of Althusser, he will plump for neither 'mechanical', 'expressive' nor 'structural' causality: all in their way answer to aspects of historical reality. For Marxist criticism to bulldoze alternative approaches would for Jameson be the merest idealism: for these other methods (myth-criticism, structuralism, semiotics, theology and the rest) must be understood as so many responses to an objectively reified history, zones of discourse which display a 'faithful consonance with this or that local law of a fragmented social life'. Marxist criticism is not to ignore these sectors but to go right through them and emerge on the other side, in that unsurpassable political dimension from which, retrospectively, these partial operations may be radically historicized. It is not a question of dismissing, say, A. J. Greimas's 'semantic rectangle' as binary rather than dialectical: it is a matter of putting such structuralism to work, as Jameson does impressively in his account of Balzac, in order to unmask it as the very model of ideological closure. For having assumed Greimas's system of logical permutations as an heuristic technique, it will then be possible to see which permutations the empirical text does not in fact realize, which possibilities have failed to become manifest in the logic of the narrative, and why such repression is for this text ideologically essential.

The strengths of Jameson's pluralism are undoubted. Behind his conception of the literary text as symbolic act, it is possible to detect at least five, incongruously diverse sources: the Freudian theory of neuroses; the Lévi-Straussian analysis of myth; the literary theory of Kenneth Burke; the 'speech act' philosophy of J. L. Austin; and Hans-Georg Gadamer's hermeneutical impulse to reconstruct the 'question' to which a given literary text is an 'answer'. If Jameson is equably at home with the caustic, demystificatory discourse of Freud, Althusser and Macherey, he is equally won by the generous humanism of an Ernst Bloch, and indeed seeks in his conclusion to maintain the faintly scandalous thesis that any form of class consciousness whatsoever, including fascism, conceals in its very collectivism a utopian moment. Such pluralism is in general more characteristic of the American intellectual left than it is of the sectarian British, where the post-Althusserian knows in advance that there is nothing in Adorno. Jameson, after all, is the Yale colleague of Paul de Man and Harold Bloom, and the influence – even if it is regrettably one-way – certainly shows through. But such pluralism is not easily separable, in the American intellectual climate, from a certain native pragmatism and eclecticism. Who but Jameson, for example, would grandly remark that he feels no great inconsistency between the concept of totality and a 'symptomal' attention to structural discontinuities? It is true, and striking, that his practical analyses – not least his admirable critique of Conrad, in some ways the book's centrepiece – take such oppositions casually in their stride; but if he is telling us that Lukács and Macherey are theoretical bed-fellows within some more global vision, he is certainly telling us news. The truth is that Jameson's pluralism is not quite as pluralist as it appears. For one thing, it has certain definite limits: it does not, at least in this work, seem to stretch to the concept of gender. That, on any political or theoretical reckoning, is a grave blindspot indeed. For another thing, it is rather deceptive: it is sometimes less a matter of working through theoretical challenges to Hegelian Marxism than of rather comfortingly folding them back into the unaltered problematic. Jameson sees shrewdly enough how Deleuzean celebrations of the 'molecular' are unavoidably parasitic on some pre-assumed ideology of unification which it is their mission to shatter and rebuke; but he stubbornly refuses to contemplate the converse possibility, one flamboyantly entertained by Jacques Derrida, that our conceptions of totality may have been all along more parasitic upon some primordial movement of difference than we care to admit. For Jameson, it would appear, everything can in the end be rerouted back through Hegel, who must be accused, not of 'some irremediable vice of "idealism"', but merely of not having been historically able to become Marx. If Jameson is launching upon the world the somewhat startling thesis that Hegel was not after all an idealist, one would expect a little more discussion of this matter to ensue. It is not that he is wrong in believing that, once we have deconstructed, we must reassemble; indeed Frank Lentricchia argues persuasively that Derrida's project, mistaken by some disciples as sheerly 'negative', is in fact a ground-clearing operation for reconstruction. It is just that Jameson seems to have a rather greater assurance that we will ultimately find ourselves standing in roughly the same place than had, perhaps, Walter Benjamin and Theodor Adorno. This assumption of an unproblematized *master*-code, and the book's failure to engage with feminism, are perhaps more related than might at first appear.

Marxist Criticism and the Class Struggle

What is clear at any rate is that in all the heady negotiations over the past decade between Marxism, semiotics and psychoanalysis, Marxism has been the first casualty; as the British class struggle sharpens, the young post-Marxist intellectuals race to deconstruct its drearily metaphysical basis. It is therefore peculiarly poignant, and a dramatic indictment of such political irresponsibility, that this remarkable book should be the product of an American intellectual, without the impetus or consolation of a militant working-class movement. That political absence leaves its scar on the study, as it does in a different way on Lentricchia's. It is not that class struggle is in the least ignored by Jameson; it is just that his ruling political concepts, inherited from Lukács and the Frankfurt school, are those of reification and commodification. The power and versatility of insight that Jameson can generate from these twin notions is little short of staggering: he can show us, for example, how the conditions of possibility of psychoanalysis become visible 'only when you begin to appreciate the extent of psychic fragmentation since the beginnings of capitalism, with its systematic quantification and rationalization of experience, its instrumental reorganization of the subject just as much as of the outside world'.[15] In his essay on Conrad, he can track the effects of reification all the way from stylistic habit to imperialist milieu. Elsewhere in the book, he can pluck from it what amounts to the outlines of a whole theory of artistic modernism.

Yet it is not only that this resourcefulness is partly the result of a spurious equation between reification and Weber's 'rationalization', uncritically inherited from Lukács. It is also that the 'question' to which the concept of reification is an 'answer' is not in the first place one of class struggle, but a dual query about the nature of capitalist economic production and the quality of lived experience within it. If reification returns a vital economic answer to the question of how we have come to experience as meagerly as we do, it promises to put cultural formation and mode of production back together only at the risk of displacing the political. If everything is mediated through the commodity, class struggle becomes an *answer* to this unhappy condition, rather than the first *question* of historical materialism. It is in this sense that Jameson's book is constrained by its historical context; it is no accident that the declared political correlative of his theoretical pluralism is the amorphousness of 'alliance' politics. There is a similar constraint at work in Lentricchia, who is able to counter a remorseless idealism, not with political answers, but with political questions.

Lentricchia's book declares at the outset that it will not encompass the work of American Marxian and para-Marxian intellectuals like Jameson and Edward Said, and the reservation, while formally acceptable, is perhaps symptomatic of a political unclarity. Yet paradoxically Lentricchia's is the more political book – not in its positions, to be sure, which remain somewhat negative and ambiguous, but in its possible effects. For the question irresistibly raised for the Marxist reader of Jameson is simply this: how is a Marxist-structuralist analysis of a minor novel of Balzac to help shake the foundations of capitalism? Jameson, to do him justice, starts out by raising exactly that sort of objection: the reader is warned not to expect 'that exploratory projection of what a vital and emergent political culture should be and do which Raymond Williams has rightly proposed as the most urgent task of a Marxist cultural criticism'. Still, it remains unclear quite how the relations between that project and the one realized in this book are to be conceived. Lentricchia's text, altogether more acerbic and polemical (Frye is a 'great' critic for Jameson but a formalist pest for Lentricchia), belongs in a full sense to the 'class struggle at the level of theory', even if it does not fully recognize itself as such. Lentricchia is out, not to produce new critical readings, but to knock the stuffing out of bourgeois criticism; it is not altogether surprising that one of his victims has already threatened, absurdly, to sue. This is not to suggest, in a current ultra-leftist wisdom, that the production of Marxist readings of classical texts is class collaborationism; for revolutionaries have little choice in the matter. As far as the uses of 'literature' for ideological reproduction are concerned, it is the ruling class who call the tune: they, not we, will largely select the literary terrain on which battle is to be engaged. Unilateral disarmament has no place here: the surest way of surrendering in advance is to define engagement with empirical texts as 'empiricist', just as a few years ago all talk of history suddenly become 'historicist' overnight. But Lentricchia's book is right in its implicit recognition (and Jameson would surely concur) that such alternative readings can never be the *primary* task of a Marxist criticism. If we cannot as yet define that primary task with any certainty, it is because its political conditions of possibility do not as yet properly exist.

Meanwhile, back in the liberal academy, the relentless 'textualization' of history goes on apace. Yet there is a simple answer to that, which in a way every child knows. History is indeed only ever textually available to us; but history is also, as Jameson reminds us, 'what hurts, it is what refuses desire and sets inexorable limits to individual as well as collective praxis'.[16] It is for this reason that 'we may be sure that its alienating necessities will not forget us, however much we might prefer to ignore them.'[17]

5.

Fredric Jameson: The Politics of Style

So it is that de Selby's text comes to resemble nothing quite so much as two great antithetical zones of signification, frozen figures of desire or paranoid oppositions which dialectical thought will strive to dissolve into some concealed masterplot or infrastructure of *Geist*. Yet nothing is quite so striking as the secret logic by which each of these antitheses may come by some trick of narrative or structuralist *combinatoire* to invert itself into the other, so that little by little we can begin to discern the shape of some new postindividualist social apparatus beneath the modernist bric-à-brac and stray allegorical fragments with which these textual superstructures or libidinal surfaces swarm. The Freudian reinvention of this impulse does not, to be sure, return to us the *hyle* or brute raw materials of the myths themselves, which as in some unimaginable feat of transcoding resist all but the most gestural of re-writings; but it comes for all that to figure as nothing less than the very metonym of late capitalism or the *société de consommation*, which in its stubborn refusal of *Aufhebung* generates a veritable explosion of narrative structures.

Fredric Jameson did not write this paragraph, though he might well have done. It is doubtful, however, that even a parody a good deal more dexterous than this could do justice to the force and centrality of style in Jameson's work, that most palpable feature of his writing which, as with some bizarrely attractive costume worn by an acquaintance, we pass over in polite silence or with a shyly admiring phrase. 'Jameson', if I may be allowed to quote myself, 'composes rather than writes his texts, and his prose . . . carries an intense libidinal charge, a burnished elegance and unruffled poise, which allows him to sustain a rhetorical lucidity through the most tortuous, intractable materials'.[1] I want in this article to press this matter a little further, inquiring into the political determinants of Jameson's style; and in this I am being faithful to his own belief, recorded on an early page of *Marxism and Form,* that 'any concrete description of a literary or philosophical phenomenon – if it is to be really complete – has an ultimate obligation to come to terms with the shape of the individual sentences themselves, to give an account of their origin and formation'.[2]

'I cannot', writes Jameson of Adorno, 'imagine anyone with the slightest feeling for the dialectical nature of reality remaining insensible to the purely formal pleasure of such sentences'.[3] For me, it is equally unimaginable that anyone could read Jameson's own magisterial, busily metaphorical sentences without profound pleasure, and indeed I must acknowledge that I take a book of his from the shelf as often in place of poetry or fiction as literary theory. Yet it is not only that this most salient, vulnerably foregrounded aspect of his work is often enough coyly suppressed by his commentators, as with some world-class actor or athlete whose technique is so predictably flawless that we all long ago tacitly agreed to stare through it to the 'content'; it is also that 'pleasure' is not the kind of word we are accustomed to encountering in Jameson's texts. Jameson's historical responsibilities, as one of the few American critics for whom 'radicalism' extends beyond the terrors of tropology or the erotic skid of the signifier to embrace the fate of the political struggles in Poland or El Salvador, prevent him from adopting the 'sumptuous and perverse' style of a Barthes,[4] even if he should secretly wish it. If 'literary criticism' is to be one day justified at the judgement seat of history – if we will be able to claim that it played a bit part in the averting of fascism or nuclear holocaust – Jameson may have the oppressive pleasure of knowing that his is one of the forlornly few names we will stammeringly evoke. Yet in the meanwhile, weighed down with these grave burdens of structural rigour and historical prognostication, he must be allowed a little for himself, and that, precisely, is style. Style in Jameson is the excess or self-delight which escapes even his own most strenuously analytical habits, that which slips through the very dialectical forms it so persuasively delineates. This, rather than the discussions of Bloch or Marcuse, is the truly utopian dimension of his work, a shadowy presence coupled at every point to his analyses, a lateral gesture so all-pervasive that, like utopia or desire itself, it refuses definitive figuration and echoes in the mind simply as the rhetorical *verso* or buzz of inexhaustible implications of his grand narrative themes.

The most predictable next step in the argument would be to claim that this constant rhetorical thickness of Jameson's writing escapes from his structural schemas only to round upon them with subversive vengeance. On the contrary, Jameson's writing seems to me to escape, and round challengingly upon, this now most compulsively repetitive of critical dogmas. Indeed what else is his essay on Wyndham Lewis than an attempt at historical-materialist explanation of those forms of discourse (of which Lewis's own flailing, hectically metonymic style is one) where such violent contestations of 'molar' and 'molecular', structure and stylistic detail, can be witnessed? This is not to say, on the other hand, that Lewis's style may not figure subliminally for Jameson as some savage caricature or nightmarish extreme of his own voracious literary energies, a sort of 'second power' version, as he might say himself, of his own restlessly 'electric' stylistic drives, a slipshod, uncouth revelation of just what might happen if this suavest of Hegelian Marxists were to let rip. There may also be in Lewis's stylistic tendency to 'smooth the most violent agitation of detail back over into a static and well-nigh visual frieze'[5] a distorted reminiscence of Jameson's own occasional 'over-totalizing', his Hegelian hunt for the master-code which will unlock all others. Whatever the value of such speculations, it seems true that in the Lewis book his own style is at its most hectic and heterogeneous, turbulently surcharged like its object-texts, just on the point of cutting loose from the sober classical lucidity of the earlier work into some altogether more jagged, impure medium. 'This is the very element of Lewis's novelistic world, this combative, exasperated, yet jaunty stance of monads on collision, a kind of buoyant truculence in which matched and abrasive consciousnesses slowly rub each other into smarting vitality'.[6] Such a sentence, in which desire breaks abruptly through as an exuberant 'overnaming', seizing the lucky chance that its theme here happens to be language itself to transform Jameson's customarily lateral stylistic message into the very 'content', bares the device and risks letting the cat out of the bag. In violating the very principle of Jameson's style, which is to moderate between *écriture* and *écrivance*, or better to problematize those very categories, it exposes it for what it is. For the impulse of Jameson's style is to stay just a hair's-breadth this side of any too flaunted or flamboyant writing, estranging but not parodying its object, subduing the brio of each rhetorical gesture to a narrative structure which will not, however, *à la* Lewis, flatten it to nothing. The excitement of reading Jameson, then, is to see each time how this trick will be pulled off – how his discourse will just escape an excessive molecular density on the one hand, and a monotonous 'molarity' or overclosure on the other. When the trick works, he avoids both the anaemic transparency of Anglo-American writing and the obscurities of European style, achieving a discourse which is paradoxically both thick and lucid. Jameson's style is less cosmopolitan than homeless: it is not just a European derivation, yet to an English eye it has almost nothing American about it either.

'Pleasure' rather than *'jouissance'*, then; and if this is so then there is doubtless a political reason for it. What distinguishes Marxism from the more debased forms of Romantic anarchism is not a refusal of *jouissance* but a recognition of its material grounds of possibility – grounds which properly exist not now but in what Marx in the *Brumaire* names the 'poetry of the future'. The poetry of the future, which we are forbidden to figure here and now on pain of utopian idolatry, furrows the present as a delectable potential in much the same way that Jameson's excess of style shadows but refuses to shatter his texts. This is perhaps the place to remark, incidentally, that what distinguishes Marxism from the various hermeneutical or post-structuralist debates about the intelligibility or otherwise of the historical past, its relation or discontinuity with the present, is that Marxism is only secondarily enthused by such issues, drawing its poetry as it does from a future to which it is simultaneously deferred. There is no historical conjuncture except from the standpoint of a desirable future. Indeed it is part of the very definition of a political conjuncture, for Marxism, that past and present are inscribed from that vantage point. If such an enterprise is 'teleological' it is no more so than reaching for a spoon. The duality of the Jamesonian sentence, at once political message and play of the signifier, seems to me an eminently dialectical figure of the relation between desire and its historical deferment, opening a space between these options in which the reader is suspended. 'Marxism and Form' is indeed a significant title in this respect, as much a comment on the *énonciation* as on the *énoncé*. It announces both identity and difference: on the one hand a Marxism which in meditating upon form cannot help thinking itself through again in that very act; on the other hand a striking divergence between the kid-gloved composure of the signifier and the raw urgency of the political signified. Trapped between the patronage of the right – 'sophisticated stuff for a

Marxist!' – and the suspicion of the left – 'not much dust and heat of class struggle here!' – Jameson's work proclaims the dilemma that we can today write neither like Brecht nor like Benjamin. Its strength is to confront that quandary in its very letter, refusing at once the chimera of a 'degree zero' political discourse and the allures of the commodified 'art sentence'. Language must be reinvested with the materiality of which one form of reification has robbed it, but the historical conditions are simply not as yet ripe to do that without the risk of fetishizing it in another direction. Discourse must be reinvested with desire, but not to the point where it confiscates the historical realizations of that desire. Jameson's style is a practice which displays such contradictions even as it strives to mediate them; and even where such mediation seems successful for whole books at a stretch, our attention can always be thrown up to the level of genre in a way which splits things apart again, confronting us with the overall strangeness of a discourse on class and modes of production which is, simultaneously, a reflection on form, trope and figure.

Style in Jameson, then, both compensates for and adumbrates pleasures historically postponed, goals as yet politically unrealizable, and is to this extent both a bleak and politically instructive displacement. But the ambivalence of Jameson's writing, stranded somewhere between *écriture* and *écrivance*, can also be read as a curious doubling of commentary and critique. Benjamin and Adorno dreamed of an exegesis which would be at once myopically immanent and utterly estranging, tenaciously faithful to its object while rewriting it with Kabbalistic boldness. It was by such scriptive acts that the old problems of 'base' and 'superstructure', text and context, were to be practically resolved. Jameson's most powerful writing seems to me to fall within this Marxist tradition, as in this passage on Lacan's concept of the imaginary:

> A description of the Imaginary will therefore on the one hand require us to come to terms with a uniquely determinate configuration of space – one not yet organized around the individuation of my own personal body, or differentiated hierarchically according to the perspectives of my own central point of view – yet which nonetheless swarms with bodies and forms intuited in a different way, whose fundamental property is, it would seem, to be visible without their visibility being the result of the act of any particular observer, to be, as it were, already-seen, to carry their specularity

upon themselves like a colour they wear or the texture of their
surface. In this – the indifferentiation of their *esse* from a *percipi*
which does not know a *percipiens* – these bodies of the Imaginary
exemplify the very logic of mirror images; yet the existence of the
normal object world of adult everyday life presupposes this prior,
imaginary experience of space.[7]

Or take the following account of the paintings of De Kooning:

> You have to imagine, I think, a process of effraction that seizes on
> the line itself, tangling it, as in the charcoal sketches, making it
> shiver and vibrate, shattering it rhythmically into pencil shadings,
> like so many overtones. Here some inner compulsion of line, some
> originary nervousness, makes it want to burst its two-dimensional
> limits and produce, out of its own inner substance, smears that
> coopt and preempt its primal adversary, the brush-stroke itself.[8]

Are these passages accounts or critiques, descriptions or re-
inventions? Jameson writes in the Preface to *The Prison-House of
Language* of his intention to 'offer an introductory survey of
these movements (formalism and structuralism) which might
stand at the same time as a critique of their basic methodology',[9]
but it is just this relation between 'survey' and 'critique', in this
book and elsewhere, which is most problematic. Once more
there would seem to me a political determinant at work in this
ambivalence of Jameson's writing, beyond the essential attempt
to rediscover a dialectical criticism which both evokes and displaces its object. The problem of deciding whether Jameson is
transcribing or free-wheeling, reining in the signifier or letting it
rip, is the stylistic index of a more fundamental dilemma, that of
his relationship as a revolutionary to bourgeois theory. One
could phrase this dilemma by claiming that Jameson tends to
appropriate the texts of such theory *at once too much and too little*.
On the one hand, he emerges in his work as one of the great
appropriators, ranging with enviable erudition over almost
every sector of the 'humanities', mobilizing their insights for his
own ends with apparently effortless skill. The most uncharitable
way of putting the point would be to say that his work resembles
nothing quite so much as some great Californian supermarket of
the mind, in which the latest flashily dressed commodities
(Hjelmslev, Barthes, Deleuze, Foucault) sit stacked upon the
shelves alongside some more tried and trusty household names
(Hegel, Schelling, Croce, Freud), awaiting the moment when

they will all be casually scooped into the Marxist basket. Alternatively, Jameson can be seen as a unrepentant *bricoleur*, reaching for a Machereyan spanner here or Greimasian screwdriver there in his patient tinkering with the faulty text. On the other hand, however, such appropriation too often leaves the texts in question relatively untransformed, intact in their 'relative autonomy', so that the strenuously *mastering* Jameson appears too eirenic, easygoing and all-encompassing for his own political good. (The fact that he is in no sense a polemical or satirical writer – essential modes, to my mind, for a political revolutionary – may be taken to confirm this impression.)

In principle, Jameson's attitude towards non-Marxist theory strikes me as properly dialectical: Marxism is not stiffly to refuse such accounts in the name of an imaginary integrity, but to go right through them and emerge on the other side, in that untranscendable dimension of material history from where alone their insights can be assembled, assessed and transformed. Marxism, as Jameson well sees, is not one 'method' among others, but an insistence that discourse should be ceaselessly referred to its material conditions of possibility. *Why* this gesture is essential, other than as a mere hobby or private predilection, can be answered only by argument over the reading and writing of history itself – by claiming, in short, that such rejoinings are constrained by the most powerful readings of history itself. Any debate over 'Marxist criticism' will thus quickly, ineluctably shift to a contention about politics. If one wished to isolate from the supermarket shelves a single source of Jameson's whole *oeuvre*, one supreme, overriding text which governs his whole work, it would surely be Lukács's great chapter on German idealism in *History and Class Consciousness*. For Jameson, one can imagine, Lukács's breathtakingly audacious gesture there, rewriting as he does the whole of that philosophical history in terms of the commodity, has the status of a moment of revelation, an intellectual apocalypse one can never go back beyond.

Still, what is claimed in principle is not always carried through in practice. As Jameson's style comes to invest in description all those dramatic intensities which one would more usually associate with argument, it sometimes becomes possible to feel that we are witnessing a mode of absorption which leaves everything just as it was. What, for example, is *The Prison-House of Language's* ultimate judgement on its formalist and structuralist objects? On the one hand, Jameson tells us, such methods are not to be ignored but to be completely worked through so that we may emerge into 'some wholly different and theoretically more satis-fying philosophical perspective'.[10] Presumably, if such a working through is not to be entirely gestural, the materials in question will have in the end contributed to that perspective; yet on another page we are warned that any theoretical approach which fails, as these do, to reckon the subject into account is bound to be sterilely self-confirming. At one point in the book Jameson justly doubts the wisdom of even provisionally bracket-ing off the 'superstructure' from the historical 'base'; he ends the study, however, with the promise of some synthesis of historical and structural approaches, retrieving the most valuable insights of the latter while 'reopen(ing) text and analytic process alike to the winds of history'.[11] Yet if structuralist insights thrive pre-cisely on a repression of history, as the book would seem to argue elsewhere, how can this not be contradictory?

One problem with respecting the 'relative autonomy of super-structures' while insisting nevertheless that there is always a dimension beyond them – history itself – is of course that the category of history itself may become rapidly drained of mean-ing. The quickest, most disreputable way for Marxism to tackle the problem of 'relative autonomy' is to hypostasize a history which is always elsewhere; in this way Marxism can reserve for itself a suitable radical home ground outside the academy while remaining on much the academy's terms in its dealings with the now safely sealed-off 'superstructures'. A history outside the superstructures has the convenient double-effect of hanging a huge sardonic question mark over bourgeois theory while leav-ing it securely as it was. There is, I think, a sporadic impulse in Jameson's work to pursue this false solution, though it is by no means what he believes and quite uncharacteristic of his best critical practice. But another alternative – to scoop up 'history' into the 'superstructures' themselves – may ironically have a similar debilitating effect: 'Where everything is historical', Jameson writes, 'the idea of history itself has seemed to empty of content'.[12] Yet he does, even so, open *The Political Unconscious* with the resounding slogan 'Always historicize!', claiming this as itself, paradoxically, a transhistorical imperative. To which one answer is surely that 'Always historicize!' is by no means a specifically Marxist recommendation; and that even though Jameson would no doubt gladly concede the point (since for him, as an Hegelian Marxist, 'Marx includes Hegel'),[13] such a concession merely blurs the specificity of Marxism itself, which is not at all to 'historicize' (any more than ideology is always and everywhere 'naturalizing'), but, in a word, to grasp history as structured material struggle. One reason why Jameson would sometimes seem to subordinate the latter emphasis to the former is that he never appears to have taken the full pressure of the Althusserian critique of Marxist historicism. Althusser, who for all his egregious limitations has at least done us the service of recalling that the 'Marxist' question is not in the first place one of historicization but of the interdeterminations of different historical practices, has no particularly prominent place on the shelves of *The Prison-House*; and the way is then open for the resolute historicism of *Marxism and Form* to re-surface almost unmodified in *The Political Unconscious* – even if the sense of history in the latter work is now, rather more bleakly, more one of closure than of horizon. The passage through and beyond Althusser is never really effected; for Jameson 'historicism' would seem to mean something like 'historical reductionism', rather than an ideology in which 'society becomes a circular "expressive" totality, history a homogeneous flow of linear time, philosophy a self-consciousness of the historical process, class struggle a combat of collective "subjects", capitalism a universe essentially defined by alienation, communism a state of true humanism beyond alienation'.[14] Because there is little evidence that Jameson has ever really thought Marxism through again within such an Althusserian problematic, if only to emerge on the other side into a 'theoretically more satisfying' perspective, his own work occasionally evinces a rather too homogeneous linear flow: the brilliant disquisition on the operation of 'transcoding' in *The Political Unconscious* is already there in essentials on p. 354 of *Marxism and Form*. Moreover, Jameson's relative stasis in this respect has prevented his work from entering so far into any very productive dialogue with post-structuralism, over and above a characteristic raiding of its concepts which remains disturbingly quiet about its overall political implications. For the Althusserian critique of historicism can provide at once a bridge and a challenge to that latter body of doctrine, as indeed can the very different Marxism of a Benjamin.

To press right through and emerge on the other side, then, is not entirely the point; it is also a question of how much of the object one finally emerges with. Jameson's Hegelian devotion to the practice of *Aufhebung* would in one sense lead him to answer 'Everything': there seems to be nothing, from Burke to Balibar, which cannot be sublated within his endlessly adroit, capacious machine. It is in this sense that he is at once intellectual appropriator and generous respecter of autonomy: for if Marxism is like *Geist*, the hidden truth of all phenomena, then all such phenomena have their allotted place within the historical totality and the task of a political hermeneutics is simply to reveal how this is secretly so. Whatever the theoretical value of this position, it would certainly seem to confiscate – rather in the manner of Jameson's regular, curiously unimpassioned style – some of those vital *political* energies – of conflict, opposition, denunciation – without which the whole Marxist project is the merest academicism.

This political tone has in turn an historical ground. 'Within the United States,' Jameson writes, 'there is no tactical or political question which is not first and foremost theoretical, no form of action that is not inextricably entangled in the sticky cobwebs of the false and unreal culture itself, with its ideological mystification on every level'.[15] In one sense, this order of priorities between 'theoretical' and 'political' could be taken as no more than a rewriting of Lenin's famous dictum 'Without revolutionary theory, no revolutionary politics', though the easy symmetry of that 'tactical or political' is perhaps a little disturbing. In another sense, however, Jameson seems to mean something rather different: not quite that political action must be saturated with political analysis, but that a *preliminary*, ground-clearing operation of demystification is necessary before we may even come to grasp what political structures we have and what political actions are possible. In order to see straight at all in the heartlands of late monopoly capitalism, we must first of all, prior to all particular political analysis and action, theorize; and since what prevents us from seeing straight is essentially reification, the most appropriate mode of theorizing will accordingly be Hegelian Marxism. 'It is in the context of . . . postindustrial Marxism that the great themes of Hegel's philosophy – the relationship of part to whole, the opposition between concrete and abstract, the concept of totality, the dialectic of appearance and essence, the interaction between subject and object – are once again the order of the day'.[16] One might be tempted to riposte that they are indeed – and that they are back on the agenda partly because a 'Western Marxism' which, confronted with severe difficulties of class struggle, has abandoned a *political* starting point, has little but reworked remnants of idealist philosophy left to it. It is ironic that an Hegelian Marxism distinguished by a concept of *praxis* which is if anything too unitary – theory as no more than self-consciousness of practice – should here be deployed to defend an essentially contemplative stance. The distance from *History and Class Consciousness* is notable indeed: the dispelling of reification which for that work was an indispensable concomitant and effect of class struggle has become, in Jameson, its theoretical prolegomenon.

For my part, it is not clear that there is anything inherent in late capitalism which spontaneously selects such philosophical issues as the relation between subject and object as the order of the day, as opposed, say, to questions of the character of the state and its repressive apparatuses, problems of proletarian organization and insurrection, or the role of the vanguard party. There seems to me nothing in monopoly capitalism which automatically selects the names of Hegel, Lukács and Adorno as relevant touchstones, rather than – those symptomatic silences in Jameson's work – Lenin, Trotsky and Gramsci. Jameson would no doubt reply that there was indeed something immanent in contemporary capitalism which enforced these options, namely the fetishism of commodities, which while not peculiar to this epoch of class-society is mightily dominant in it. Indeed that classical Marxist doctrine has been a shaping motif of all his work, all the way from discussions of *Trauerspiel* to post-modernism, Cervantes to Conrad. But as I have argued elsewhere, too great an attention to 'commodification' links the economical to the experiential only at the cost of displacing the political; and in this sense it must be grasped as itself a political option, a partial displacement occasioned by the intractable problems of class struggle in the contemporary United States. The unusual popularity of the various Hegelian inflections of Marxism in the US is surely to be seen, not only as a particularly appropriate 'answer' to a thoroughly commodified society, but as part of the problem – the reflex of a condition in which the commodity bulks so large that it threatens to obfuscate, not only bourgeois social relations, but a specifically political and institutional understanding in areas of the left.

The risks of privileging such philosophical concerns as the interaction of subject and object can be shown in a particular way. Jameson has always properly insisted on that dimension of dialectics which reckons the subject into its own practice, hostile from the outset to such counter-revolutionary chimeras as Althusser's transcendental subject of knowledge. At the same time, of course, he has firmly upheld that related feature of dialectical thought which grasps the material, independent activity of the object itself. Certain trends in post-structuralism, however, have embraced and caricatured the first proposition only thereby to liquidate the second. What right-thinking person would now not rush to topple the transcendental subject? And how many of them now in doing so would triumphantly demolish the independent existence of the object, as a mere fiction of the subject's power and desire! Jameson, naturally, would not agree; but you cannot situate your major argument on the terrain of subject and object, shot through as it is with all that idealist history, and then be wholly surprised, or innocent, when others press that issue through to what is really just the most fashionable form of idealism. To *start* with class struggle; to begin, theoretically, from the political; to take off from institutions rather than from discourse or 'consciousness': though all this will of course be dismissed as 'metaphysical' by those who have much to lose, it cannot be *incorporated* in quite the way that an epistemological critique can be.

I have been arguing that Jameson's style displays an intriguing ambivalence of commentary and critique; that this springs from a similarly ambivalent relation to bourgeois culture, at once over-appropriative and over-generous; and that all of this in turn may be illuminated by the essentially Hegelian cast of Jameson's Marxism, which tends to subordinate political conflict to theoretical *Aufhebung*. This, finally, may be related to a Western Marxism whose primary category, in practice if not always in theory, would seem to be reification or commodity fetishism; and there are definite historical conditions, consequent upon the current relative quiescence of the class struggle in the US, for this theoretical choice. For what appears wrong with the world, from the standpoint of such a theory, is not so much this or that phenomenon but the fact that we cannot see all these phenomena together and see them whole – the fact that they are isolated, fragmented, compartmentalized. So it was that the German Romantic anti-capitalist heritage passed over, partly via Max Weber, into Georg Lukács, and on in some of its aspects to Fredric Jameson. What is wrong with capitalism on this reckoning is its power to disconnect; and Marxism will accordingly become a hermeneutics, in outright violation of Marx's eleventh thesis on Feuerbach, deciphering the submerged grammar of bourgeois society, explaining how all of these disconnected phenomena are secretly totalized. Thus it is that Marxism is moved towards that 'truth of the whole' which, precisely in so far as it is that, comes like the Almighty himself to impinge less and less on any particular quarter. In dealing with Hegel or Northrop Frye, it seems less important to interrogate the contents of their systems than to indicate the historical appropriateness of the systems themselves, their formal status within history. In this sense also, 'Marxism and Form' comes to assume new significance.

'Only connect': Jameson would not of course agree that this liberal panacea was anything but a feeble piece of mystification, but there is a sense in which it comes to supply some of the driving force of his own work, in faithful consonance with the Hegelian-Marxist critique of reification. For Jameson is a master of coruscating connections and brilliant analogies, whose primarily intellectual habit is metaphor; his texts form a kind of immense *combinatoire* into which others' ideas are duly fed only to emerge as strikingly novel insights of his own. Here again, that tension which we have traced stylistically as one between commentary and critique can be seen at work. Jameson can transform a connection into an idea in its own right with all the creativity with which he imbues description with the force of analysis; yet the fact that it is largely the ideas of others which are being connected remains as evident as the fact that, even at his most 'original', he is simply explicating another's text. In structuralist fashion, his intellectual creativity seems to inhere more in the act of connecting than in the individual units combined; and this, once more, has its historical ground. Jameson is a Marxist intellectual inhabiting a society which, like Britain, is not remarkable for its original work in Marxism – a fact which has of course nothing to do with individual capability and everything to do with political conditions. He is thus inevitably, like some of us in Britain, a client of Europe. But if his historical position constrains him to such clientage, there is also no doubt that he is a powerfully creative thinker in his own right, easily the equal in this respect of some of his European *confrères*. The tension between clientage and creativity, then, is yet another version of the hesitation between commentary and critique; and it is style which regulates this tension in his writing.

In transcoding European thought so fluently into his own magisterial periods, re-routing it through his own rhetoric, Jameson 'reinvents' these materials to the point where he appears master of what, officially speaking, he is mediator. A measured Anglo-American equability supervenes upon European exoticism, preserving it in all its scandalous theatricality while subjecting it to a coolly analytical gaze.

'Even if ours is a critical age', Jameson writes, 'it does not seem to me very becoming in critics to exalt their activity to the level of literary creation'.[17] One reason why he holds this view, no doubt, is that he belongs with those of us who cling churlishly to the case that cognition and the referent have their place, and do not feel any particular impulse to relegate to metaphysical darkness those who from time to time remark that a proposition is true. The ideology of criticism as creation implies another sort of epistemology altogether, which does not strike me as in the best interests of the masses of Poland and El Salvador. Criticism as creation is of course one answer, at once slightly desperate and faintly ludicrous, to the historical and political crisis of criticism itself; but Jameson's work points to another kind of response. I once heard it said of him, in a familiar piece of liberal patronage, that he 'wasn't just a Marxist critic'. But it all depends on where you place the emphasis. Not just a *Marxist* critic: I have tried here to explore some of the strengths and limits of that. But the proper emphasis, surely, is 'not just a Marxist *critic*'. The difference between Jameson and most other Anglo-American critics is not in the end a matter of ideological criticism *versus* deconstruction *versus* careful scholarship *versus* the words on the page. It is a matter of political struggle over the meaning and function of criticism itself. For there is no resting place in criticism for those who take their poetry from the future.

6.

Frère Jacques:
The Politics of Deconstruction

That there is a left- and right-wing of American deconstruction has for some time been apparent. On the one hand, there are those who, to quote Michael Ryan in *Marxism and Deconstruction*,[1] have translated a complex philosophy 'into an old-model new criticism from which the muffler has been removed, creating more noise without noticeably improving the speed'. On the other hand, there are those like Gayatri Spivak, Samuel Weber and Michael Ryan himself who seek to stay faithful to Derrida's remark (no doubt intended to put a degree of daylight between himself and the first set of acolytes) that 'it is by touching solid structures, "material" institutions, and not merely discourses or significant representations, that deconstruction distinguishes itself from analysis or "criticism"'.[2] Both parties could stake a claim to the true faith, if either believed in such a concept: the former because, whatever his more recent pronouncements, Derrida himself has hardly been remarkable for his 'institutional' as opposed to discursive analyses, and is thus performatively askew to what he claims in ways of interest to deconstructive criticism. It is Michel Foucault, not Jacques Derrida, who has occupied the 'institutional' area. The latter party can lay claim to authentic inheritance because Derrida, whatever his practice, is quite evidently some kind of Marxist sympathizer; indeed Michael Ryan actually refers to a colloquium at which Derrida declared himself to be a communist. '*Some kind* of Marxist sympathizer' is of course the appropriate indeterminacy; one might say, with 'proper' deconstructive provisionality, that whatever Marxism is, Jacques Derrida is something to do with it. His polite silence about the more rebarbative metaphysical claims of his friend Louis Althusser must surely be understood as a strategically admirable refusal to pronounce a post-Marxist front in political conditions where this could only have had reactionary effects. The ambiguous relationship between Derrida and Marxism, then, can be summarized by saying that it is as easy to imagine how distasteful Derrida must find the appropriation of his work to prop up Reagan's America as it is hard to imagine why he appears happy to collude with it.

What comes through superbly in Michael Ryan's excellent (if irritatingly fragmentary and repetitive) book is the inherently *historical* and *materialist* nature of deconstructive thought, and this in ways which far outstrip in their profundity the modish, purely gestural uses of that most euphoric of radical buzz-words 'materialist'. In a fluently condensed opening chapter, Ryan charts the remorselessly anti-idealist bias of deconstruction, its insistence that truth, presence, meaning and identity are 'a product of numerous histories, institutions and processes of inscription which cannot be transcended by consciousness conceived as a domain of pure ideality' (p. 24). 'Textuality' is to be understood not (as with the Yale rhetoricians) as a privileging of the discursive or 'literary', but as the resituating of otherwise idealistically perceived entities within the 'weave of differential relations, institutions, conventions, histories, practices' of which they are always the internally conflictual effects. In a later chapter, Ryan is able convincingly to demonstrate the parallels between this historical sense of textuality – the precise *antithesis* of the muddled proposition that Derrida ousts 'history' for 'the text' – and the classical Marxist reinscription of otherwise reified phenomena (labour, capital, the state, commodities and the rest) within the relational, differential social process itself. To 'deconstruct', then, is to reinscribe and resituate meanings, events and objects within broader movements and structures; it is, so to speak, to reverse the imposing tapestry in order to expose in all its unglamorously dishevelled tangle the threads constituting the well-heeled image it presents to the world. Ryan's understanding of deconstruction is in this sense in line with Fredric Jameson's bold equation in *The Prison-House of Language* between Derrida's *'toujours déjà'* and Marx's 'material conditions'. For both modes of inquiry, whenever we are confronted with a sign, object or event, something else must always already have happened for this to be possible – something which has not, moreover, simply gone away. For the inscription of this otherness may be traced in the very phenomenon which represses it, as its material condition of possibility; whenever we have a sign or a superstructure, *there* – and yet not quite *there* – we have a history or a base.

This seems to me a fertile, accurate (whatever that might mean) reading of Derrida, though it is not without its difficulties. For one thing, Ryan's deconstructed Marxism, with its insistence on process, relationality and the identity of identity and non-identity, sounds very Hegelian, which is paradoxical in one sense but not in another. I mean that while it is obviously ironic to make the author of *Glas* sound like Hegel, it is not at all surprising that an American Marxist should sound like an Hegelian, given the pervasive influence of that particular Marxist lineage in the United States. One reason why Hegelian Marxism has been so dominant in the United States is, if I may speak bluntly, that in certain of its aspects it tends to defuse the less comfortable political realities of Marxism itself – realities of which one is likely to be kept constantly mindful only in a society with a more militant working-class movement and richer culture of political struggle than the United States has for a long time had. Talk of the inherently processual and relational character of social reality is both essential and understandable in such a grievously reified environment; but though such talk is both historical and materialist it is not in itself historical materialist, and neither is Michael Ryan's deconstructionist recycling of it. Many a good liberal can concede with embarrassing readiness that everything lives pregnant with its other; there is no very obvious route through from this radical contextualism to the victory of the proletariat. If Marxism is simply some insistence that everything is conflictually or contradictorily related to everything else, then it is merely one of the many classical systems of dialectics, with no further distinguishing claims or call on our attention than that. Hegelian and deconstructive Marxism *are*, of course, radically at odds – the former proposes just the kind of holism that the latter refuses – but they are alike at least in this.

Marxism cannot, by definition, be distinguished by what it shares in common with 'dialectics' as such. It cannot be merely an historicism, or merely a materialism, even though Ryan's account tends precisely in this sense to deconstruct the hyphen in historical-materialism. The specificity of Marxism is in my view at least twofold: it lies, first, in its claim that material

production is the ultimately determinant factor of social existence, and, secondly, that the class struggle is the central dynamic
of historical development. I am tempted to add a third distinguishing feature, one which perhaps belongs more properly
to Marxism-Leninism, and which concerns the *revolutionary*
nature of the doctrine: Marxism is among other things a theory
and practice of political *insurrection*.

Now Ryan is notably uneasy about all three of these uniquely
distinguishing claims. His book scornfully rejects the classical
Marxist thesis of economic determination, discerning in this
doctrine no more than a form of left economism, and correctly
stressing the always-already-political character of the economic
to the point where (incorrectly, in my view) the two categories
are simply conflated together. To argue that '"the political"
and "the economic" cannot even be considered as separate categories for the sake of theoretical exposition' is not only empiri-
cally implausible (there are many distinguished works of Marxist
economic theory which 'bracket' the political), but collapses
dialectics into identity. Ryan fails to recognize that what differen-
tiates the Marxist from the Hegelian dialectic is precisely its
'loaded' or asymmetrical character: the political and the economic may well be mutually imbricated, but their relation is not
one of simple *equivalence*. A certain spontaneous Hegelianism
converges here with a deconstructive distaste for 'hierarchies': it
is undeconstructive to assert that men are superior to women or
professors to truck drivers, so it seems to follow that it is equally
'elitist' or 'exclusivist' to claim that economic production is more
historically determinant than political forms. Or than literary
texts? Does this charitable anti-hierarchalism have its limits? As
for class struggle, Ryan certainly allots this a central role, but it
usually crops up in his text as one component of the contemporary Holy Trinity of 'class, race and gender'. Once again, with
the most gracious kind of theoretical good manners, he seems
anxious to exclude nothing or nobody, reluctant to privilege
anything or anybody over anything else. This may be an admirable gesture; but it is a liberal, not a Marxist, one. Perhaps Ryan
is right always to equalize class and other modes of struggle;
but I do not think, for good or ill, that he can be right on this
score and a Marxist too, since Marxism has traditionally been
distinguished from beliefs in 'struggle in general' by the historical centrality it has accorded to this one in particular.

I suspect that Ryan himself might be a little impatient with this appeal to Marxist tradition, which seems to figure for him as a suspiciously 'normative', potentially terroristic gesture. I do not share this suspicion: a Marxist, in my view, is always a traditionalist, respecting Trotsky's affirmation that 'We Marxists have always lived in tradition'. To say of a particular line of 'Marxist' argument that it is untraditional is not automatically to banish it to the outer darkness, but to note that it is not in line with what many hundreds of thousands of men and women engaged in active struggle have found it possible or necessary to believe. Classical Marxist doctrines are not simply abstract theoretical formulations: they are also living indices of this 'real history'; marks of a collective historical wisdom which is almost always richer than our own individual theoretical resources. To be wary in this sense of wandering from tradition is not servility, and only a liberal-individualist society which has repressed its history for the barren Protestantism of the 'present conjuncture' could see it as such. Tradition frequently needs to be modified, transformed or abandoned; but the socialist, as opposed to the liberal, will always do this with a certain sense of awe. Ryan's impatience with 'tradition' bears the trace of a society which is hardly rich in Marxist lineages, and needs to be understood in this light.

As far as the revolutionary character of Marxist politics goes, Ryan quite consciously displaces attention from the moment of insurrection – the fact that, for classical Marxism, the complex, drawn-out, multiple revolutionary process includes within itself a punctual crisis of decisive confrontation with the armed might of the bourgeois state. This is not just a question of 'preferring' one kind of political strategy to another; a materialist understanding of the nature of bourgeois hegemony itself entails such an insurrectionary politics. Derrida himself has dismissed the concept of revolution as metaphysical; but it is curiously hard to find revolutionists who, as this accusation seems to demand, obediently trust to some moment at which everything we know will stop and something entirely new will start. Such people stubbornly continue to designate themselves revolutionaries, to differentiate themselves not from tough-minded anti-metaphysicians but from those who hold that somewhere along the line, if we all push hard enough in all directions, things might get rather better. Michael Ryan is not of course one of this latter group; but he fails in my view to appreciate the necessary relation between 'revolution' and 'insurrection', concerned as he appears to be with imputing every conceivable betrayal and distortion of Marxism to Lenin. His account of Leninism, it must be said, is drastically undialectical and wholly in line with conventional liberal wisdom on the topic. His entirely appropriate criticisms of the centralist, authoritarian facets of Leninism would come more acceptably from one who did not speak so distastefully of 'disciplinarian' political organizations, or applaud a 'rejection of the logic of power and domination in all their forms'. This, one is tempted to say, may be stirring stuff in the University of Virginia, but it has something of a hollow ring in the jungles of Vietnam or Guatemala. For discipline, power, unity and authority are the utterly indispensable characteristics of any revolutionary movement with the faintest hope of success, as anyone who has taken the briefest of glances at the power structures of imperialism may understand; and to interpret these characteristics as domination, centralization and elitism is to lapse directly into the discourse of anarchism and liberal pluralism. It is true that the most pressing strategic problem for the revolutionary left today is precisely how such revolutionary virtues are to be rendered compatible with democracy, difference and multiplicity; but anyone who takes a steady look at the capitalist state and concludes that discipline and unity are somehow irrelevant to its defeat has 'resolved' this problem at a stroke merely by abolishing one set of its terms. Ryan has much of great value to say of difference, conflict and non-identity; but he is largely silent on the issue of revolutionary *solidarity* (is this yet another shabbily undeconstructed shibboleth?), of the kind that, as I write, is being rather impressively demonstrated by the British miners, dockers and transport workers in opposition to Thatcherite oppression.

To take up Ryan's critique of Leninism in the historical detail it would require would take us too far afield in the compass of a brief review. It would also entail the kind of 'philosophical' or full-dress theoretical discourse of which Ryan is significantly disapproving. For he does not believe that there is such a thing as 'Marxist philosophy' – this provides another point of contact between Marxism and deconstruction – and can actually write that Marxist thought should address 'concrete issues' rather than such 'abstract categories' as 'mode of production' or 'determination in the last instance'. He does not, one notes, refuse to address himself to such abstract categories as 'difference' and 'non-identity'; the concepts he chooses to disdain here are, conveniently enough, the very 'Althusserian' ones he anyway rejects. But the gesture is none the less telling. For it is characteristic of Hegelian Marxism, and one of its points of complicity with commonplace liberal or pragmatist anti-intellectualism, that it dissolves 'theory' into 'practice' at a stroke, with its rallying cry of 'concrete issues' and vote-catching suspicion of the cerebral. For Marx, a mode of production was actually a *more* concrete phenomenon than, say, a handloom, since 'the concrete is the product of many determinations'; Marx inverts the empiricist hierarchy of concrete and abstract which Ryan here obediently reproduces. Such 'anti-theoreticism' goes hand in hand with a purely 'conjunctural' politics; if everything is connected with everything else, what does it matter where you politically begin? Nothing is now less fashionable in left-deconstructive circles than 'general theories'; it seems that we are being constantly offered a Hobson's choice between such theories, which are of course 'terroristic', and pure conjunctures or micropolitics, which have the advantage of not being terroristic because they have the disadvantage of not being very effective either. I do not see why Marxists, or anybody else for that matter, should indulge the masochistic urge to put their heads into this particular cleft stick.

Deconstruction, as Derrida and Ryan understand it, insists not that truth is illusory but that it is institutional. Metaphysician and 'wild' deconstructionist are alike in suspecting that unless you have the 'whole truth' you have no truth at all, specular images of each other in this as in much else. Ryan rightly refuses this bind: he does not believe that the radical contextualization he advocates is the subversion of truth, rather that it is the only adequate understanding of it. There is, even so, a problem with this advocacy of context. For Ryan, it would seem, capitalism is contextless thought; and to reinscribe meanings and objects in their material contexts thus becomes at times almost *equivalent* to Marxism. It is not so much that Marxism involves viewing social phenomena in a *particular* material context; it is rather that it involves viewing them in a material context. There is a strange residual empiricism at work here: what is problematic is not so much which context to construct for the object as the fact that, under capitalism, its 'given' context is suppressed. Once this context is made to appear again, then the truth of the object will appear along with it. This is, once more, a modified form of Hegelianism, a more full-blooded variety of which can be found in the work of Fredric Jameson; and it evades rather than encounters the challenge of that right-wing (sceptical) deconstruction which would say to Ryan, with its customary blending of tolerance and put-down, 'Well, that's *your* narrative.' His own reading of deconstruction, like any other, is a selective one: roughly speaking, it shifts emphasis from *aporia* and undecidability to history, process, relationality and materiality. But in so far as this involves inscribing the object in a potentially inexhaustible text, the issue of undecidability can always be made to return, smuggled in by the back door by those sceptical of Ryan's politics. It is not so much that there are no counter-moves to such a ploy – if you really believe in any old story, then just try it on – but that Ryan seems insufficiently alert to the complex relations of identity and non-identity between his own 'good object' of political deconstruction and the 'bad object' being fashioned at Yale. Both, after all, are possible readings of Derrida, and cannot be simply severed from one another in some wish-fulfilling binary opposition. The same habit of stringent opposition marks Ryan's discrimination between a 'good' (that is, 'critical') Marxism and a 'bad' (that is, 'scientific', positivistic) one. Things are not, unfortunately, so simple: not all scientific Marxism is metaphysical, and not all 'critical' – for which read 'humanistic' – Marxism is by any means invulnerable to vigorous theoretical and political critique. If Ryan suspects Althusser's doctrine of 'relative autonomy' to be a bit of metaphysical claptrap, he ought to think hard about the history of political blunders and blindnesses which springs from the lack of such a concept.

Deconstructive Marxism, Ryan writes, 'comes out on the side of those who emphasize the necessity of "interactive adaptation", the role of uncertainty, the modifications imposed by diverse situations and different contexts, the need for inclusion, rather than exclusion, of variables, the wisdom of choosing policies over monolithic programs, and the impossibility of mapping a whole reality'. This is all rather like the man who said he was in favour of virtue. Hands up all those who disagree. To term such a Marxism 'deconstructive' is surely to risk theoretical overkill; every right-thinking socialist the world over holds such views, though most of them have never heard of Jacques Derrida and would not be excessively enthralled if they had. This, indeed, touches upon a genuine problem. For if the liaison between Marxism and deconstruction is to be more than an idly theoreticist affair, it would seem necessary for it to make some difference to political practice; yet whenever Ryan sketches out a possible 'deconstructive politics' it seems instantly assimilable to the well-meaning, flexible, participatory if somewhat theoretically diffuse political programmes of the traditional New Left. Is there to be a Deconstructive Party alongside the Democrats, or is the encounter between Marxism and deconstruction not that kind of thing at all? Is 'deconstructing' an institution just a more modish name for traditional forms of socialist transformation, or does it imply practical strategic differences? These are questions prompted, rather than tackled, by Ryan's study.

One of the major strengths of *Marxism and Deconstruction* is that it turns against the muffler-removers aspects of their own theory. It reminds us forcibly of just what deliberate blindness and amnesia, what violence, suppression and marginalisation have been active in the effort to make Derrida's thought serve the cause of an elitist rhetoric. I once had a conversation with a member of the 'Yale School' about Derrida's politics, which ran slowly aground on my gathering recognition that, as far as my interlocutor was concerned, we might have been discussing Derrida's taste in antique snuffboxes. Perhaps it will be less easy, after the forthrightness, intelligence and originality of Michael Ryan's study, for such misunderstandings to occur.

7.

Marxism, Structuralism and Post-structuralism

In *Considerations on Western Marxism* (1976), Perry Anderson proposed a number of theses which have since passed into the general wisdom of the Marxist left. Western Marxism, he argued, sprang essentially from proletarian defeat in the post-Bolshevik era; the predominantly aesthetic and philosophical biases of its thought, in marked contrast to the political and economic preoccupations of classical Marxist theory, reflected a damaging dislocation of historical materialism from a blocked and thwarted working-class movement. For all its undoubted theoretical fertility, Western Marxism remained a largely academic phenomenon, drawing deeply upon idealist philosophical sources and marked by a most untraditional pessimism and melancholia. At the turn of the 1970s, Anderson claimed, this ambivalently creative and crippled heritage was on the wane, as renewed socialist militancy in the advanced capitalist societies appeared to herald the possibility of a Marxism less aloof from political practice.

That, in effect, was the situation when Anderson wrote his book; and his latest book begins by assessing in hindsight the accuracy of the predictions which *Considerations* advanced.[1] Two of these predictions – that Western Marxism itself would generate no more substantial work, and that there would be a return to the crucial political and economic issues which it had suppressed – Anderson believes to have been justified by the past decade. Since 1974, some decisive, even pioneering bodies of work (by Mandel, Braverman, Aglietta, Poulantzas, Miliband, Therborn, Olin Wright, Bahro, Cohen and others) have signalled a reversion to the classical problems of historical materialism in a range of theoretical areas. At the same time such work has represented an intriguing geographical shift, away from the heartlands of Western Marxism (France, Germany, Italy) towards the Anglophone world. The rise of a powerful Marxist historiography in that region, since the appearance of *Considerations*, is one major sign of this geographical displacement. The traditional relation between British and Continental Marxism, then, seems for the moment to have been effectively reversed.

Another of his predictions Anderson acknowledges to have been strikingly unvalidated: this resurgence of traditional Marxist *topoi* in the realm of theory did not lead to a reunification of theory and popular practice in a mass revolutionary movement. Strategic thinking remained immune from the 1970s theoretical renaissance; contemporary Marxism continues to share a 'poverty of strategy' with its Western Marxist precursors. Moreover, the shift in Marxist theory to the English-speaking world was coupled with a grave crisis of Marxism in the Latin societies, tantamount often enough to an abrupt renunciation of historical materialism as a whole. The apostasy of Lucio Colletti in Italy, and the squalid degeneration of the erstwhile Maoist *Tel Quel* group in France into strident anti-Sovietism and portentous mysticism, are signal instances. The paradox, then, is plain:

> At the very time when Marxism as a critical theory has been in unprecedented ascent in the English-speaking world, it has undergone a precipitous decline in the Latin societies where it was most powerful and productive in the post-war period (p. 30)

'Paris today', Anderson claims, 'is the capital of European intellectual reaction'; and it is to an exploration of this phenomenon that his first chapter is devoted.

The hypothesis which Anderson entertains here, to account for the French Marxist decline, is a striking and simple one: French Marxism is in crisis because it has been routed by structuralism. Shorn of an adequate theory of the subject, Althusserianism was unable to offer any coherent response to the mass insurgency of 1968; the consequence was a progressive effacement and dissolution of this current by the mid-1970s. Structuralism in general, however, passed through the ordeal of 1968 and out the other side, though in significantly transmogrified form. The post-structuralism of Lacan, Derrida, Foucault, Deleuze and others outstripped Marxist thought, and can be characterized, so Anderson argues, by three major intellectual themes: the exorbitation of language, the attenuation of truth and the randomization of history. Linguistics rashly extended its jurisdiction to imperialize all major structures of society, culminating in Derrida's flamboyant claim that 'there is nothing outside of the text'. Parallel with this inflation of the signifier went an attenuation of its referent, breeding the various neo-Nietzschean scepticisms about the very possibility of determinable truth, and the consequent elimination of the very grounds of rational knowledge. History was accordingly scattered into a purely aleatory phenomenon, in which adjacency eclipsed sequentiality. An implacable structural determinism gave birth, ironically, to a sheer contingency of historical change, which is no more than the chance outcome of a synchronic combinatory. Such a paradox is inscribed in the dualistic model of structuralism's founding father Saussure, for whom the language system as a whole is structurally predetermined and individual speech random and contingent; but it also mapped itself chronologically in the transition from the 'ascetic objectivism' of 'high' structuralism to the 'saturnalian subjectivism', the 'subjectivism without a subject' of the mid-1970s. Post-structuralism, Anderson writes in an agreeable rhetorical flourish, 'strafed meaning, over-ran truth, outflanked ethics and politics, and wiped out history'. Its themes can be found echoed in the work of Jürgen Habermas, whose initial insistence on the centrality of symbolic communication slides into an assertion of its primacy over production. Discourse, once more, is steadily inflated over all other social structures, although with Habermas in 'angelic' rather than 'diabolic' form: language assures the foundations of society and political consensus, restores order to history and is somehow naturally wedded to truth.

At this stage in the book, the reader is firmly convinced that the editor of *New Left Review* has undergone an inexplicable degeneration into idealism. Was Latin Marxism really rolled back and routed by the Saussurean sign? The answer, of course, is that it was not; in a carpet-pulling compositional device, Anderson explores this hypothesis only to reject it. Led gullibly up the garden path for an entire chapter, the reader is now decisively returned to the firm terrain of historical materialism. The explanation for the crisis in Latin Marxism lies in its 'external' rather than 'internal' history: if Marxist political disarray was particularly evident in the Latin societies, it was because they more than others endured the disillusionments of what appeared at the time two viable alternatives to Stalinism, namely Maoism and Eurocommunism. It was precisely in these societies, with their mass communist parties, that the chances of Eurocommunism seemed most favourable, and the bitter deflation of those chances thus most disorientating. In the Anglophone societies, by contrast, as well as in Scandinavia and West Germany, such hopes and projections had never been so vigorously generated, and the prospects of a reformist administration of capitalism held few novelties. In these nations, 'a steadier and more tough-minded historical materialism proved generally capable of withstanding political isolation or adversity, and of generating increasingly solid and mature work in and through them'. The culprit for the Marxist crisis is not, after all, the vagaries of the signifier but the vicissitudes of Eurocommunism.

One of the major virtues of *Considerations* was its deft articulation of the theoretical and political histories of Western Marxism. At every point, the limitations and lacunae of the theoretical work itself were grasped in relation to the historical situations of Western Marxist intellectuals. In this study, by contrast, any such significant articulation is effectively denied. The story of structuralism and its progeny, and the narrative of recent European political history, are both delivered with the intellectual acuity, bold synoptic sweep and formidable erudition which we have come to associate with Perry Anderson's work; but they are in no sense to be linked. In a kind of *trompe l'oeil* or conjuror's flourish, structuralism is waved alluringly before the reader only to disappear again, dismissed as any significant element of the Marxist crisis. It never, in brief, presented Marxism with any real challenge. This is a highly implausible claim, and in its way an idealist one. Structuralism, according to Anderson, was never significantly imbricated with the material political history he identifies as the true cause of Latin Marxism's dilemmas. Was it, then, merely a set of fashionable ideas conducting its own intellectual life in stately isolation from that historical context? Where did it come from, and what secured its intellectual tenacity and durability? Does Anderson not risk the very aleatory model of history he rightly denounces in Parisian post-structuralism? And if his study rightly rejects one kind of idealism – the fantasy that structuralism in itself could have defeated the Latin socialist movements – does it not run the risk of keeling over into another, sealing the complex historical phenomenon of structuralism into its own hermetic space, in a gesture curiously reminiscent of its own intellectual habits?

The fundamental reason why Anderson is unable to relate structuralism at all significantly to the historical context he analyses is because his view of it is unremittingly negative. In one sense, to be sure, one might argue that no critique of certain features of post-structuralism in particular could be negative enough. Its grosser political and philosophical absurdities, which have managed to turn the heads of a whole younger generation of potentially valuable militants now arrogantly confident that they have deconstructed a Marxism many of them have not even encountered, merit the most implacable opposition. From one viewpoint, post-structuralism certainly emerges from a political history: in some of its aspects it articulates a massive, pervasive failure of political nerve consequent upon the disillusionments of post-1968. Its profound pessimism (power is ubiquitous, the law inescapable, the ego impotent and derisory, truth and communication inconceivable, general theories of society terroristic, only marginal political activity feasible) is sure to be tracked to that source, as a later, more theatrical version of Western Marxist melancholia. Similarly, the euphoria of post-structuralism – its paradoxical other face – is at once displacement and recreation of the revolutionary moment: the orgasmic crisis of *jouissance*, the thrills and spills of the skidding signifier, the *éclat* of *écriture*, Lyotard's ageing-hippie points of libidinal intensity.

It is not that Anderson's book is not aware of post-structuralism as in these aspects a political retreat. But the connections are not made in detail, for structuralism is wheeled on stage only to be rolled instantly back into the wings. One could imagine, indeed, a parody of this book which began by gravely entertaining the notion that Zen Buddhism was responsible for Thatcher's re-election, proceeded to deliver a proper materialist denunciation of Zen Buddhism and then concluded that it had in fact been of nugatory significance for the event in question. The theoretical and compositional question which the book thus raises is simply: why discuss structuralism at all? Just because it happens to be there? The unqualifiedly negative treatment of the topic is curious for a writer like Anderson, than whom (after a little youthful intemperateness common to us all) there is no more generous-minded, intellectually charitable, impeccably

judicious British Marxist. Anderson's work is distinguished not
only by its theoretical brilliance but by its moral conscientious-
ness – its readiness to concede what it can to an opponent's case,
its swiftness to engage in self-criticism, its striking intellectual
humility and fair-dealing. His treatment of structuralism, by
contrast, is notably undialectical, failing as it does to attribute the
least grain of intellectual worth to its tenets, and failing in
consequence to grasp its essentially *contradictory* nature. A
properly dialectical assessment has yet to be made of how the
'high' or classical structuralism of the 1960s was *at once*, in its
scientism, idealism, compulsive holism, elimination of subjectivity, reification of social process and synchronic arresting of
history, an ideology eminently suitable to late capitalist society,
and *also*, in its extreme philosophical conventionalism, its disdain for triumphalistic historicisms and the pieties of bourgeois-
humanist subjectivity, its ruthlessly 'de-naturalizing' impulse and
exposure of truth as *production*, its resistance to the bourgeois
divisions of academic labour, a limitedly subversive strategy.

The same contradictory character can be found in the bodies
of writing which flowed from this 'classical' period. The denunciation of all global theorizing as epistemologically indefensible
meta-discourse is certainly an assault on Marxism; but it was also
a potentially valuable deconstruction of certain 'overtotalizing'
theories (not least certain versions of Marxism) which did indeed
ride roughshod over difference, conflict and specificity. The
'saturnalian subjectivism' Anderson scorns is indeed often
enough a politically despairing hedonism, but it has also engaged (in the work of Julia Kristeva, for example) more authentically Bakhtinian themes of the carnival of the oppressed.
Foucaultean 'micro-politics' represent at once a politically disas-
trous dispersal of traditional Marxist forms of political organization, and a recovery of vital, twilight regions of political work
which traditional Marxism has often brutally suppressed. The
'attenuation of truth' is certainly one of the more irresponsible
features of post-structuralism; but Anderson writes as though
the correspondence theory is quite unproblematic and in good
working order, despite the grievous difficulties with which it is
beset.

Anderson's summary treatment of Jacques Derrida exempli-
fies his seriously one-sided approach to his topic. Language, as
Anderson interprets Derrida's view of it, is 'a system of floating
signifiers pure and simple, with no determinable relation to any

extra-linguistic referents at all' (p. 46). This is indeed the ridiculous case touted by many of Derrida's less canny acolytes, on both sides of the Atlantic, but Derrida himself has specifically defended the place of authorial intentionality in discourse, acknowledged the determinate forces of productive matrix and historical conditions in the construction of meaning, and firmly denied that he is a pluralist.[2] The statement that 'there is nothing outside of the text' is not to be taken, absurdly, to suggest that, for example, Jacques Derrida does not exist, but to deconstruct empiricist or metaphysical oppositions between discourse and some 'brute' reality beyond it. Derrida has insisted in recent years that deconstruction is a political rather than textual operation – that 'it is by touching solid structures, "material" institutions, and not merely discourses or significant representations, that deconstruction distinguishes itself from analysis or "criticism"'.[3] He has refused to ally himself unequivocally (so far at least) with post-Marxism, criticized the American appropriation of his work as confirming dominant political and economic interests, and denounced the attack on the teaching of philosophy in French schools as an assault on Marxism.[4] Anderson's polemic quite fails to distinguish between 'left' and 'right' deconstruction – between those for whom the theory merely offers an opportunity for hermetic textualism and self-indulgent word-play, and those who have discerned in it (not least within the women's movement) political possibilities. Nor can the work of Michel Foucault be as airily, abrasively dismissed as Anderson would appear to wish. For if anyone has presented traditional Marxism with a powerful challenge, one with immense influence upon a whole younger generation of radicals from Sydney to San Diego, it is precisely Foucault. It is not that the challenge is always by any means a productive one; the work of Foucault well deserves many of Anderson's scornful strictures. But it can by no means be evaded or ignored; and the tone of this book invites us, in effect, to do precisely that. The blank puzzlement evinced by Etienne Balibar and Pierre Macherey at how exactly to respond to Foucault's work is one index of the fact that (post)-structuralism, *pace* Anderson, has indeed played its subordinate part in the crisis of French Marxism.[5]

It is symptomatic of Anderson's too sweeping excoriation of structuralism that while many of his points are superbly just and effectively unanswerable, others are off the mark. He chides

Lacan's famous formula that 'the unconscious is structured like a language' on the Freudian grounds that the unconscious 'is a stranger to all syntax'; but while this is true, Lacan is referring here specifically to the mechanisms of (metaphorical) substitution and (metonymic) displacement, which are not dependent upon a well-ordered grammar. He makes a casual, scathing reference (a familiar bugbear, this) to Lacan's 'ten-minute' psychoanalytic sessions; in fact, these are sessions in which the analyst, having failed to establish himself as 'Other' to an analysand who insists on seeing him in the 'imaginary', prematurely forecloses the dialogue on that account. Anderson rightly upbraids linguistic or discursive imperialism, but he is himself too uncritical of Saussure, appearing to endorse his view of *parole* as some form of free individual contingency. On the contrary, discourse theory (and not least that of Voloshinov, in his *Marxism and the Philosophy of Language*) has revealed the rigorously constrained social determinations of all speech, the subject of which is never, as Anderson asserts, 'axiomatically individual' but always, as Bakhtin has shown, a *dialogic* subject.

Several of these points are minor in themselves; but they betray a certain unfocusedness of analysis, and accumulate to a point where Anderson's language grows exorbitant and its truth-value attenuated. The book's refusal to allow structuralism any significant role in the crisis of Marxism, and its unmodifiedly inimical treatment of the topic, are significantly related. For if Anderson had more judiciously assessed the positive aspects of structuralism, he would have been more sensitive to their appeal to the left; he would have thus been less inclined to intimate a purely negative relation between structuralism and political society, in which the two are either bluntly disconnected or the former is viewed simply as a flight from the realities of the latter.

Anderson's failure to take the full positive measure of these intellectual developments reproduces itself, in the book's postscript, in a seriously flawed account of feminism. He rightly emphasizes the greater historical and social weight of sexual as against class oppression, and while insisting that only the forces of organized labour can finally produce the social transformations which might bring patriarchy down, in no way denies the autonomy of feminist political practice. But his estimation of the potential power of the women's movement is curiously

defective. He is unwarrantably sceptical about the possibilities of
collective resistance among women, stressing what he sees as
the typically 'individual' character of women's rebellion. Having
made this point, he seems to remember the power and solidarity
of the women's movement, and hastily qualifies himself: 'None
of this means, of course, that joint action by women for their
liberation is impossible' (p. 92). It would indeed demand the
most full-blooded post-structuralist sceptic to survey the historical record and deny that! Having inserted this saving clause,
Anderson then reassumes a critical position; but now his
argument has subtly shifted to an essentially different one concerning the ultimate (socialist) forces of emancipation. He
regards the biologically based interdependence of the sexes as
a serious stumbling block in the movement to women's liberation, generating as it does ties of 'sentiment and support'; yet
there is no reason in principle why the functions of biological
reproduction could not be fulfilled without such ties, in a world
where men and women had severed all emotional relationship
with each other. These emotional gratifications, so Anderson
argues, provide women with (politically counterproductive)
'compensations' within the structures of sexist oppression, which
he claims have no strict equivalent in the economic relationships
between workers and capitalists. No *strict* equivalent, perhaps; but the process of hegemony is among other things the
generating of gratifications and compensations in the labour
process too, and there is no reason to believe that these are
necessarily less tenaciously rooted than the fulfilments derived
from sexual relationship. Women, Anderson argues, tend to
concentrate their rebellion on a 'particular partner' rather than
a whole gender – a speciously universalizing claim which (even
were it true) merely effaces the whole hard-bought experience
of consciousness-raising and collective political activity within
the women's movement. Women 'do not possess either the same
positional unity or totalized adversary' as the working class;
yet they do indeed of course possess a 'totalized adversary' –
men! – and the capitalist class is quite as physically dispersed
as the male sex. It is true that women do not share the same
positional unity as the proletariat, but neither, for example, does
the peasantry, which has none the less manifested itself as a
socially transformative force from time to time. The 'peculiarity'
of women's condition, Anderson argues, is the absence of any
specialized agencies for their regulation and repression; but this

is not in fact a feature peculiar to women, as the case of homosexuals and ethnic groups well enough reveals. If there is 'never any overall *centralization* of the structures of women's oppression', this is quite as true of certain structures of racist oppression; yet powerfully collective movements have shaken such structures in their time.

The lapses in Anderson's account of the women's movement are at once serious enough in themselves, and significantly related to the one-sidedness of his critique of structuralism. For there has been, of course, a certain historic alliance between feminism and post-structuralism, as radical, oppositional movements gravely sceptical of certain central features of classical Marxist politics. Anderson rightly stresses the need for a socialist movement 'various and plural in composition', within which feminists will 'muster under their own banners'; and it would therefore be quite mistaken to view his account of feminism as a politically appropriating one. It is rather a politically *belittling* one: by no means in its entirety, but in its curious insensitivity to the historical realities and future potential of collective feminist action. The analyses of structuralism are, as I have argued, similarly insensitive to its more constructive and subversive aspects. I am afraid that it is already possible to foresee the feminist and post-structuralist reviews of this book which read it as a mere re-statement of a classical Marxist position which, they feel, has nothing in it for them. Its most damaging effect would be to confirm the sometimes warrantable, sometimes complacent assumption that Marxism has remained merely unscathed by feminist and post-structuralist developments. Anderson is certainly a 'traditional' Marxist, but he is by no means an uncritical one; the final pages of this book are devoted to a brilliant exposé of some of the intractable problems of socialist construction which, as Anderson recognizes, much Marxist thought has left studiously vague. The account of feminism, while flawed in the ways I have suggested, also contains some powerfully positive, politically suggestive elements; the account of structuralism, while brilliantly accomplished, is much more seriously belittling. Jacques Derrida once wrote that as far as he was concerned, the encounter with Marxism was 'still to come'. I am afraid that, after this book, the same must be said by Marxism about post-structuralism.

8.

Wittgenstein's Friends

Searching for an epigraph to his *Philosophical Investigations*, Ludwig Wittgenstein considered using a quotation from *King Lear*: 'I'll teach you differences.' 'Hegel', he once told a friend, 'always seems to me to be wanting to say that things which look different are really the same. Whereas my interest is in shewing that things which look the same are really different.'[1] Perhaps one should not invest too much in this remark. One way in which Wittgenstein kept his distance from classical philosophy was by not reading it: as Professor of Philosophy at Cambridge he had not read a word of Aristotle; and as far as Hegel goes, he was once told by a professor in Russia that he ought to read more of him.[2] Yet it is surely remarkable that Wittgenstein should consider choosing as a way of summarizing the project of the *Investigations* the term which more than any has become hallmark and totem of contemporary post-structuralism. Remarkable in one way, maybe, but not in another: the influence of Wittgenstein's work on Anglo-Saxon linguistic philosophy has served partly to obscure its deep-seeted affinities with a body of thought which has also shaped post-structuralism, that of Martin Heidegger.[3] The Wittgenstein of Geach and Strawson seems largely to have lost that distinctively European timbre, that dimension of sheer strangeness and intractability, as one might claim that the Derrida of some Anglo-American deconstructionists has forfeited a certain rigorous circumspection and political resonance notable in the work of the master.

I. Everyday Language Versus Metaphysics

Russell and the Parsons

Meeting his friend F. R. Leavis one day in Cambridge, Wittgenstein stepped up and commanded him unceremoniously to give up literary criticism. We have Leavis's reaction in an ambiguous, posthumously published memoir.[4] Perhaps Wittgenstein thought that Leavis should give up literary criticism because, like philosophy, it changed nothing. Wittgenstein's well-known claim that philosophy leaves everything exactly as it is has often been quoted as an index of social and intellectual reaction, a complacent consecration of existing 'language games', and there is surely some truth in this. The friend who once took him aback by telling him to his face that Marxism was nothing like so discredited as his own antiquated political opinions was as shrewd as she was bold.[5] But Wittgenstein's attitude to philosophy is not after all very different from that of Marx's eleventh thesis on Feuerbach, not that that formulation is impervious to criticism. How absurd to imagine that *philosophy* could change anything! If deep-seated conceptual change is to be possible, it can only be the result of transformations in 'forms of life'. Wittgenstein was thus presumably quite serious in urging his acolytes to abandon philosophy altogether. Philosophy might have a certain therapeutic value for the badly mystified, but it hardly seemed to warrant a lifetime's labour. Wittgenstein had a fine knack for philosophy but little respect for it, like someone who finds himself embarrassingly adept at juggling or playing the Jew's harp.

'Russell and the parsons between them have done infinite harm, infinite harm,' Wittgenstein complained to a friend.[6] The metaphysical, as for Jacques Derrida, is the main enemy: that hunt for the crystalline structure of all speech which obsesses the early *Tractatus Logico-Philosophicus*: 'The more narrowly we examine actual language, the sharper becomes the conflict between it and our requirement. (For the crystalline purity of logic was, of course, not a *result of investigation*: it was a requirement.) The conflict becomes intolerable; the requirement is now in danger of becoming empty. – We have got on to slippery ice where there is no friction and so in a certain sense the conditions are ideal, but also, just because of that, we are unable to walk. We want to walk: so we need *friction*. Back to the rough ground!

. . . A *picture* held us captive. And we could not get outside it, for it lay in our language and language seemed to repeat it to us inexorably' (107, 115).[7]

The structure of our grammar holds out illusory representations to us, tempts us to assimilate kinds of discourse which have quite different uses. This is not some kind of knockabout anti-metaphysical iconoclasm, any more than it is for Jacques Derrida, who has constantly emphasized the inescapability of the meta-physical, 'Don't think I despise metaphysics,' Wittgenstein warned. 'I regard some of the great philosophical systems of the past as among the noblest productions of the human kind. For some people it would require an heroic effort to give up this sort of writing.'[8] For some people, indeed! It can't have been much less than heroic for Ludwig Wittgenstein to abandon the icily metaphysical *Tractatus*, the very bible of such thought for a whole coterie of philosophers, even though as a man he was adept at abandoning, often with casual brutality, any friend, belief or habit which seemed to him to block the path to personal purity. The personal fanaticism of this intensely repressed émigré patrician contrasts curiously with the generous pluralism of the *Investigations*.

Wittgenstein and Derrida are alike in suspecting all philo-sophy of immediacy, all grounding of discourse in the experi-ence of a subject.[9] The sign for Wittgenstein is not the mark of an inward sensation (intending, for example, is not an experi-ence); meaning is an effect of the signifier, which must always already be in play, traced through with its history of hetero-geneous uses, for the meaning of the subject to emerge at all. For Wittgenstein, as for post-structuralism, the subject is 'written' from the outset, an effect of the play of the signifier; any 'fullness' he or she may experience over and above this is no more than a rhetorical emphasis: 'I have seen a person in a discussion on this subject strike himself on the breast and say: "But surely another person can't have THIS pain!" – The answer to this is that one does not define a criterion of identity by emphatic stressing of the word "this"' (253).

The 'private' sign, leashed by a supposedly internal bond to a pure sensation, is a metaphysical chimera, an instance of that philosophy of phenomenological self-presence which both Witt-genstein and Derrida are out to fracture by the disseminating force of language. Nor for either thinker can this force be recuperated or evaded by some unassailable notion of identity.

Difference and identity are equally effects of discourse: how do I know that this is the 'same' sensation as I was having last Wednesday unless I have learnt to deploy words in a particular rule-governed way? Perhaps I can privately invent names for my experiences and use the 'same' name each time the 'same' one comes up, as A. J. Ayer once argued[10] – a ceremony which for Wittgenstein would be precisely equivalent to my left hand giving my right hand money (268); or to someone exclaiming 'But I know how tall I am!' and placing his hand on top of his head (279); or to a man buying himself several copies of the daily newspaper to assure himself that what the first copy said was true (265).

How can I invent names for my experiences unless I am already inscribed in a discourse which includes the practice of naming experiences? How could I get somebody to understand the name of an object by pointing to it, unless he or she already grasped the social institution of pointing, looked away from my fingertip to the object rather than up my arm? If only *I* know whether I used a word to identify the 'same' experience then the ceremony is empty, as nothing here would count as going wrong (and thus of going right). The man who buys several copies of the newspaper fails to see that the first text was a copy too – that there was no 'original' text, that there is no privileged originary sign which grounds all the others. Wittgenstein as much as Derrida is 'opposed to the idea that certain forms of language are specially privileged, meaningful in some unique, fundamental way'.[11] The person who uses the same privately invented sign each time an experience comes up has grasped the point that signs, to be signs at all, must be in Derrida's term 'iterable', but not the point that it is just this iterability which fissures their self-identity[12] – that since there is no 'pure' repetition, the question of what counts as difference or identity is a social question to be contended over within discourse and forms of life, not a problem resolvable by 'experience'.

Rules of the Game

'A thing is identical with itself.' There is no finer example, Wittgenstein says, of a useless proposition (216). 'We seem to have an infallible paradigm of identity in the identity of a thing with itself' (215). So I know that two things are the same when they are what one thing is! And how did I apply what I knew of one thing to two things? Anyone cay *say* that 'It is five o'clock on the sun' means the same as 'It is five o'clock here', but this is no more informative than saying that what it means for me to have a pain is what it means for you to have one (350). In the *Remarks on the Foundations of Mathematics*, Wittgenstein considers how we would respond to someone who when following a rule seems suddenly to change its application but on being told that he is now doing something different denies it.[13] This would not necessarily be perverse, for rules are not commands and do not carry their interpretations on their faces. What counts as a different way of proceeding under one rubric may count as the same under another. Wittgenstein is not a 'structuralist' out to decentre the subject into some set of unbreachably determining codes: for 'what does a game look like that is everywhere bounded by rules? . . . Can't we imagine a rule determining the application of a rule, and a doubt which *it* removes – and so on?' (84).

Such an infinitely regressive recourse to meta-rules in order to eradicate indeterminacies is for Wittgenstein as for Derrida merely one more metaphysical illusion: 'But when the use of the word is unregulated, the "game" we play with it is unregulated. – It is not everywhere circumscribed by rules; but no more are there any rules for how high one throws the ball in tennis, or how hard; yet tennis is a game for all that and has rules too' (68). If someone has been taught to master an arithmetical series, 'how far need he continue the series for us to have the right to say that [he had done so]?' 'Clearly', Wittgenstein says, 'you cannot state a limit here' (145).

'But still, it isn't a game, if there is some vagueness *in the rules*,' muses Wittgenstein ironically (100). Perhaps, once we admit such indeterminacies, the whole definition (of 'game', 'text', 'mode of production') collapses. This, indeed, is the illicit move made by certain strains of post-structuralism. Once we have seen through the chimera of ideality, recognized with Wittgenstein or Derrida that the play of our discourses is potentially unbounded and the metonymic chains of the signifier unstoppable, then we are plunged into an abyss in which nothing is certain except 'undecidability'. But concepts of 'certainty', 'exactness', 'indeterminacy' and so on, like concepts of identity and difference,[14] operate within practical forms of social life and take their force from that. It is just as transcendentally unhistorical to assert that all discourse is undecidable as it is to claim that all language is luminously clear. The post-structuralist devotee of undecidability is to this extent merely the prodigal child of the metaphysical father. 'Without exact boundaries we don't know where we are!' It is the *tone* in which one says this – anxious or euphoric – which indicates whether one is a metaphysician or a deconstructionist. But what that indicates in turn is a certain complicity between the two. *Of course* language is 'indeterminate': how could it work, how could we walk, if it were not? Can't it 'work perfectly', Wittgenstein asks, to say 'stand roughly there'? Is Frege right to claim that an area with vague boundaries isn't an area at all? Is an indistinct photograph not a picture of a person at all, and is it always an advantage to replace an indistinct picture by a sharp one? (71). 'Am I inexact because I do not give our distance from the sun to the nearest foot?' (88).

Perhaps discourse is groundless, the transcendental signified illusory, in the sense that there isn't a 'last' definition; but what would count as this in the first place? 'Last' for whose and what purpose, within what practical forms of life? 'Do not say: "There isn't a last definition". That is just as if you chose to say: "There isn't a last house in this road; one can always build an additional one"' (29). Indeed one can: just as new language games can always emerge into existence; for there are no transcendentally fixed bounds to discourse, and language is productive precisely because of, not despite, this indeterminacy.[15] (The criticism that Wittgenstein consecrates the linguistic status quo, though accurate in one sense, is mistaken in another, since if it is in the nature of language to be dynamically indeterminate it can have no high degree of stability to be consecrated.) But the fact that one can always build a new house, reinscribe a piece of discourse in a new context, or develop new forms of discourse altogether, does not strike the concept of 'the last house' or 'the last definition' meaningless in a *particular* use of it. What counts as an adequate or ultimate definition 'will depend on the circumstances under which it is given, and on the person I give it to' (29); and we should remember in any case that we sometimes demand definitions 'for the sake not of their content, but of their form. Our requirement is an architectural one; the definition a kind of ornamental coping that supports nothing' (217).

An explanation does not 'hang in the air unless supported by another one' (87). And if there is no ultimate ground to explanation, no immovable bedrock of sense, then it is still metaphysical to believe that this renders an explanation any less of an explanation. There is a form of post-structuralist thought which makes much the same mistake in this respect as that made by the Christian Brothers who tried to teach me, at the age of eleven, Aquinas's demonstration of the existence of God from causality. What was the cause of the water boiling? It was clearly no kind of answer to reply, 'The heat of the gas', for what caused this? And then that? And so on. To avoid an infinite regress here you must finally posit a first uncaused cause, God.

Post-structuralism is not theistic, but some modes of it have not thereby ceased to preserve the metaphysical structure of this argument. In removing the end-stop of the Almighty, such theories weave the metonymic chains tied to his throne into the inexhaustible operations of the *text*, in which every element is invaded, disrupted and rendered undecidable by every other. One simple response to this is that 'The heat of the gas' is indeed the answer to 'What causes water to boil?' It counts within certain discursive criteria as the answer to *that* question. You may then choose to raise a further question, or you may not. 'An explanation may indeed rest on another one that has been given, but none stands in need of another – unless *we* require it to prevent a misunderstanding' (87). What will determine whether we need to give another explanation is the social context in which we are arguing. Whether this explanation is found exact or desperately indeterminate depends on what we are doing.

'Doubting has an end,' Wittgenstein writes (180). This, too, would seem at odds with a certain post-structuralist bent, despite the affinities between such thought and Wittgenstein's that I am trying to suggest. Surely nothing could be more metaphysical than claims to certainty? Let us consider one such claim: the claim that in certain circumstances I can be certain of what you are feeling. When I see you rolling at my feet with your hair on fire then I can be certain that the utterances you are producing signify pain, rather than simply being able to infer or surmise that you are in pain. I cannot say, 'I can know that I am in pain but can only guess that you are,' since as Wittgenstein comments the sentence 'I know that I am in pain' is meaningless. I can be as certain of someone else's sensations in certain circumstances as I can be of any fact, Wittgenstein remarks – as certain as I am that twice two is four. If this does not mean that I am 'mathematically certain' of your sensations, it is only because mathematical certainty is not a psychological concept, and that such a claim merely conflates two different language games (224). But the fact is that I can be, if you like to use the term, 'absolutely' certain in such situations of what you are feeling.[16] Those who doubt this do so because they are the captives of traditional forms of metaphysical dualism. It is metaphysical to doubt that we can sometimes know with certainty what others are feeling. Those post-structuralists who believe that in subverting concepts of certainty they are putting the skids under metaphysics should perhaps consider that in this respect at least they are doing exactly the opposite.

Discourse and 'Forms of Life'

Wittgenstein's argument here rests on a particular view of the relations between discourse and its material conditions; and this is also an issue of relevance to contemporary debates between post-structuralists and historical materialists. The former appear to the latter to be idealists in their suppression of the material conditions of discourse, or in the discursive imperialism whereby they would translate such conditions into yet more undecidable 'text'. The latter appear to the former as discursive reductionists, smuggling in some 'transcendental signified' (history, the 'real') in order to lend discourse yet another metaphysical underpinning. For all practical purposes it would appear that there was a choice between the two approaches: some discourse theorists refer texts to their material conditions of possibility, while others do not. But if Wittgenstein is right then there is not in fact a choice in the matter: discourse is *internally* related to its social conditions. If a lion could talk we would not be able to understand him (223), not simply because he was speaking a foreign language (we might always get to translate it), but because his language would be as necessarily inaccessible to us as his form of life. If you spend your life on four legs roaring and chasing after raw meat then you could not speak intelligibly to beings like ourselves. As Norman Malcolm puts it: 'If we want to understand any concept we must obtain a view of the human behaviour, the activities, the natural expressions, that surround the words for that concept.'[17] The relation between discourse and forms of life is necessary, not contingent; for Wittgenstein the language of sensation in particular would be incomprehensible if it were not closely bound up with actual behaviour.

It follows that 'what has to be accepted, the given, is – so one could say – *forms of life*' (226). This is not an expression of political conservatism: there is no reason why what has to be accepted are *these particular* forms of life, and indeed little reason to believe that Wittgenstein himself was in the least content with his own society. It is just that even if existing forms of life were to be revolutionized, those transformed practices and institutions would still in the end provide the only justification for why people spoke and thought as they did. Such practices would not thereby be *self*-justifying: you could always get people to see that they were in some way at fault, and thus to change them. When someone is inclined to say: 'This is simply what I do' to justify his or her beliefs and utterances (217), you can always say: 'Well, do something else!'

Where Wittgenstein's philosophy is reactionary is not in its referring of beliefs and discourses to social activity, but in its assumption that such referring constitutes a liberation from the metaphysical. 'When philosophers use a word – "knowledge", "being", "object", "I", "proposition", "name" – and try to grasp the *essence* of the thing, one must always ask oneself: is the word ever actually used in this way in the language-game which is its original home? – What we do is to bring words back from their metaphysical to their everyday use' (116).

And where, for Marxism and post-structuralism, could metaphysics be more at home than in the everyday? For Wittgenstein, metaphysical mystifications seem to arise for purely linguistic reasons – from 'a tendency to sublime the logic of our language' (38), from 'the bewitchment of our intelligence by means of language' (109). The task of philosophy is consequently 'not to advance any kind of theory' (109), but to familiarize surroundings which have suddenly become alien, to *remind* us of our whereabouts. In a way we were seeing through the metaphysical all the time: philosophy will simply 'arrang(e) what we have always known' (109), articulate what everyone admits, and we have only to take the metaphysical spectacles off our nose in order to see reality straight. 'The ideal, as we think of it, is unshakable. You can never get outside it; you must always turn back. There is no outside; outside you cannot breathe. – Where does this idea come from? It is like a pair of glasses on our nose through which we see whatever we look at. It never occurs to us to take them off' (103).

The specular image, suggestive of certain Marxist notions of 'false consciousness', is interestingly undermined by Wittgenstein's arguments elsewhere in the *Investigations*. For if metaphysical mystification arises out of the very structures of our grammar, how can *these* be 'taken off'? Perhaps this is why Wittgenstein does not write here that the *ideal* is the pair of glasses, but that the *idea* of it is – a kind of double refraction. But what is freeing ourselves from the idea of the ideal other than freeing ourselves from the ideal, and how could this possibly be done if the ideal is embedded in the very forms of our daily discourse? Are these glasses idealizing ones, such that if we took them off we could see reality for what it is, or is it that if we took them off we would see the *ideal* steadily for what it is? Is this idealization just a form of astigmatism, corrigible at will (we can always decide to take the glasses off if it occurs to us to do so), or does this ideal picture 'lie in our language' (115), out there beyond our noses, such that the mere correct perception of it will not make it go away? Is seeing the ideal the same as seeing through it? Why *doesn't* it occur to us to take the glasses off? Because the ideal is closer to us than the mere idea of it, part of the structure which allows us to produce ideas (of the ideal) in the first place, inside the head rather than perched outside on the nose?

It is the ideal itself, Wittgenstein tells us, which deceives us into thinking that we can never get outside it, that there is no outside, that outside you cannot breathe. But how could you even think of breathing in the first place in an outside which is no place at all, which is not the outside of anything and which is not an inside either? The ideal seems at once to intimate and deny an outside to itself, cannot indeed deny it without intimating it in that very act. Caught on this problematic frontier between an outside which does not exist and an inside which is therefore not an inside at all, Wittgenstein will escape not by 'always turning back', but by turning *away* to ordinary language itself: fleeing from prison to home, from ice to the rough ground, from thin air to the living, breathing world. But this outside is an inside too, for it is here, after all, in the rough-and-ready forms of our speech, that philosophico-grammatical illusions are continually generated; the very instruments with which the metaphysical will be safely defused are themselves metaphysically contaminated. If 'ordinary language' contains the perpetual possibility of metaphysical illusion, if its logic is sublimable, then such operations cannot be contingent to it but must be part of its very character. Metaphysical distortions are not 'external' contaminations implanted from above by philosophy, but products of an internal 'defectiveness' of which metaphysical philosophy itself is merely the most dramatic.

Derrida and Nietzsche

'What we are destroying is nothing but houses of cards and we are clearing up the ground of language on which they stand' (118). Now the inside/outside metaphor has shifted to one of base and superstructure: the metaphysical houses of cards rest on the ground of ordinary language but can be demolished in a way which leaves that ground intact. In clearing away these flimsy edifices, philosophy 'may in no way interfere with the actual use of language . . . It leaves everything as it is' (124). One can see well enough, then, why Wittgenstein needs his houses to be made of *cards*: it would not be so easy to demolish a building of brick or stone and leave the ground on which it was standing unseared, for such a building has *foundations* which might also need to be uprooted, foundations which render the binary distinction between 'above' (or 'outside') the ground, and the ground itself, between 'air' and 'earth', considerably less stable. For Wittgenstein philosophy 'cannot give (actual uses of language) any foundations' (124), for such language games have their foundation already in forms of life. It would be superfluous for philosophy to try to ground these forms of life in hypostasized essences: that is the metaphysical error.

But what if it was superfluous because these forms of life were in some sense metaphysical already? Wittgenstein would seem to believe that it is traditional philosophy which is the metaphysical villain, 'exterior' to the unimpeachable ground of social life; but if philosophy, like any other discourse, can itself be explained only in terms of certain concrete social practices, his case simply deconstructs itself. He must find himself arguing, rather like Derrida's Plato and his *pharmakon*,[18] that 'everyday linguistic use' is both source and prophylactic of metaphysical disorder. Paul Feyerabend has argued that Wittgenstein, contrary to his usual way of thinking, does indeed want to draw a sharp line between philosophy and social life, for unless he did so he would be forced to admit that philosophy is itself a 'language game', that there is no determinate border between it and other discourses, and that its existence, far from being a mere therapeutic response to linguistic disorders, thus poses a serious historical problem in its own right.[19] One might argue similarly that deconstruction's refusal to pose itself as a *theory* is in practice a suppression of its historical conditions of existence.

Feyerabend also suggests that Wittgenstein does not want his reader to discover that reading is *not* a mental process. For if 'mental process' is used in a metaphysical way in 'reading is a mental process', it is used just as metaphysically in 'reading is not a mental process'.[20] He is not out to provide us with a different theory of such metaphysical entities as 'mental processes' but to induce the problem to self-destruct, as it were, by referring such uses of language back to their quotidian home. In this sense, as Feyerabend recognizes, there is a continuity between the Wittgenstein of the *Investigations* and the mystic of the *Tractatus*, for whom 'he who understands [the author] must finally recognize [these sentences] as senseless . . . [He must so to speak throw away the ladder, after he has climbed up on it]. He must surmount these [sentences] . . . then he sees the world rightly.'[21] Religious illumination breaks upon the reader of the *Investigations* when he or she realizes that there are no metaphysical problems, that everything lies open to view and that the world is the way it is; such illumination strikes the reader of the *Tractatus* when he or she is somehow *shown* how language pictures the world, a relation which language itself cannot state.

Jacques Derrida, rather similarly, is not out to advocate a *theory* of the metaphysical. He sees, as Wittgenstein does not, that there is no escape from the prison-house of metaphysics into 'ordinary language'; that indeed 'ordinary language' is itself a metaphysical illusion, and that any conception of an 'outside' to metaphysics, sublimely uninfected by its propositions, is itself a metaphysical opposition. The fly is not to be let out of the fly-bottle quite so easily. Nevertheless, for Derrida too, there are moments when through the disruptive force of textual dissemination we may show – not state or conceptualize – a fissure in the metaphysical enclosure, moments which in the sense of the *Tractatus* have something mystical about them.[22] If what a certain form of deconstruction predicates of all discourse – that it is ultimately undecidable – must logically be predicated of itself, then we are back to that self-destructing moment of the *Tractatus* in which the impossible 'truth' of language is disclosed at the very point of its annihilation.

Aware that the death of God has left metaphysics securely in place, Wittgenstein and Derrida seek to complete the task which Nietzsche began, and in doing so risk moving into an alternative form of religion. The strength and weakness of deconstruction is that it seeks to position itself at the extreme limit of the thinkable. This rocks the foundations of metaphysical knowledge to the precise extent that, posed at the extreme edge as it is, it threatens like Wittgenstein to leave everything exactly as it was. To affirm that because of the nature of discourse and the movement of the signifier no analysis can be exhaustible, no interpretation ultimately grounded, valuably demystifies the metaphysical but is, as I have tried to use Wittgenstein to demonstrate, quite compatible with talk of 'truth', 'certainty', 'determinacy' and so on. To make a stronger claim – that because of the nature of discourse no truth or certainty is possible at all – does indeed make a dramatic difference to everything as it is, but is itself no more than a negative metaphysic.

Wittgenstein returns a disreputable answer to the question of the practical foundations of the metaphysical; Derrida is wholly silent upon the question. The former would dissolve metaphysics by recourse to 'popular' discourse; the latter remains locked within certain textual strategies. The former's 'popular' language remains largely metaphysical; the latter's strategies remain distinctly unpopular. We may now turn to a third thinker, whose work strikingly combines and surpasses both positions.

II. Language as Carnival

The Brothers Bakhtin

One of Wittgenstein's closest friends, in so far as he had any, was Nikolai Bakhtin, lecturer in classics at the University of Birmingham, and later the first professor of linguistics there. Born in Russia in 1896, the son of a civil servant who was an untitled member of the nobility, Bakhtin studied classics at Petersburg University, where he associated with the Russian Symbolists, was deeply influenced by Nietzsche and hoped for an Hellenic renaissance. He volunteered to fight in the First World War, and on the outbreak of the Bolshevik revolution seems at first to have assumed a fairly neutral posture; but roused by reports of Red atrocities he joined the White Army in 1918 and saw some fighting. Sometime later he emigrated from

Russia, spent four years in the French Foreign Legion where he was wounded in action and was invalided out to a bohemian life of semi-starvation in Paris. Here he gave occasional lectures on ancient Greece, and became a member of the editorial board of the literary journal *Zveno*. From Paris he came to England and in 1935 was appointed assistant lecturer in classics at University College, Southampton. In 1938 he became lecturer in classics at Birmingham University, and in 1945 founded the department of linguistics there. In his later years he was engaged on a study of Plato's *Cratylus* – a doomed project, the drafts of which are held in the Birmingham University library.

Bakhtin was apparently unable to organize his ideas into a coherent statement: he privately published one book in 1945, an introduction to the study of modern Greek; and a collection of rather unremarkable essays and lectures of his, on such topics as Tolstoy, Pushkin, Mayakovsky, realism in theatre and Russian Symbolism, was edited in 1963 by Austin Duncan-Jones.[23] By the time of the Second World War, this erstwhile Russian aristocrat and White Guard had become, in his friend Fanya Pascal's words, a 'fiery Communist';[24] his memoir of the Russian Revolution – 'The Russian Revolution as seen by a White Guard' – makes it plain that he regarded himself as having fought on the wrong side, and that the White Army 'fully deserved destruction'.[25] He joined the Communist Party before his death in 1950.

According to all reports, Nikolai Bakhtin was an extraordinary character, passionate, flamboyant and exuberant, and exerted a deep influence on Wittgenstein. His widow, Constance Bakhtin, reports that 'Wittgenstein loved Bakhtin',[26] and the two men apparently conducted 'interminable discussions'. According to Fanya Pascal, Wittgenstein was 'unusually happy and gay in [Bakhtin's] presence, and never dropped him as easily as he did others.'[27] Bakhtin was the friend to whom Wittgenstein, as he notes in the Preface to his *Philosophical Investigations*, explained the ideas of the *Tractatus*.[28] Exactly what the two men discussed is not known; but Bakhtin fiercely espoused what he took to be an Aristotelian sense of the particular over Plato's tyranny of the universal, and one can see well enough in a general way how this would fit with Wittgenstein's own philosophy of language.

In his essay 'Aristotle versus Plato', Bakhtin sees Plato, much after the manner of contemporary deconstruction, as a remorselessly 'binary' theorist, concerned with separation, opposition and division, and opposes to this 'tyranny of abstract ideas and dogmas over life' an Aristotelian engagement with 'continuous transitions of shades and qualities', a 'living multiplicity of moral values' which runs counter to the univocal metaphysics of a Plato.[29] His notion of thought is pragmatist and dynamic: ideas in Russian literature are 'bits of condensed energy to be converted into action . . . A work that counts is a generator of force, a rule of conduct, an appeal to action, a battle cry, an order, a challenge.'[30]

It is not difficult to feel the consonance of this cast of thinking with the outlook of a Wittgenstein. Bakhtin has high praise for Mayakovsky and the Russian Futurists as the revolutionists of the word appropriate to a Bolshevik age, much as he feared and opposed Mayakovsky when a White Russian school student. His essays on poetry disclose a consistently populist strain: 'Literature', he argues, was an historically late conception in Russia, distinct from a 'poetry' which had its roots in the oral practice of the people. In what might now be termed a characteristically 'phonocentric' gesture, he writes of the 'deadening effects of the printing press' on poetry,[31] and cultivates against this a concept of linguistic energy and passionate particularity which for him typifies Russian literature at its greatest.

The most important literary historical fact about Nikolai Bakhtin, however, has yet to be mentioned. For he was the elder brother by a year of Mikhail Mikhailovich Bakhtin, one of the major Marxist philosophers and aestheticians of the twentieth century. It is Mikhail, not Nikolai, who combines and surpasses the positions I have sketched above. There is apparently no evidence that the two brothers remained in contact after 1918, when their ways parted in the midst of post-revolutionary turmoil. We know, however, that Nikolai came across a copy of Mikhail's work on Dostoevsky in Paris in 1930.[32] We also know that though the brothers never met again after 1918, they had been extraordinarily close as children and were later to contend that they had never encountered anyone else in their lives who had been so important in their development.[33] The two men were influenced by much the same literary and intellectual context: as students, they were contemporaries at Petersburg University during one of the most stimulating and turbulent periods of twentieth-century Russian cultural life. Both men were to embark upon careers which took the philosophy of language as their basis, and there are some affinities between Nikolai's essays and lectures and Mikhail's 'Discourse and the Novel', surely one of the most superb documents of Marxist literary criticism of the century.[34] By a curious historical quirk, then, it may be that the thought of Ludwig Wittgenstein is indirectly related to the mainstream of Marxist aesthetics.

The Novel and Semantic Subversion

This does not seem an exaggerated claim, considering the book Mikhail Bakhtin published in 1929 under the name of his colleague V. N. Voloshinov, *Marxism and the Philosophy of Language*. Like Wittgenstein, Bakhtin insists in this text on the concrete uses of languages rather than on some metaphysical notion of essences; unlike Wittgenstein, however, he sees such concrete uses to be inseparable from the realm of ideology. The sign must be viewed not as Saussurean abstraction, definable by its exchange-value with other signs, but as concrete utterance unintelligible outside the material conditions and social relations in which it is caught up. For Bakhtin, the sign is material and 'multi-accentual', a shifting nexus of ideological struggle which is never stable or self-identical but lives only in its 'dialogic' orientation to other material signs. His literary interests are accordingly in those genres – 'carnival', Menippean satire, and indeed for Bakhtin the 'novel' as such – which embody some mighty 'polyphonic' contestation of discourses, genres whose sociality is inscribed in their very form; one language inhering within, relativizing and decentring another; one form of discourse invading, subverting, citing, framing, parodying or dismantling another.

Epic, for Bakhtin, is a type of that metaphysical 'monologism' in which truth is determinate and self-identical, transcendentally guaranteed by the aura and authority of an unimpeachable mythological past; the novel, which he sees as inherently multiple and disruptive, a 'dialogic' parody and deconstruction of other literary forms, destroys this epical aura rather as mechanical reproduction does for Walter Benjamin, unleashing a heterogeneity of language which is always unbounded and untotalized, in which 'there is no first word (ideal word), and the final word has yet to be spoken'.[35] What Bakhtin has done in fact is to take the terms drawn up by Georg Lukács in his *Theory of the Novel* – the epic as lost totality, the novel as doomed to 'transcendental homelessness' – and boldly invert their values. In the inconclusive context of the novel, 'all the semantic stability of the object is lost'; there is always 'an unrealized surplus of humanness' (37) within which the human subject itself is radically divided, and 'man ceases to coincide with himself'.

Bakhtin, as Michael Holquist argues, gives the name 'novel' to whatever force is at work within a literary system to reveal its artificial constraints.[36] 'Discourse lives, as it were, on the boundary between its own context and another, alien context' (284), and in this way authoritative or meta-linguistic language, which 'permits no play with the context framing it, no play with its borders' (243), is forced by a set of satirical alienation effects to render up its concealed relativism. In this explosive 'heteroglossia', this 'Galilean' linguistics which decentres all metaphysical signifiers, 'no living word relates to its object in a *singular* way: between the word and its object, between the word and the speaking subject, there exists an elastic environment of other, alien words about the same object, the same theme . . . Indeed any concrete discourse (utterance) finds the object at which it was directed already as it were overlain with qualifications, open to dispute, charged with value' (276).

Words, as for Derrida, are always-already inscribed, dense with the tangled traces of other historical uses. This direction of speech to and reception of it from an Other is true also for the emergence of the human subject: 'consciousness awakens to independent ideological life precisely in a world of alien discourses surrounding it, and from which it cannot initially separate itself' (345). In this sense there is no language which is not, in Jacques Lacan's terms, refracted through the Other: 'All direct meanings and expressions are false' (401), and the unity of the subject is in consequence an ideological construct: 'The unity of a man and the coherence of his acts . . . are of a rhetorical and legal character' (407). The novel for Bakhtin destroys 'any absolute bonding of ideological meaning to language', which is the very condition of magical and mythological thought (369); and its heteroglossia is enabled by the disintegration of stable verbal-ideological systems at certain key points (the Hellenistic era, Imperial Rome, the Middle Ages) of historical conflict. When class, regional, national and other discourses collide and are confounded through the breaching of some discrete ruling-class language, the socially productive soil for the novel is laid down.

The Anticipation of Post-structuralism

It is surely striking how Bakhtin's work seems to recapitulate, long before they had started, many of the dominant motifs of contemporary post-structuralism and to lend them moreover an historical basis. The division and dispersion of the human subject within language; the disseminating force of a 'centrifugal' language which fractures all authoritative codes; the recognition, now perhaps most closely linked to the name of Michel Foucault, that what is at stake in discourse is not only the signified but who speaks it and under what conditions; a Derridean concern with iteration, citability and 'framing', such that 'the speech of another, once enclosed in a context, is – no matter how accurately transmitted – always subject to certain semantic changes' (401): all of these are notable proleptic gestures.[37]

Yet it is equally striking how this affinity with post-structuralism has already been brusquely refused by certain exponents of that approach. David Carroll dismisses Bakhtin's notion of the novel as 'empiricist', yet another hapless prisoner of the illusion that discourse can 'represent' historical reality.[38] In one sense, perhaps, this comes down to arguing that it is empiricist to claim that the Artful Dodger speaks a kind of Cockney. But it also overlooks the extent to which Bakhtin's aesthetics, while doubtless 'representational' and certainly 'logocentric',[39] nevertheless promise to throw the whole metaphysical conception of representation into a certain disarray. If truth is never direct but always dialogic, intertextual, then this, as Bakhtin sees in his comments on Rabelais, may offer itself as 'a parody of the very act of conceptualizing anything in language' (309). What is 'represented' for Bakhtin in the novel is less 'historical reality' than 'images of language'; it is simply *in* this great turbulence and antagonism of historically determined discourses, not by some unmediated reflection of a real object, that literary texts are for him most deeply historical.

Post-structuralist denigrations of Bakhtin are themselves historically understandable,[40] for the whole force of his work is to unite what we might now rhetorically call certain Derridean and Lacanian positions with a politics revolutionary enough to make much post-structuralism nervous. In 1972, in *Positions*, Jacques Derrida remarked that as far as he was concerned the encounter with Marxism was 'still to come'.[41] One decade and one global capitalist crisis later, Derrida is, as the actress said to the bishop, a long time coming. Gayatri Spivak has sought to defend this silence on the grounds that Derrida takes a long time to work his way through texts, as though revolutionary politics were a question of library opening hours.[42].

By the time of his great work on Rabelais, Bakhtin's 'deconstructive' strategies are fully harnessed to that popular subversion of ruling-class metaphysics which is carnival, that 'temporary liberation from the prevailing truth' which 'marks the suspension of all hierarchical ranks, privileges, norms, and prohibitions.'[43] The 'gay relativity' of popular carnival, 'opposed to all that [is] ready-made and completed, to all pretence at immutability' (11), is the political materialization of Bakhtin's poetics, as the blasphemous, 'familiarizing' language of plebeian laughter destroys monologic authoritarianism with its satirical estrangements. The Nietzschean playfulness of contemporary post-structuralism leaves the academy and dances in the streets, as a somatic superabundance which mocks, materializes and transgresses the metaphysical pieties of the medieval and Renaissance state.[44] Among the modern names which Bakhtin cites as sustaining this tradition of grotesque metamorphosis is that of Bertolt Brecht.

Materialist Poetics and the 'Dialogic'

Perhaps one could situate Bakhtin's achievements within the coordinates of the present essay in the following way: Derrida is much preoccupied with the materiality of the signifier, but only at the price of violently severing it from the material conditions within which it moves. Wittgenstein rightly returns our attention to such conditions, but in his studied linguistic 'ordinariness' displays little sense of semiotic potential. For a third possibility – a writer who united the two projects only at the risk of parodying both – we might turn to Walter Benjamin. Benjamin's magical, mimetic theory of language certainly couples word and script in intimate correspondence (he early perceived a relation between his own Kabbalistic linguistics and Marxism), and restores to the signifier its full resonance and density. But Benjamin's correspondences of word and thing are too little mediated, while the signifier is sometimes naively rematerialized as emblem and hieroglyph. (*The Origin of German Baroque Drama* depicts a world in which the signifier may be rematerialized only as fetish, as magical sign; the Wittgenstein of the *Tractatus* betrays a similar nostalgia for the hieroglyph as against verbal language.) Bakhtin, by contrast, produces what could genuinely be termed, with equal stress on both words, a materialist poetics. It is not a question of choosing between semiosis and social conditions: to analyse the ideological force of an utterance is, inseparably, to interpret its precise rhythm, inflection, intonality, and to refer it to its determining social context.

One of the earliest historical instances of the 'dialogic' for Bakhtin is Socratic irony; and it is interesting that this is in some sense too the implicit genre of Wittgenstein's *Investigations*. The *Investigations* are a voice in dialogue with itself and an implied other, digressing and doubling back, so that the reader is not supplied with ready-made truth as in the monologism of a Russell, but invited to share in the unfoldings, quickenings and arrestings of the discursive process, with its jokes, aphorisms, unanswered questions, parables, exclamations and wonderings aloud.[45] It is less consent to discrete propositional truths which Wittgenstein demands, than consent to a way of seeing; his work has the form of the classic Leavisian question 'This is so, isn't it?', recalling us *à la* Leavis to do what we intuitively knew all along.

But whereas Wittgenstein appeals in this way to what 'we' know, to *ordinary* language, Bakhtin appeals to the language of the *people*. His work is populist in the most productive Marxist sense of the term, politicizing Wittgenstein's antimetaphysical opening to everyday language and finding in its carnivalesque forms what Gramsci would call a 'spontaneous' political philosophy. For Wittgenstein, the task of philosophy is to re-familiarize an everyday landscape made strange by metaphysics, leading words patiently back to their homes in practical life. For Bakhtin, it is a certain mode of practical life – the discourse and practice of carnival – which grotesquely defamiliarizes the metaphysical truths of routine social existence.

For Wittgenstein, it is the metaphysical which is abnormal, disruptive, estranging; for Bakhtin the metaphysical is what is normative and the language of the people disruptive and estranging. For Wittgenstein, 'philosophical problems arise when language *goes on holiday*' (38); for Bakhtin it is the holiday of carnival which promises to dismantle them. The unboundedness of Wittgenstein's language games becomes in Bakhtin's hands a transgression of political limits; the Anglo-Saxon appeal to the 'concrete' becomes in the Russian's work a celebration of the licentious politics of the body. Post-structuralism knows something of that libidinal, transgressive power but can give it little or no historical home; Wittgenstein can give language an historical home only at the cost of leaving its metaphysical base intact. He does not see that if metaphysics are to be abolished at all, it could only be by a *transformation* of practical life, not by a mere return to it. And in the process of such transformation, philosophy, *pace* both Wittgenstein and Marx's eleventh thesis on Feuerbach, does indeed have a role to play.

III. Language as Fetishized Exchange

For Jacques Derrida, what forestalls the sealing of precise meaning in an equitable exchange of signs is the fact that each signifier has a history of use-values whose traces disrupt such a contract. The productive forces of language threaten to burst and disseminate beyond the social relations of meaning. The Saussurean sign, in short, is the sign as commodity, repressing its traces of production, its value defined by abstract exchange rather than by social use.[46]

The point need not in fact remain purely metaphorical. For there is a major tradition of Marxist thought which derives philosophy itself from exchange-value and commodity production. The key text here is Lukács's *History and Class Consciousness*, for which commodity production is 'the model of all the objective forms of bourgeois society, together with all the subjective forms corresponding to them.'[47] Theodor Adorno, whom Lukács's book greatly influenced, wrote that 'the exchange principle, the reduction of human labour to its abstract universal concept of average labour-time, is fundamentally akin to the principle of identification. Exchange is the social model of the principle, and exchange would be nothing without identification'.[48] For Adorno, indeed, 'identity is the primal form of ideology'; and the tortuousness of his own writing, struggling to avoid at once the 'bad immediacy' of irrationalism and the false self-identity of the concept, finds some parallel in the acrobatics whereby Derrida deliberately poses himself on the frontier between some unusable metaphysics and its inconceivable beyond. Both Adorno and Derrida strive to grasp 'whatever is heterogeneous to thought' as a moment of thought itself; but since such heterogeneity must inevitably be *thought*, 'reproduced in thought itself as its immanent contradiction',[49] the enterprise is always teetering on the brink of blowing itself up. For both men, it can only be writing itself – 'style' – which ceaselessly rescues the project from self-destruction.

Adorno and Strategies of De-reification

I have suggested elsewhere that many of the apparently novel themes of Derridean deconstruction are anticipated by Adorno. 'Long before the current fashion, Adorno was insisting on the power of those heterogeneous fragments that slip through the conceptual net, rejecting all philosophy of identity, refusing class consciousness as objectionable "positive" and denying the intentionality of signification.'[50] The list could be extended: in his *Zur Metakritik der Erkenntnistheorie* (1956), Adorno, like Derrida, rejects as illicit any philosophy which depends on a first principle or ground; and elsewhere he extends his critique of identity in Derridean fashion to language itself: 'Language becomes a measure of truth only when we are conscious of the non-identity of an expression with what we mean'.[51]

But for all the similarities I have tried to show between Derrida's and Wittgenstein's notions of identity, Adorno's point here is firmly anti-Wittgensteinian. Indeed for Adorno the Wittgensteinian view of language (not that he discusses it directly) is literally childish: for the child, 'the meaning of words and their truth content, their "attitude towards objectivity", are not yet sharply distinguished from each other. To know what the word "bench" means and to know what a bench really is . . . is one and the same to that consciousness.'[52] For Wittgenstein, of course, to know how the word 'bench' is variously used simply *is* to know 'what a bench really is'. For Adorno, such a view of language is fetishistic, wielding a totemic name as a substitute for the truth of the object. But such fetishism is not easy to undo, for the language in which we might undo it is equally tainted. 'At the outset there is fetishism, and the hunt for the outset remains always subject to it. That fetishism is hard to see through, of course, since whatever we think is also a matter of language. Unreflective nominalism is as wrong as the realism that equips a fallible language with the attributes of a revealed one.'[53] The final phrase could be a direct comment on Wittgenstein's endorsement of existing language games: in seeking to defetishize metaphysical meanings, Wittgenstein has converted fallible everyday language into a 'revealed' one and thereby succumbed to a fetishism of common usage.

But just as Wittgenstein's own project is self-defeating, in hoping to 'see through' metaphysical fetishism with the commodified language of daily life, so for Adorno the opposite strategy is equally ironic: philosophy must de-reify routine life in a discourse which is reifying from the outset. Philosophy's problem is on the one hand to avoid identifying the truth of a concept with its mystified daily uses, and on the other hand to avoid reifying the concept beyond all such uses, thus rendering them purely nominalistic. Language and truth must be at once identified and non-identified: 'It is in Heidegger's favour that there is no speechless "in-itself" – that language, therefore, lies in truth, not truth in language, as something merely signified by language. But the constitutive share of language in truth does not establish an identity of truth and language.'[54]

Perhaps there is a sleight of hand here with the word 'language'. If Adorno means 'particular uses of language', then these may indeed be non-identical with truth; if he means 'language as a whole', then it is hard to see how there could be any question of a truth which lay outside this. Adorno has himself momentarily fallen victim to a reified concept of language, conflating different uses, and a Wittgensteinian move here may help to clarify the problem. What Adorno wants to avoid – truth as empirical consensus – is a point which Wittgenstein anticipates: 'So you are saying that human agreement decides what is true and what is false? – It is what human beings *say* that is true and false; and they agree in the *language* they use. That is not agreement in opinions but in forms of life' (241).

What Wittgenstein means, presumably, is that what 'human agreement' decides is not what is true or false, but the criteria as to what is to count as truth or falsity. Agreements or disagreements in opinion are possible only because of some primordial pact struck in the very structures of our language, which are in turn embedded in social practices. Without such a fundamental contract we could not say what would count as a proposition at all, let alone what would count as a proposition's being true. And this contract, unlike the mythical social contract, is not one legislatable at will: it is already inscribed in social activities and institutions. Adorno, then, does not have to salvage the concept of truth by reifying it outside of language: he simply has to point out, against the whole grain of Wittgenstein's numbingly consensual thought, that disagreements are possible not only between opinions but *between forms of life themselves* . For Mikhail Bakhtin, truth is itself a 'dialogic' concept; but the 'dialogue' in his case is a sharp, unremitting struggle between antagonistic class idioms and interests.

Wittgenstein's belief that an appeal to ordinary language may defetishize our thought is at one point interestingly illustrated by a monetary metaphor: 'You say: the point isn't the word, but its meaning, and you think of the meaning as the thing of the same kind as the word, though also different from the word. Here the word, there the meaning. The money, and the cow that you can buy with it. But contrast: money and its use' (120).

In seeking to overturn one fetishized version of language – meaning as a mental entity mysteriously linked with a sign – Wittgenstein runs unwittingly into another. His implication is that money, like language, derives its value from its multiple social uses; but the value of my money is not of course determined by what I use it for. Money is metaphysics incarnate, as treacherously homogenizing as the structures of grammar: 'Just as every qualitative difference between commodities is extinguished in money, so money, on its side, like the radical leveller that it is, does away with all distinctions.'[55]

It is deeply ironic that Wittgenstein should offer as an image of use-value the 'universal equivalent' (Marx). By trusting to money as *difference* – you can do many varied things with it, he hints – he merely obscures its function as an extinguisher of difference; just as, in highlighting the use-values of language, he obscures the fact that such uses none the less remain prisoners of metaphysical assumptions. For Wittgenstein, however, what is concealed is quite unimportant: 'Philosophy simply puts everything before us, and neither explains nor deduces anything. – Since everything lies open to view there is nothing to explain. For what is hidden, for example, is of no interest to us' (126). If what is concealed in class-society by the fetishism of commodities had in fact been of interest to Wittgenstein, he might have come to recognize that metaphysical obscurities are not the passing products of social transparency, but social 'transparency' the effect of an essential obscurity. He might have discovered, to extend the 'pathological' metaphor he occasionally used of his own work, that he was dealing not merely with a distorted text but, like Freud, with the meaning of text-distortions themselves.[56]

Walks with George Thomson

One man who might have helped Wittgenstein to this recognition was George Thomson, Marxist professor of classics at Birmingham University, and perhaps best known today as the author of a pathbreaking materialist work on ancient Greek tragedy, *Aeschylus and Athens* (1941). Thomson had first come to know Wittgenstein while a Fellow of King's College, Cambridge, and the two men became close friends; it was Thomson who invited Nikolai Bakhtin to move to Birmingham to teach classics there, and his *Greek Language* is dedicated to Bakhtin. Bakhtin was Thomson's best friend and exerted a strong intellectual influence on him, not least upon *Aeschylus and Athens*; conversely, Thomson influenced Bakhtin politically and had an important hand in his moving to the left.

It would be interesting to know whether Thomson, who accompanied Wittgenstein on long walks, ever discussed with him the ideas later embodied in his book *The First Philosophers* (1955), published four years after Wittgenstein's death.[57] For Thomson's argument there is of direct relevance to Wittgenstein's own attempts to demystify philosophy, and the materialist theory of language outlined in his first chapter, with its insistence on the imbrication of speech with bodily gesture, could well owe something to conversations with Wittgenstein.[58] Unlike both Wittgenstein and Derrida, however, Thomson is concerned to give an account of the historical conditions which brought metaphysical thought into existence in the first place. This is not only a question of the historical division of manual and intellectual labour, with thought's consequent illusory trust in its own autonomy; it is more particularly a question of the growth of commodity production. The formalizing, abstracting, quantifying, homogenizing and universalizing characteristics of philosophy, so Thomson claims, are the product of the generalization of commodity exchange and the invention of coinage in the Greece of the seventh and sixth centures BC.

'Philosophy, as distinct from mythology, emerged for the first time in Greece and China with the invention of the coinage.'[59] In the thought of Anaximenes, Pythagoras and other early Greek thinkers, 'the world was by implication stripped of quality and presented as a quantitative abstraction . . . [Parmenides's] pure being, stripped of everything qualitative, is a mental reflex of the abstract labour embodied in commodities, [as] his pure reason, which rejects everything qualitative, is a fetish concept reflecting the money form of value.'[60] Thomson's book is in part indebted to Alfred Sohn-Rethel's later published *Intellectual and Manual Labour* (1978), which finds in the Galilean laws of inertial motion a reflection of the movement of the circulation of commodities, and draws parallels between the 'empty' time and space of exchange relations and the dematerialized time and space of Newtonian physics.

This whole argument has a distinctively reductionist flavour. Philosophy for Thomson is 'the ideological reflex of commodity production',[61] and at one point Sohn-Rethel flatly names Parmenides's 'One' as money.[62] It is not easy to find a balance in this kind of theorizing between vague homologies on the one hand and crudely direct causality on the other. Both Lukács's and Adorno's derivations of thought-forms from commodity fetishism are notably essentialist – indeed Adorno writes more than once of the commodity as the 'essence' of bourgeois society, and his obsession with the doctrine of commodity fetishism has itself, one might claim, something fetishistic about it. Nevertheless, it is remarkable how post-structuralist awareness of the tenacity and pervasiveness of the metaphysical, as an unbreachable inner structure and outer limit of all thought, has in recent years largely ignored this suggestive line of enquiry, first touched on in Marx's own celebrated comment in *Capital* that the commodity is 'a very queer thing, abounding in metaphysical subtleties and theological niceties'.[63]

For the Marx of the *Eighteenth Brumaire*, bourgeois society constricts the potential heterogeneity of history within empty, falsely formalizing images; here, he remarks, 'the phrase [goes] beyond the content'. The aim of socialist revolution is to release that repressed historical content from those fetishized mythological or metaphysical forms in a ceaseless semiotic process which will outstrip and overturn any particular signifier, in which 'the content [will go] beyond the phrase'.[64] History will then begin, liberated from the metaphysics of repetition, and men and women will be able to live in the plural, heterogeneous play of their productive forces. The post-structuralist who celebrates such play now is not so much wrong as somewhat premature.

IV. Wittgenstein and the 'Captive' Gramsci

In *New Left Review* 73, John Moran assembled some previously unavailable (or suppressed) evidence about Wittgenstein's sympathies for the Soviet Union. It is known that Wittgenstein visited the Soviet Union in 1935 with the idea of studying medicine in England and then returning to Russia to practise as a doctor. There seems little doubt that in some ways he looked favourably on the Stalinist regime, and more recently published evidence would tend to confirm Moran's conclusions. 'People have accused Stalin of having betrayed the Russian Revolution,' Wittgenstein told a friend in 1939, 'but they have no idea of the problems that Stalin had to deal with; and the dangers he saw threatening Russia. I was looking at a picture of the British Cabinet and I thought to myself, "a lot of wealthy old men".'[65] The philosopher Rush Rhees records Wittgenstein's opinion that the Soviet regime at least provided work for the people, which he believed the most important consideration, and states that he was unimpressed by talk of labour camps or tyranny.[66] 'If anything could destroy my sympathy with the Russian regime,' he told Rhees in 1945, 'it would be the growth of class distinctions.'[67]

Wittgenstein's leanings towards Stalinist Russia, as the *New Left Review* editorial introduction to Moran's article points out, are if anything evidence of his ignorance of Marxism rather than his affinities with it. Though he was apparently a good deal more politically conscious than has sometimes been made out, his attraction to the Soviet Union at its most draconian and repressive period is probably explicable in terms of his 'extreme personal asceticism, and fixed belief in the regenerative powers of manual labour as such.'[68] Wittgenstein began his professional life as an engineer, and punctuated his philosophical career with flights into seminary gardening, village school-teaching and solitary self-communings in Norway and the west of Ireland. His deep respect for manual labour, at which he was personally unusually adept, is perhaps best seen as a form of intellectual suicide, the fetishism of a self-torturing Tolstoyan. It differs perhaps in this respect from the carnival spirit which Mikhail Bakhtin discerns in that other religious tradition of reverence for manual labour, Franciscanism.[69] Wittgenstein's personal response to the division of manual and mental labour was to live as a reluctant prisoner of the academy while harbouring a

Heideggerian impulse for peasant toil.

Piero Sraffa

Yet there is more to be said about Wittgenstein's relations with Marxism than that. We have yet to mention his third and most influential friend, the economist Piero Sraffa, friend and supporter of the imprisoned Antonio Gramsci. Wittgenstein acknowledges Sraffa in the preface to the *Investigations* as one who has 'for many years unceasingly practised on my thoughts', and declares him to be the source of 'the most consequential ideas' of the book. We do not know whether Sraffa discussed Gramsci with Wittgenstein, though given the two men's personal closeness it seems possible. Wittgenstein and Gramsci would seem strange bed fellows, and it may well be that Sraffa locked them into separate compartments of his life. Yet Gramsci was like Wittgenstein concerned to demystify philosophy: 'It is essential to destroy the widespread prejudice that philosophy is a strange and difficult thing just because it is the specific intellectual activity of a particular category of specialists or of professional and systematic philosophers. It must first be shown that all men are "philosophers", by defining the limits and characteristics of the "spontaneous philosophy" which is proper to everybody.'[70]

For Gramsci, the difference between the philosopher and other individuals is primarily 'quantitative' rather than qualitative: the former thinks with a greater degree of rigour, coherence and logicality than do the latter, but that is simply to say that he or she has amassed a greater 'quantity of qualitative elements'.[71] The philosopher's primary quantitative advantage over the people, moreover, is that unlike them he is capable of surveying the entire history of thought. 'Modern theory' (Marxism) and the 'spontaneous' beliefs of the masses, Gramsci claims, are not in opposition to each other: between the two there is a 'quantitative difference of degree, not one of quality. A reciprocal "reduction", so to speak, a passage from one to the other and vice versa, must be possible.[72] Like Wittgenstein also, Gramsci views even the most apparently sublime concepts in an essentially *practical* light: his radical – indeed excessive – historicism leads him to regard ideas as 'the ever-new expression of real historical development . . . Every truth, even though it may be universal and expressible in an abstract formula of the mathematical type, owes its efficacy to being expressed in the language of particular, concrete situations; if it cannot be so expressed it is a Byzantine, scholastic abstraction for phrase-mongers to toy with.'[73]

The Critique of 'Common Sense'

The parallel with Wittgenstein, however, stops precisely there. For in the first place, Gramsci's historicist theory of thought rounds dialectically upon itself, in a way that Wittgenstein's philosophizing, as we have seen, dares not do: philosophy is itself a class-bound, historically determined activity, whatever the befuddled faith of ideas that they are merely the products of previous ideas. In the second place, Gramsci's assertion of a continuity between philosophy and popular experience is as far removed as possible from the patrician amateurism with which the 'Narodniks of North Oxford' (Ernest Gellner) disdain any distasteful professionalism, discerning a bland continuum between examining acts of promising and shopping at Harrods. Gramsci's demystification of philosophy does not entail a corresponding mystification of popular consciousness: on the contrary, as Alberto Maria Cirese has argued, his attitude towards such 'folkloric' consciousness is almost always negative.[74] Gramsci's insistence of a continuity beween scientific and spontaneous thought – the latter, however amorphous and implicit, can also be described as a 'conception of the world' – never underestimates the typical backwardness of such world-views, even when their characteristic difference from and conflict with 'official' ideologies is under scrutiny in his text. Popular ideology, which for Gramsci is always socially stratified, is to a great extent a client territory of the hegemonic culture, a domain into which certain 'official' scientific and philosophical concepts, distorted and displaced from context, are forever falling, to be assimilated in strange ways.

This is not to say, as Cirese points out, that Gramsci ascribes no positive value whatsoever to such *doxa*: the strength and tenacity of certain popular conceptions can outstrip hegemonic moralities, the class instinct of the people can be constructive, and if some elements of popular consciousness are the mere fossilized residues of past conditions, others display 'a range of often creative and progressive innovations, spontaneously determined by the forms and conditions of life as it is developing.'[75] If the masses are seduced by a 'Ptolemaic' common sense – itself, in Gramsci, a carefully differentiated concept – they also have the resources of that 'good sense' which springs from popular thought's spontaneous adherence to the actual conditions of life. Indeed the masses, Gramsci argues, may be said to have two 'theoretical consciousnesses', or at least one contradictory one: one is implicit in the activity of workers in their practical transformation of the world, the other is a superficially explicit or 'verbal' consciousness uncritically inherited from the past.[76]

There is some similarity here, perhaps, to Wittgenstein's counterposing of practical and metaphysical forms of knowledge. But for Gramsci, unlike Wittgenstein, implicit and explicit knowledges are in dialectical relationship: 'A philosophy of praxis . . . must be a criticism of "common sense", basing itself initially, however, on common sense in order to demonstrate that "everyone" is a philosopher and that it is not a question of introducing from scratch a scientific form of thought into everyone's individual life, but of renovating and making "critical" an already existing activity . . . It is a matter therefore of starting with a philosophy which already enjoys, or could enjoy, a certain diffusion, because it is connected to and implicit in practical life, and elaborating it so that it becomes a renewed common sense possessing the coherence and sinew of individual philosophies. But this can only happen if the demands of cultural contact with the "simple" are continually felt.'[77]

There is no question for Gramsci, then, of philosophy leaving everything exactly as it was. The particularly virulent brand of metaphysics he confronted – Roman Catholicism – could be uprooted only by a materialist philosophy systematized and elaborated in the structures of popular culture themselves. Gramsci neither dissolves philosophy into social practice, nor like much post-structuralism displaces political radicalism into philosophy; his response to the problem of the relation between philosophy and material life is neither 'textual' nor epistemological but political, centred on those 'organic' intellectuals whose role is to materialize such a relation in their own practice. 'The relationship between common sense and the upper level of philosophy is assured by "politics".'[78]

'The Fly in the Fly-bottle'

The question Gramsci poses is still one of the most urgent for socialist intellectuals today. What are the mechanisms by which popular ideologies combine (progressive or reactionary) elements of the hegemonic culture with (progressive or reactionary) aspects of the life-experience of the the masses, to produce forms of consciousness which for the most part sustain rather than challenge ruling-class hegemony? How are the chauvinism, racism, sexism and political quietism or conformism of broad sections of the masses combined with, related to or disjoint from the more creative aspects of their consciousness: a certain 'spontaneous' materialism, a distrust of and resistance to authority, a stubborn defence of 'rights' and of a margin of autonomy, a traditional habit of tolerance (the expression 'it takes many sorts to make a world' was, Wittgenstein commented, 'a very beautiful and kindly saying'),[79] a scorn of ruling-class arrogance and parasitism, a debunking of formalism and pretentiousness, a suspicion of propaganda and paternalism, a non-obsequious respect for learning, a distaste for extravagance and the more flagrant forms of competitiveness, and a spirit of mutual support and solidarity? If a 'socialist common sense' is to be constructed, Gramsci's theses will need to be carried into specific analyses of such ambiguities.

Listing the formal qualities which Gramsci associates with folklore or popular belief, Alberto Cirese includes contradictoriness, fragmentation, dispersal, multiplicity, unsystematicness and difference.[80] These qualities, which might have been drawn from a dictionary of highly valued post-structuralist and Bakhtinian terms, must for Gramsci be combated by conceptual elaboration and political systematization. His work, that is to say, not only offers an implicit rebuke to Wittgenstein; it also contains an essential corrective to the Bakhtinian notion of carnival. For carnival is, of course, a spasmodic, officially licensed affair, without the rancour, discipline and organization essential for an effective revolutionary politics. Any politics which predicates itself on the carnivalesque moment alone will be no more than a compliant, containable libertarianism. Bakhtin is too little attentive to the incorporating, politically defusing effects of popular humour; Gramsci, theorist of revolutionary strategy, offers a perspective within which carnival may be seen as a crucial yet partial element.

Sitting with a friend in Trafalgar Square sometime during the war, Wittgenstein pointed to Canada House and observed that such architecture took over certain rhetorical forms but said nothing in them: 'That's *bombast*; that's Hitler and Mussolini.'[81] His aim in philosophy, he remarks in the *Investigations*, is to 'teach you to pass from a piece of disguised nonsense to something that is patent nonsense' (464): to demystify bombast, to return from the slippery ice where we cannot walk to the rough ground. Bertolt Brecht, in conversation with Walter Benjamin, referred to fascism as the 'new ice age'. The icy language of metaphysics, which includes the *Tractatus Logico-Philosophicus*, produces a picture which 'held us captive'. Who is held captive here? 'Russell and the parsons have done infinite harm, infinite harm.' But not only Russell and the parsons. Does Wittgenstein make reparation in the *Investigations* for the metaphysics, including the *Tractatus*, which have helped to hold captive Antonio Gramsci? 'What is your aim in philosophy? – To shew the fly the way out of the fly-bottle' (309). Who is this fly imprisoned in a fly-bottle, and how is he to be let out?

9.

Capitalism, Modernism and Postmodernism

In his article 'Postmodernism, or the Cultural Logic of Late Capitalism' (*New Left Review* 146), Fredric Jameson argues that pastiche, rather than parody, is the appropriate mode of postmodernist culture. 'Pastiche', he writes, 'is, like parody, the imitation of a peculiar mask, speech in a dead language; but it is a neutral practice of such mimicry, without any of parody's ulterior motives, amputated of the satiric impulse, devoid of laughter and of any conviction that alongside the abnormal tongue you have momentarily borrowed, some healthy linguistic normality still exists.' This is an excellent point; but I want to suggest here that parody of a sort is not wholly alien to the culture of postmodernism, though it is not one of which it could be said to be particularly conscious. What is parodied by postmodernist culture, with its dissolution of art into the prevailing forms of commodity production, is nothing less than the revolutionary art of the twentieth-century avant-garde. It is as though postmodernism is among other things a sick joke at the expense of such revolutionary avant-gardism, one of whose major impulses, as Peter Bürger has convincingly argued in his *Theory of the Avant-Garde*, was to dismantle the institutional autonomy of art, erase the frontiers between culture and political society and return aesthetic production to its humble, unprivileged place within social practices as a whole.[1] In the commodified artefacts of postmodernism, the avant-gardist dream of an integration of art and society returns in monstrously caricatured form; the tragedy of a Mayakovsky is played through once more, but this time as farce. It is as though postmodernism represents the cynical belated revenge wreaked by bourgeois culture upon its revolutionary antagonists, whose utopian desire for a fusion of art and social praxis is seized, distorted and jeeringly turned back upon them as dystopian reality. Postmodernism, from this perspective, mimes the formal resolution of art and social life attempted by the avant-garde, while remorselessly emptying it of its political content; Mayakovsky's poetry readings in the factory yard become Warhol's shoes and soup-cans.

I say it is *as though* postmodernism effects such a parody, because Jameson is surely right to claim that in reality it is sometimes blankly innocent of any such devious satirical impulse, and is entirely devoid of the kind of historical memory which might make such a disfiguring self-conscious. To place a pile of bricks in the Tate gallery once might be considered ironic; to repeat the gesture endlessly is sheer carelessness of any such ironic intention, as its shock value is inexorably drained away to leave nothing beyond brute fact. The depthless, styleless, dehistoricized, decathected surfaces of postmodernist culture are not meant to signify an alienation, for the very concept of alienation must secretly posit a dream of authenticity which postmodernism finds quite unintelligible. Those flattened surfaces and hollowed interiors are not 'alienated' because there is no longer any subject to be alienated and nothing to be alienated from, 'authenticity' having been less rejected than merely forgotten. It is impossible to discern in such forms, as it is in the artefacts of modernism proper, a wry, anguished or derisive awareness of the normative traditional humanism they deface. If depth is metaphysical illusion, then there can be nothing 'superficial' about such art-forms, for the very term has ceased to have force. Postmodernism is thus a grisly parody of socialist utopia, having abolished all alienation at a stroke. By raising alienation to the second power, alienating us even from our own alienation, it persuades us to recognize that utopia not as some remote *telos* but, amazingly, as nothing less than the present itself, replete as it is in its own brute positivity and scarred through with not the slightest trace of lack. Reification, once it has extended its empire across the whole of social reality, effaces the very criteria by which it can be recognized for what it is and so triumphantly abolishes itself, returning everything to normality. The traditional metaphysical mystery was a question of depths, absences, foundations, abysmal explorations; the mystery of some modernist art is just the mind-bending truth that things are what they are, intriguingly self-identical, utterly shorn of cause, motive or ratification; postmodernism preserves this self-identity, but erases its modernist scandalousness. The dilemma of David Hume is surpassed by a simple conflation: fact *is* value. Utopia cannot belong to the future because the future, in the shape of technology, is already here, exactly synchronous with the present. William Morris, in dreaming that art might dissolve into social life, turns out, it would seem, to have been a true prophet of late capitalism: by anticipating such a desire, bringing it about with premature haste, late capitalism deftly inverts its own logic and proclaims that if the artefact is a commodity, the commodity can always be an artefact. 'Art' and 'life' indeed interbreed – which is to say that art models itself upon a commodity form which is already invested with aesthetic allure, in a sealed circle. The *eschaton*, it would appear, is already here under our very noses, but so pervasive and immediate as to be invisible to those whose eyes are still turned stubbornly away to the past or the future.

The productivist aesthetics of the early twentieth-century avant-garde spurned the notion of artistic 'representation' for an art which would be less 'reflection' than material intervention and organizing force. The aesthetics of postmodernism is a dark parody of such anti-representationalism: if art no longer reflects, it is not because it seeks to change the world rather than mimic it, but because there is in truth nothing there to be reflected, no reality which is not itself already image, spectacle, simulacrum, gratuitous fiction. To say that social reality is pervasively commodified is to say that it is always already 'aesthetic' – textured, packaged, fetishized, libidinalized; and for art to reflect reality is then for it to do no more than mirror itself, in a cryptic self-referentiality which is indeed one of the inmost structures of the commodity fetish. The commodity is less an image in the sense of a 'reflection' than an image of itself, its entire material being devoted to its own self-presentation; and in such a condition the most authentically representational art becomes, paradoxically, the anti-representational artefact whose contingency and facticity figures the fate of all late capitalist objects. If the unreality of the artistic image mirrors the unreality of its society as a whole, then this is to say that it mirrors nothing real and so does not really mirror at all. Beneath this paradox lies the historical truth that the very autonomy and brute self-identity of the postmodernist artefact is the effect of

its thorough *integration* into an economic system where such autonomy, in the form of the commodity fetish, is the order of the day.

To see art in the manner of the revolutionary avant-garde, not
as institutionalized object but as practice, strategy, performance,
production: all of this, once again, is grotesquely caricatured by
late capitalism, for which, as Jean-François Lyotard has pointed
out, the 'performativity principle' is really all that counts. In his
The Postmodern Condition, Lyotard calls attention to capitalism's
'massive subordination of cognitive statements to the finality
of the best possible performance'; 'The games of scientific
language', he writes, 'become the games of the rich, in which
whoever is wealthiest has the best chance of being right.'[2] It is
not difficult, then, to see relation between the philosophy of J. L.
Austin and IBM, or between the various neo-Nietzscheanisms of
a post-structuralist epoch and Standard Oil. It is not surprising
that classical models of truth and cognition are increasingly out
of favour in a society where what matters is whether you deliver
the commercial or rhetorical goods. Whether among discourse
theorists or the Institute of Directors, the goal is no longer truth
but performativity, not reason but power. The CBI are in this
sense spontaneous post-structuralists to a man, utterly disen-
chanted (did they but know it) with epistemological realism and
the correspondence theory of truth. That this is so is no reason
for pretending that we can relievedly return to John Locke or
Georg Lukács; it is simply to recognize that it is not always easy
to distinguish politically radical assaults on classical epistemology
(among which the early Lukács must himself be numbered,
alongside the Soviet avant-garde) from flagrantly reactionary
ones. Indeed it is a sign of this difficulty that Lyotard himself, having grimly outlined the most oppressive aspects of the
capitalist performativity principle, has really nothing to offer in
its place but what amounts in effect to an anarchist version of
that very same epistemology, namely the guerrilla skirmishes of
a 'paralogism' which might from time to time induce ruptures,
instabilities, paradoxes and micro-catastrophic discontinuities
into this terroristic techno-scientific system. A 'good' pragmatics,
in short, is turned against a 'bad' one; but it will always be a
loser from the outset, since it has long since abandoned the Enlightenment's grand narrative of human emancipation, which
we all now know to be disreputably metaphysical. Lyotard is in
no doubt that '[socialist] struggles and their instruments have
been transformed into regulators of the system' in all the

advanced societies, an Olympian certitude which, as I write, Mrs Thatcher might at once envy and query. (Lyotard is wisely silent on the class struggle outside the advanced capitalist nations.) It is not easy to see how, if the capitalist system has been effective enough to negate all class struggle entirely, the odd unorthodox scientific experiment is going to give it much trouble. 'Postmodernist science', as Fredric Jameson suggests in his introduction to Lyotard's book, is here playing the role once assumed by high modernist art, which was similarly an experimental disruption of the given system; and Lyotard's desire to see modernism and postmodernism as continuous with one another is in part a refusal to confront the disturbing fact that modernism proved prey to institutionalization. Both cultural phases are for Lyotard manifestations of that which escapes and confounds history with the explosive force of the Now, the 'paralogic' as some barely possible, mind-boggling leap into free air which gives the slip to the nightmare of temporality and global narrative from which some of us are trying to awaken. Paralogism, like the poor, is always with us, but just because the system is always with us too. The 'modern' is less a particular cultural practice or historical period, which may then suffer defeat or incorporation, than a kind of permanent ontological possibility of disrupting all such historical periodization, an essentially timeless gesture which cannot be recited or reckoned up within historical narrative because it is no more than an atemporal force which gives the lie to all such linear categorization. As with all such anarchistic or Camusian revolt, modernism can thus never really die – it has resurfaced in our own time as paralogical science – but the reason why it can never be worsted – the fact that it does not occupy the same temporal terrain or logical space as its antagonists – is precisely the reason why it can never defeat the system either. The characteristic post-structuralist blend of pessimism and euphoria springs precisely from this paradox. History and modernity play a ceaseless cat-and-mouse game in and out of time, neither able to slay the other because they occupy different ontological sites. 'Game' in the positive sense – the ludic disportings of disruption and desire – plays itself out in the crevices of 'game' in the negative sense – game theory, the techno-scientific system – in an endless conflict and collusion. Modernity here really means a Nietzschean 'active forgetting' of history: the healthy spontaneous amnesia of the animal who has wilfully repressed its own sordid determinations and so is free.

It is thus the exact opposite of Walter Benjamin's 'revolutionary nostalgia': the power of active remembrance as a ritual summoning and invocation of the traditions of the oppressed in violent constellation with the political present. It is no wonder that Lyotard is deeply opposed to any such historical consciousness, with his reactionary celebrations of narrative as an eternal present rather than a revolutionary recollection of the unjustly quelled. If he could remember in this Benjaminesque mode, he might be less confident that the class struggle could be merely extirpated. Nor, if he had adequately engaged Benjamin's work, could he polarize in such simplistic binary opposition – one typical of much post-structuralist thought – the grand totalizing narratives of the Enlightenment on the one hand and the micropolitical or paralogistic on the other (postmodernism as the death of metanarrative). For Benjamin's unfathomably subtle meditations on history throw any such binary post-structuralist schema into instant disarray. Benjamin's 'tradition' is certainly a totality of a kind, but at the same time a ceaseless detotalization of a triumphalistic ruling-class history; it is in some sense a given, yet is always constructed from the vantage point of the present; it operates as a deconstructive force within hegemonic ideologies of history, yet can be seen too as a totalizing movement within which sudden affinities, correspondences and constellations may be fashioned between disparate struggles.

A Nietzschean sense of the 'modern' also informs the work of the most influential of American deconstructionists, Paul de Man, though with an added twist of irony. For 'active forgetting', de Man argues, can never be entirely successful: the distinctively modernist act, which seeks to erase or arrest history, finds itself surrendered in that very moment to the lineage it seeks to repress, perpetuating rather than abolishing it. Indeed literature for de Man is nothing less than this constantly doomed, ironically self-undoing attempt to make it new, this ceaseless incapacity ever quite to awaken from the nightmare of history: 'The continuous appeal of modernity, the desire to break out of literature toward the reality of the moment, prevails and, in its turn, folding back upon itself, engenders the repetition and the continuation of literature.'[3] Since action and temporality are indissociable, modernism's dream of self-origination, its hunger for some historically unmediated encounter with the real, is internally fissured and self-thwarting: to write is to disrupt a tradition which depends on such disruption for its very self-reproduction. We are all, simultaneously and inextricably, modernists and traditionalists, terms which for de Man designate neither cultural movements nor aesthetic ideologies but the very structure of that duplicitous phenomenon, always in and out of time simultaneously, named literature, where this common dilemma figures itself with rhetorical self-consciousness. Literary history here, de Man contends, 'could in fact be paradigmatic for history in general'; and what this means, translated from de-Manese, is that though we will never abandon our radical political illusions (the fond fantasy of emancipating ourselves from tradition and confronting the real eyeball-to-eyeball being, as it were, a permanent pathological state of human affairs), such actions will always prove self-defeating, will always be incorporated by a history which has foreseen them and seized upon them as ruses for its own self-perpetuation. The daringly 'radical' recourse to Nietzsche, that is to say, turns out to land one in a maturely liberal Democrat position, wryly sceptical but genially tolerant of the radical antics of the young.

What is at stake here, under the guise of a debate about history and modernity, is nothing less than the dialectical relation of theory and practice. For if practice is defined in neo-Nietzschean style as spontaneous error, productive blindness or historical amnesia, then theory can of course be no more than a jaded reflection upon its ultimate impossibility. Literature, that aporetic spot in which truth and error indissolubly entwine, is at once practice and the deconstruction of practice, spontaneous act and theoretical fact, a gesture which in pursuing an unmediated encounter with reality in the same instant interprets that very impulse as metaphysical fiction. Writing is both action and a reflection upon that action, but the two are ontologically disjunct; and literature is the privileged place where practice comes to know and name its eternal difference from theory. It is not surprising, then, that the last sentence of de Man's essay makes a sudden swerve to the political: 'If we extend this notion beyond literature, it merely confirms that the bases for historical knowledge are not empirical facts but written texts, even if these texts masquerade in the guise of wars and revolutions.' A text which starts out with a problem in literary history ends up as an assault on Marxism. For it is of course Marxism above all which has insisted that actions may be theoretically informed and histories emancipatory, notions capable of scuppering de Man's entire case. It is only by virtue of an initial Nietzschean dogmatism – practice is necessarily self-blinded, tradition necessarily impeding – that de Man is able to arrive at his politically quietistic aporias.[4] Given these initial definitions, a certain judicious deconstruction of their binary opposition is politically essential, if the Nietzschean belief in affirmative action is not to license a radical politics; but such deconstruction is not permitted to transform the metaphysical trust that there is indeed a single dominant structure of action (blindness, error), and a single form of tradition (obfuscating rather than enabling an encounter with the 'real'). The Marxism of Louis Althusser comes close to this Nietzscheanism: practice is an 'imaginary' affair which thrives upon the repression of truly theoretical understanding, theory a reflection upon the necessary fictionality of such action. The two, as with Nietzsche and de Man, are ontologically disjunct, necessarily non-synchronous.

De Man, then, is characteristically rather more prudent about the possibilities of modernist experiment than the somewhat rashly celebratory Lyotard. All literature for de Man is a ruined or baffled modernism, and the institutionalization of such impulses is a permanent rather than political affair. Indeed it is part of what brings literature about in the first place, constitutive of its very possibility. It is as though, in an ultimate modernist irony, literature masters and pre-empts its own cultural institutionalization by textually introjecting it, hugging the very chains which bind it, discovering its own negative form of transcendence in its power of rhetorically naming, and thus partially distantiating, its own chronic failure to engage the real. The modernist work – and all cultural artefacts are such – is the one which knows that modernist (for which read also 'political') experiment is finally impotent. The mutual parasitism of history and modernity is de Man's own version of the post-structuralist deadlock of Law and Desire, in which the revolutionary impulse grows heady and delirious on its meagre prison rations.

De Man's resolute ontologizing and dehistoricizing of modernism, which is of a piece with the steady, silent anti-Marxist polemic running throughout his work, does at least give one pause to reflect upon what the term might actually mean. Perry Anderson, in his illuminating essay 'Modernity and Revolution' (*New Left Review* 144), concludes by rejecting the very designation 'modernism' as one 'completely lacking in positive content . . . whose only referent is the blank passage of time itself'. This impatient nominalism is to some degree understandable, given the elasticity of the concept; yet the very nebulousness of the word may be in some sense significant. 'Modernism' as a term at once expresses and mystifies a sense of one's particular historical conjuncture as being somehow peculiarly pregnant with crisis and change. It signifies a portentous, confused yet curiously heightened self-consciousness of one's own historical moment, at once self-doubting and self-congratulatory, anxious and triumphalistic together. It suggests at one and the same time an arresting and denial of history in the violent shock of the immediate present, from which vantage point all previous developments may be complacently consigned to the ashcan of 'tradition', and a disorientating sense of history moving with peculiar force and urgency within one's immediate experience, pressingly actual yet tantalizingly opaque. All historical epochs are modern to themselves, but not all live their experience in this ideological mode. If modernism lives its history as peculiarly, insistently *present*, it also experiences a sense that this present moment is somehow of the *future*, to which the present is nothing more than an orientation; so that the idea of the Now, of the present as full presence eclipsing the past, is itself intermittently eclipsed by an awareness of the present as deferment, as an empty excited openness to a future which is in one sense already here, in another sense yet to come. The 'modern', for most of us, is that which we have always to catch up with: the popular use of the term 'futuristic', to denote modernist experiment, is symptomatic of this fact. Modernism – and here Lyotard's case may be given some qualified credence – is not so much a punctual moment in time as a revaluation of time itself, the sense of an epochal shift in the very meaning and modality of temporality, a qualitative break in our ideological styles of living history. What seems to be moving in such moments is less 'history' than that which is unleashed by its rupture and suspension; and the typically modernist images of the vortex and the abyss, 'vertical' inruptions into temporality within which forces swirl restlessly in an eclipse of linear time, represent this ambivalent consciousness. So, indeed, does the Benjaminesque spatializing or 'constellating' of history, which at once brings it to a shocking standstill and shimmers with all the unquietness of crisis or catastrophe.

High modernism, as Fredric Jameson has argued elsewhere, was born at a stroke with mass commodity culture.[5] This is a fact about its internal form, not simply about its external history.

Modernism is among other things a strategy whereby the work of art resists commodification, holds out by the skin of its teeth against those social forces which would degrade it to an exchangeable object. To this extent, modernist works are in contradiction with their own material status, self-divided phenomena which deny in their discursive forms their own shabby economic reality. To fend off such reduction to commodity status, the modernist work brackets off the referent or real historical world, thickens its textures and deranges its forms to forestall instant consumability, and draws its own language protectively around it to become a mysteriously autotelic object, free of all contaminating truck with the real. Brooding self-reflexively on its own being, it distances itself through irony from the shame of being no more than a brute, self-identical thing. But the most devastating irony of all is that in doing this the modernist work escapes from one form of commodification only to fall prey to another. If it avoids the humiliation of becoming an abstract, serialized, instantly exchangeable thing, it does so only by virtue of reproducing that other side of the commodity which is its fetishism. The autonomous, self-regarding, impenetrable modernist artefact, in all its isolated splendour, is the commodity as fetish resisting the commodity as exchange, its solution to reification part of that very problem.

It is on the rock of such contradictions that the whole modernist project will finally founder. In bracketing off the real social world, establishing a critical, negating distance between itself and the ruling social order, modernism must simultaneously bracket off the political forces which seek to transform that order. There is indeed a political modernism – what else is Bertolt Brecht? – but it is hardly characteristic of the movement as a whole. Moreover, by removing itself from society into its own impermeable space, the modernist work paradoxically reproduces – indeed intensifies – the very illusion of aesthetic autonomy which marks the bourgeois humanist order it also protests against. Modernist works are after all 'works', discrete and bounded entities for all the free play within them, which is just what the bourgeois art institution understands. The revolutionary avant garde, alive to this dilemma, were defeated at the hands of political history. Postmodernism, confronted with this situation, will then take the other way out. If the work of art really is a commodity then it might as well admit it, with all the *sang froid* it can muster. Rather than languish in some intolerable conflict between its material reality and its aesthetic structure, it can always collapse that conflict on one side, becoming aesthetically what it is economically. The modernist reification – the art work as isolated fetish – is therefore exchanged for the reification of everyday life in the capitalist marketplace. The commodity as mechanically reproducible exchange ousts the commodity as magical aura. In a sardonic commentary on the avant-garde work, postmodernist culture will dissolve its own boundaries and become coextensive with ordinary commodified life itself, whose ceaseless exchanges and mutations in any case recognize no formal frontiers which are not constantly transgressed. If all artefacts can be appropriated by the ruling order, then better impudently to pre-empt this fate than suffer it unwillingly; only that which is already a commodity can resist commodification. If the high modernist work has been institutionalized within the superstructure, postmodernist culture will react demotically to such elitism by installing itself within the base. Better, as Brecht remarked, to start from the 'bad new things', rather than from the 'good old ones'.

That, however, is also where postmodernism stops. Brecht's comment alludes to the Marxist habit of extracting the progressive moment from an otherwise unpalatable or ambivalent reality, a habit well exemplified by the early avant-garde's espousal of a technology able both to emancipate and enslave. At a later, less euphoric stage of technological capitalism, the postmodernism which celebrates kitsch and camp caricatures the Brechtian slogan by proclaiming not that the bad contains the good, but that the bad *is* good – or rather that both of these 'metaphysical' terms have now been decisively outmoded by a social order which is to be neither affirmed nor denounced but simply accepted. From where, in a fully reified world, would we derive the criteria by which acts of affirmation or denunciation would be possible? Certainly not from history, which postmodernism must at all costs efface, or spatialize to a range of possible styles, if it is to persuade us to forget that we have ever known or could know any alternative to itself. Such forgetting, as with the healthy amnesiac animal of Nietzsche and his contemporary acolytes, *is* value: value lies not in this or that discrimination within contemporary experience but in the very capacity to stop our ears to the Siren calls of history and confront the contemporary for what it is, in all its blank immediacy. Ethical or political discrimination would extinguish the contemporary simply by mediating it, sever its self-identity, put us prior or posterior to it; value is just that which *is*, the erasure and overcoming of history, and *discourses* of value, which cannot fail to be historical, are therefore by definition valueless. It is for this reason that postmodernist theory is hostile to the hermeneutic, and nowhere more virulently than in Gilles Deleuze and Félix Guattari's *Anti-Oedipus*.[6] In post-1968 Paris, an eyeball-to-eyeball encounter with the real still seemed on the cards, if only the obfuscatory mediations of Marx and Freud could be abandoned. For Deleuze and Guattari, that 'real' is desire, which in a full-blown metaphysical positivism 'can never be deceived', needs no interpretation and simply *is*. In this apodicticism of desire, of which the schizophrenic is hero, there can be no place for political discourse proper, for such discourse is exactly the ceaseless labour of *interpretation* of desire, a labour of interpretation which does not leave its object untouched. For Deleuze and Guattari, any such move renders desire vulnerable to the metaphysical traps of meaning. But that interpretation of desire which is the political is necessary precisely because desire is not a single, supremely positive entity; and it is Deleuze and Guattari, for all their insistence upon desire's diffuse and perverse manifestations, who are the true metaphysicians in holding to such covert essentialism. Theory and practice are once more ontologically at odds, since the schizoid hero of the revolutionary drama is by definition unable to reflect upon his own condition, needing Parisian intellectuals to do it for him. The only 'revolution' conceivable, given such a protagonist, is disorder; and Deleuze and Guattari significantly use the two terms synonymously, in the most banal anarchist rhetoric.

In some postmodernist theory, the injunction to glimpse the good in the bad has been pursued with a vengeance. Capitalist technology can be viewed as an immense desiring machine, an enormous circuit of messages and exchanges in which pluralistic idioms proliferate and random objects, bodies, surfaces come to glow with libidinal intensity. 'The interesting thing', writes Lyotard in his *Economie libidinale*, 'would be to stay where we are – but to grab without noise all opportunities to function as bodies and good conductors of intensities. No need of declarations, manifestos, organizations; not even for exemplary actions. To let dissimulation play in favour of intensities.'[7] It is all rather closer to Walter Pater than to Walter Benjamin. Of course capitalism is not uncritically endorsed by such theory, for its libidinal flows are subject to a tyrannical ethical, semiotic and juridical order; what is wrong with late capitalism is not this or that desire but the fact that desire does not circulate freely enough. But if only we could kick our metaphysical nostalgia for truth, meaning and history, of which Marxism is perhaps the prototype, we might come to recognise that desire is here and now, fragments and surfaces all we ever have, kitsch quite as good as the real thing because there is in fact no real thing. What is amiss with old-fashioned modernism, from this perspective, is just the fact that it obstinately refuses to abandon the struggle for meaning. It is still agonizedly caught up in metaphysical depth and wretchedness, still able to experience psychic fragmentation and social alienation as spiritually wounding, and so embarrassingly enmortgaged to the very bourgeois humanism it otherwise seeks to subvert. Postmodernism, confidently postmetaphysical, has outlived all that fantasy of interiority, that pathological itch to scratch surfaces for concealed depths; it embraces instead the mystical positivism of the early Wittgenstein, for which the world – would you believe it? – just is the way it is and not some other way. As with the early Wittgenstein, there cannot be a rational discourse of ethical or political value, for values are not the kind of thing which can be *in* the world in the first place, any more than the eye can be part of the field of vision. The dispersed, schizoid subject is nothing to be alarmed about after all: nothing could be more normative in late capitalist experience. Modernism appears in this light as a deviation still enthralled to a norm, parasitic on what it sets out to deconstruct. But if we are now posterior to such metaphysical humanism there is really nothing left to struggle against, other than those inherited illusions (law, ethics, class struggle, the Oedipus complex) which prevent us from seeing things as they are.

But the fact that modernism continues to struggle for meaning is exactly what makes it so interesting. For this struggle continually drives it towards classical styles of sense-making which are at once unacceptable and inescapable, traditional matrices of meaning which have become progressively empty, but which nevertheless continue to exert their implacable force. It is in just this way that Walter Benjamin reads Franz Kafka, whose fiction inherits the form of a traditional storytelling without its truth contents. A whole traditional ideology of representation is in crisis, yet this does not mean that the search for truth is abandoned. Postmodernism, by contrast, commits the apocalyptic error of believing that the discrediting of this particular representational epistemology is the death of truth itself, just as it sometimes mistakes the disintegration of certain traditional ideologies of the subject for the subject's final disappearance. In both cases, the obituary notices are greatly exaggerated. Postmodernism persuades us to relinquish our epistemological paranoia and embrace the brute objectivity of random subjectivity; modernism, more productively, is torn by the contradictions between a still ineluctable bourgeois humanism and the pressures of a quite different rationality, which, still newly emergent, is not even able to name itself. If modernism's underminings of a traditional humanism are at once anguished and exhilarated, it is in part because there are few more intractable problems in the modern epoch than of distinguishing between those critiques of classical rationality which are potentially progressive, and those which are irrationalist in the worst sense. It is the choice, so to speak, between feminism and fascism; and in any particular conjuncture the question of what counts as a revolutionary rather than barbarous break with the dominant Western ideologies of reason and humanity is sometimes undecidable. There is a difference, for example, between the 'meaninglessness' fostered by some postmodernism, and the 'meaninglessness' deliberately injected by some trends of avant-garde culture into bourgeois normality.

The contradiction of modernism in this respect is that in order valuably to deconstruct the unified subject of bourgeois humanism, it draws upon key negative aspects of the actual experience of such subjects in late bourgeois society, which often enough does not at all correspond to the official ideological version. It thus pits what is increasingly felt to be the phenomenological reality of capitalism against its formal ideologies, and in doing so finds that it can fully embrace neither. The phenomenological reality of the subject throws formal humanist ideology into question, while the persistence of that ideology is precisely what enables the phenomenological reality to be characterized as negative. Modernism thus dramatises in its very internal stuctures a crucial contradiction in the ideology of the subject, the force of which we can appreciate if we ask ourselves in what sense the bourgeois humanist conception of the subject as free, active, autonomous and self-identical is a workable or appropriate ideology for late capitalist society. The answer would seem to be that in one sense such an ideology is highly appropriate to such social conditions, and in another sense hardly at all. This ambiguity is overlooked by those post-structuralist theorists who appear to stake all on the assumption that the 'unified subject' is indeed an integral part of contemporary bourgeois ideology, and is thus ripe for urgent deconstruction. Against such a view, it is surely arguable that late capitalism has deconstructed such a subject much more efficiently than meditations on *écriture*. As postmodernist culture attests, the contemporary subject may be less the strenuous monadic agent of an earlier phase of capitalist ideology than a dispersed, decentred network of libidinal attachments, emptied of ethical substance and psychical interiority, the ephemeral function of this or that act of consumption, media experience, sexual relationship, trend or fashion. The 'unified subject' looms up in this light as more and more of a shibboleth or straw target, a hangover from an older liberal epoch of capitalism, before technology and consumerism scattered our bodies to the winds as so many bits and pieces of reified technique, appetite, mechanical operation or reflex of desire.

If this were wholly true, of course, postmodernist culture would be triumphantly vindicated: the unthinkable or the utopian, depending upon one's perspective, would already have happened. But the bourgeois humanist subject is not in fact simply part of a clapped-out history we can all agreeably or reluctantly leave behind: if it is an increasingly inappropriate model at certain levels of subjecthood, it remains a potently relevant one at others. Consider, for example, the condition of being a father and a consumer simultaneously. The former role is governed by ideological imperatives of agency, duty, autonomy, authority, responsibility; the latter, while not wholly free of such strictures, puts them into significant question. The two roles are not of course merely disjunct; but though relations between them are practically negotiable, capitalism's current ideal consumer is strictly incompatible with its current ideal parent. The subject of late capitalism, in other words, is neither simply the self-regulating synthetic agent posited by classical humanist ideology, nor merely a decentred network of desire, but a contradictory amalgam of the two. The constitution of such a subject at the ethical, juridical and political levels is not wholly continuous with its constitution as a consuming or 'mass cultural' unit. 'Eclecticism', writes Lyotard, 'is the degree zero of contemporary general culture: one listens to reggae, watches a

western, eats MacDonald's food for lunch and local cuisine for
dinner, wears Paris perfume in Tokyo and "retro" clothes in
Hong Kong; knowledge is a matter of TV games.'[8] It is not just
that there are millions of other human subjects, less exotic than
Lyotard's jet-setters, who educate their children, vote as responsible citizens, withdraw their labour and clock in for work; it is
also that many subjects live more and more at the points of
contradictory intersection between these two definitions.

This was also, in some sense, the site which modernism occupied, trusting as it still did to an experience of interiority which
could, however, be less and less articulated in traditional ideological terms. It could expose the limits of such terms with styles
of subjective experience they could not encompass; but it also
remembered that language sufficiently to submit the definitively
'modern' condition to implicitly *critical* treatment. Whatever the
blandishments of postmodernism, this is in my view the site of
contradiction we still inhabit; and the most valuable forms of
post-structuralism are therefore those which, as with much of
Jacques Derrida's writing, refuse to credit the absurdity that we
could ever simply have jettisoned the 'metaphysical' like a cast-
off overcoat. The new post-metaphysical subject proposed by
Bertolt Brecht and Walter Benjamin, the *Unmensch* emptied of
all bourgeois interiority to become the faceless mobile function-
ary of revolutionary struggle, is at once a valuable metaphor for
thinking ourselves beyond Proust, and too uncomfortably close
to the faceless functionaries of advanced capitalism to be
uncritically endorsed. In a similar way, the aesthetics of the
revolutionary avant-garde break with the contemplative monad
of bourgeois culture with their clarion call of 'production', only
to rejoin in some respects the labouring or manufacturing
subject of bourgeois utilitarianism. We are still, perhaps, poised
as precariously as Benjamin's Baudelairian *flâneur* between the
rapidly fading aura of the old humanist subject, and the ambivalently energizing and repellent shapes of a city landscape.

Postmodernism takes something from both modernism and
the avant-garde, and in a sense plays one off against the other.
From modernism proper, postmodernism inherits the fragmentary or schizoid self, but eradicates all critical distance from it,
countering this with a pokerfaced presentation of 'bizarre' experiences which resembles certain avant-garde gestures. From
the avant-garde, postmodernism takes the dissolution of art into
social life, the rejection of tradition, an opposition to 'high'

culture as such, but crosses this with the unpolitical impulses of modernism. It thus unwittingly exposes the residual formalism of any radical art form which identifies the de-institutionalization of art, and its reintegration with other social practices, as an intrinsically revolutionary move. For the question, rather, is under what conditions and with what likely effects such a reintegration may be attempted. An authentically political art in our own time might similarly draw upon both modernism and the avant-garde, but in a different combination from post-modernism. The contradictions of the modernist work are, as I have tried to show, implicitly political in character; but since the 'political' seemed to much modernism to belong precisely to the traditional rationality it was trying to escape, this fact remained for the most part submerged beneath the mythological and metaphysical. Moreover, the typical self-reflexiveness of modernist culture was at once a form in which it could explore some of the key ideological issues I have outlined, and by the same stroke rendered its products opaque and unavailable to a wide public. An art today which, having learnt from the openly committed character of avant-garde culture, might cast the contradictions of modernism in a more explicitly political light could do so effectively only if it had also learnt its lesson from modernism too – learnt, that is to say, that the 'political' itself is a question of the emergence of a transformed rationality, and if it is not presented as such will still seem part of the dead tradition from which the adventurously modern is striving to free itself.

10.

The Critic as Clown

All propaganda or popularization involves a putting of the complex into the simple, but such a move is instantly deconstructive. For if the complex *can* be put into the simple, then it was not as complex as it seemed in the first place; and if the simple can be an adequate medium of such complexity, then it cannot after all be as simple as all that. A mutual transference of qualities between simple and complex takes place, forcing us to revise our initial estimate of both terms, and to ponder the possibility that a translation of the one into the other was made possible only by virtue of a secret complicity between them. If one has a cultural form in which simple characters are made to voice highly-wrought rhetorical discourse, or sophisticated figures to articulate simple feelings, then the political effects of the form are likely to be ambiguous. On the one hand, it will obviously enact a certain class collaborationism: how reassuring that aristocrats have common human emotions (how much more real and credible it makes them seem), and, conversely, how complimentary to ruling-class discourse that even peasants, once gripped by fundamental passions, can rise spontaneously to such eloquence. On the other hand, the class structure is momentarily destabilized by such dialogism: if the simple can discourse refinedly without detriment to their simplicity, then they are equal to aristocrats in their sophistication – not as simple as we thought – and superior to them in what simplicity they do have. And if the refined speak a language of simple feeling, then their suavity elevates such common passions at the same time as its ironic excess of them threatens to render it redundant. You cannot really have this dialogical situation other than ironically, since we know that Cockneys do not actually speak like Etonians, but the irony, once more, is a politically unstable one. For the very self-conscious artifice which allows us to bracket all this as a charming fiction also threatens to spread over into, and put in question, the artifice of upper-class discourse itself, which is estranged by its earthy contents at precisely the moment it seeks to defuse and appropriate them. The strange, solemn children of Ivy Compton-Burnett's novels speak exactly the grave, measured, juridical discourse of their elders and betters, which at once confirms that language's authority – even the children speak it! – and threatens to discredit it: even a child can speak it!

The name of the cultural form I am describing is of course pastoral; and William Empson's classic study of it, *Some Versions of Pastoral*, culminates precisely with a chapter on the child (Lewis Carroll's Alice). The child is a type of the critic in all kinds of ways: because of its incessant questioning, because it is parasitically dependent on a language it none the less finds baffling and alien, because, being an outsider, it can see both more and less than the insiders, because it is an isolated 'intellectual' not fully conversant with common practices of feeling yet also more emotionally sensitive than most, because its social marginality is the source at once of its blindness and insight. Pastoral is Empson's way of coming to terms with the fraught relations between critic and text, intellectual and society; its ironic interchanges of refinement and simplicity are an allegory of the critic's own dilemma. This is evident enough in Empson's literary style, a version of pastoral all of its own. His airy, flattened, colloquial prose, with sub-clause slung casually on to sub-clause, at once reproduces a distinctively English ruling-class tone – brisk but subduedly genial, cavalierly unbuttoned, the garrulous, gossipy, faintly facetious discourse of throw-away brilliance appropriate to an Oxbridge high table – and at the same time subverts in its insistent ordinariness the belle-lettristic preciosities or metaphysical solemnities of orthodox critical writing. The racy, underplayed speech of the patrician, in a familiar English paradox, makes implicit alliance with the tongue of the 'people' over the heads of a linguistically pretentious bourgeoisie. Reading Empson, one is meant to gather the impression that he understands you rather as the daredevil landlord understands the poacher, as opposed to the petty-bourgeois farm bailiff; the Etonian (or in this case the Wykehamist) is not after all so remote from the Cockney. In a characteristically English way, Empson's style enforces its own brilliance by casually disowning it, only occasionally betraying itself by a too studiously placed quip or epigram; his writing is strikingly depthless, plucking insight after insight from a text in an inexhaustible metonymic movement but notably nervous of metaphorical density. He is like us in everything except that he is more clever, but even the cleverness is of the *kind* we could aspire to; and there is perhaps an ironic implication, shadowing the prose, that he is clever because he is like us only more thoroughly so, more shrewdly versed in our common wisdom than we are ourselves.

If there is a 'pastoral' irony between critic and reader, the same can be said of the relationship between critic and text. Empson's outrageously rationalistic paraphrases of sacred literary documents, which I distil here by parody, are intended in one sense to parade the grotesque disparity between literary and critical discourses, in a flamboyant gesture of dissociation:

Oh go not to the war, my love,
For you will ne'er return.

> The sense is: 'I am telling you not to have your head turned by military glory, you little idiot, not because you will take my advice, since the fact that I have to plead with you in the first place reveals just the insensitivity which will deafen you to it, but because if I do not advise you thus you will impute to me just the kind of indifference I am asking you not to impute to yourself, and so give yourself an excuse for denying your own finer instincts, which you have anyway done by putting me in this humiliating situation in the first place.' (There is probably some sort of smack here at Puritanism.)

The interplay between poetic statement and critical commentary forms a kind of pastoral indeterminacy, in which the question of which party has the upper hand is left deliberately ambiguous. In one sense the prose commentary humbly flattens itself before the poetry, caricaturing in its breezy colloquiality its helpless incapacity to adequate it, wryly acknowledging an unsurpassable rift between the two registers. In another sense the commentary is considerably more elaborate than the text, tempting us by its commonsensical tone to believe that its own subtle turns are merely derivative of the poem in the very act of outdoing it in intricacy. The two discourses seem at once continuous and incommensurate: the literary text is both enriched and demystified by the criticism, left poorer but more honest in one sense, but impressively complicated in another. A pastoral transference of qualities has been effected: 'If my criticism can have something of the subtlety of the text, then the text may have something of the straightforwardness of my criticism, in which case neither piece of writing is exactly what we thought it was.' The critic is both richer and poorer than the poem, something of a jester in his heavy-footed cavortings before the majesty of the literary, yet also superfluously cerebral and refined in contrast with the simple passionate spontaneity he analyses.

All cultural critics for Empson are pastoralists, since they cannot escape the occasionally farcical irony of being fine, delicate and excessively complex about writing whose power lies ultimately in its embodiment of a 'common humanity'. They are continually haunted by the irony that the very instruments which give them access to those powers also threaten to cut them off from them. This for Empson is a permanent rather than historical condition: *Some Versions of Pastoral* opens with a chapter on proletarian literature which denies the real possibility of the genre since 'the artist never is at one with any public'. But this liberal-Romantic mystification (what exactly is meant here by 'at one'?) is surely undercut by a glance at the social history which produced the early Empson. *Seven Types of Ambiguity* was published between the Wall Street crash and the financial collapse of Austria and Germany, when British unemployment stood at around two million; *Some Versions of Pastoral* appeared in the year of the Italian invasion of Abyssinia, the re-election of a National Government in Britain and the founding of the Left Book Club. It is not difficult in this situation to see why the literary intellectual might have felt somewhat less than at one with his public, or why one fascinated by the verbal cavillings of minor seventeenth-century poets might have experienced some slight need to justify his enterprise. Pastoral is in a sense Empson's political self-apologia, as a form which exposes the ironic contradictions of intellectual sophistication and common wisdom; it is an implicit reflection on the dazzling pyrotechnics of *Seven Types* in a darkening political scene. The real swains, now, are the hunger marchers. In so far as the pastoral form is generously capacious, good-humouredly *containing* the conflicts it dramatizes, it is of course, as Raymond Williams has protested, a flagrant mystification;[1] but what Williams fails to see (understandably enough, for one from the rural proletariat) is that this spurious harmonization of class struggle is the heavy political price Empson has momentarily to pay for a politically well-intentioned aesthetic which, in the epoch of wars and revolutions, seeks to return the increasingly fine-drawn analyses of literary critics to their roots in a practical social wisdom. Empson's life-long guerrilla campaign against the whole portentous gamut of formalisms and symbolisms, his brusque dismissal of all metaphysical poetics, is the fruit of a profoundly sociable theory of language which grasps the literary text as discourse rather than *langue*, refusing purely textual (or 'organically contextual') notions of meaning for an insistence that meanings are inscribed in practical social life before they come to be distilled into poetry. The literary text for Empson is no organicist mystery but a social enunciation capable of rational paraphrase, open to the routine sympathies and engagements of its readers, turning around terms which crystallize whole social grammars or practical logics of sense. The Empsonian reader is always an active interpreter: ambiguity itself is defined as any verbal nuance 'which gives room for alternative reactions to the same piece of language',[2] and the act of reading depends upon certain tacit social understandings, certain 'vague rich intimate' apprehensions carried in collective social practice. Interpretation rests upon the humanist-rationalist assumption that the human mind, however baffled, complex and divided, is essentially 'sane'; to interpret is to make as large-minded, generous allowance as one can for the way a particular mind, however self-broodingly idiosyncratic, is striving to work through and encompass its own conflicts, which can never be wholly inscrutable precisely because they inhere in a shared social medium – language itself – inherently patient of public intelligibility. If criticism is a mug's game it is because such conflicts, 'life' being the multiple, amorphous affair it is, will never endure definitive formulation, never submit to the boundaries of a single sense; but this 'pastoral' sense of the loose, incongruous character of history dignifies human reason rather than tragically defeating it, providing it with the most recalcitrant materials on which to exercise its powers and arrive at the most fulfilling type of (in)adequation. The 'aristocratic' refinements of complex analysis, that is to say, are at once at odds with and enhanced by the basic, unfinished stuff on which critical acumen goes to work – just as that 'common' stuff at once ironizes the critical gesture itself and, in being revealed by it as in truth inexhaustibly subtle, comes to be on terms with it. Empson,

like the Freud by whom he is nervously fascinated, is the kind of
rationalist who constantly allows reason to press up against its
own stringent limits without for a moment ceasing to trust in its
force. In this sense he fits awkwardly into the straw-target
category of rationalism ideologically requisite for the fashionable irrationalism of our own time.

Responding to a question about his attitude towards Leavis
and New Criticism, Raymond Williams makes an acute comment
on the politics of English criticism:

> I said to people here at Cambridge: in the thirties you were passing
> severely limiting judgements on Milton and relatively favourable
> judgements on the metaphysical poets, which in effect redrew the
> map of 17th-century literature in England. Now you were, of
> course, making literary judgements – your supporting quotations
> and analysis prove it, but you were also asking about ways of living
> through a political and cultural crisis of national dimensions. On
> the one side, you have a man who totally committed himself to a
> particular side and cause, who temporarily suspended what you
> call literature, but in fact not writing, in that conflict. On the other,
> you have a kind of writing which is highly intelligent and elaborate,
> that is a way of holding divergent attitudes towards struggle or
> towards experience together in the mind at the same time. These
> are two possibilities for any highly conscious person in a period of
> crisis – a kind of commitment which involves certain difficulties,
> certain naiveties, certain styles; and another kind of consciousness,
> whose complexities are a way of living with the crisis without being
> openly part of it. I said that when you were making your judge-
> ments about these poets, you were not only arguing about their
> literary practice, you were arguing about your own at that time.[3]

The dilemma outlined by Williams here – one between a
highly specialized mode of critical intelligence which in fore-
grounding ironic complexity evades certain necessarily univocal
social commitments, and a plainer, committed writing prepared
to sacrifice such ambivalences in the cause of political responsibility – is a modern version of the contradictions which, as I
have argued elsewhere, fissure the English critical institution
throughout much of its history.[4] Criticism has lurched between
a 'professional' sophistication which sequesters it from collective
social life, and a political intervention into that life which at its
best (as with Milton) lends it a substantive function, at its worst
(as with Arnold) degenerates into an ineffectually 'amateur'
liberal humanism. Williams, one suspects, would place Empson's

work firmly on the second side of his antithesis, and there is much truth in such a judgement. But this would also be to overlook the ironies of pastoral which, while conscious of the socially determined distance between the language of developed consciousness and a common *Lebenswelt*, nevertheless seeks a basis of dialogue between them. If Empson's pastoral model is transferred, as it would seem to ask to be, from the anodyne artifice of a courtly drama to the problem of the critical intellectual in modern bourgeois society, it can be made to yield up significances akin rather than alien to Williams's own political case. The author of *Seven Types of Ambiguity*, that supposed classic of New Criticism, is also the author of *Milton's God*, a work quite prepared to negotiate its way in most unEliotic or un-Leavisian fashion through the twists and turns of Milton's religious ideology, powered as it is by a ferociously debunking Voltairean humanism but steadfast in its acknowledgement of Milton's magnificence. One can trace indeed in the radically divided character of *Paradise Lost* – its rational humanism and religious transcendentalism – a veritable allegory of Empson's own critical battles with literary reaction. Empson the ironist and ambiguist is, after all, the critic who writes in *Milton's God* that he feels he can well understand the God of *Paradise Lost* from the inside, having been a propaganda specialist himself during the Second World War. The insult is directed against the Christian God, not against propaganda or political rhetoric.

Empson's criticism, that is to say, offers a partial deconstruction of Williams's polarity. That the deconstruction is only partial is surely plain: he is obviously not a 'committed' critic in the style of a Milton, or a Williams. But those features of his critical approach which look most lemon-squeezingly Wimsattian are in fact nothing of the sort; his relentless unravelling of finer and finer shades of verbal meaning is no aridly evasive enterprise of the kind Williams is right to denounce, but itself a political position, inscribed by a whole range of militantly humanistic beliefs – a trust in the intelligibility and sense-making capacities of the mind even at its most divided, a dogged refusal of symbolistic mystifications, a recognition of conflicts and indeterminacies – which are a necessary, if not sufficient, condition of any more politically radical criticism. Christopher Norris, in his excellent study of Empson, describes his pastoral as 'lift[ing] the subtleties of poetic argument into a larger, essentially social air';[5] but, while this is true, 'ambiguities' for

Empson were in a way this all along, not sealed structures of New Critical ambivalence but interpretative struggles and enigmas consequent upon language's ineradicable sociality and correlative roughness, its multipurpose functioning in practical life, its intrinsic openness to alternative social histories and tonalities. Poetry is not for Empson, as for New Criticism and some contemporary deconstruction, the privileged locus of ambiguity or indeterminacy; *all* language is indeterminate, and this, precisely, is how it is fruitful and productive. Empson's Cambridge is also the Cambridge of Wittgenstein, who reminds us in the *Blue and Brown Books* that 'We are unable clearly to circumscribe the concepts we use; not because we don't know their real definition, but because there is no "real" definition to them.'[6] Those who seem suddenly to have discovered that the essence of 'literary' language lies in its indeterminacy have obviously not been listening for some years to how the people around them actually talk.

Empson's ambiguities, moreover, were never purely rhetorical affairs. They root down into conflicts of impulse and allegiance, in what seems to him the mixed, contradictory character of social being itself, in the friction of competing ideologies and social valuations. Paul de Man is not wrong to claim that Empson's work thus manifests a 'deep division of Being itself'; he is mistaken rather in appearing to assimilate Empson's category of 'contradictory meanings' (the seventh type of ambiguity) to his own model of semantic deadlock (Empson in fact writes breezily that 'any contradiction is likely to have some sensible interpretations'),[7] and in appropriating the English critic's essentially *social* notions of conflict to his own ontologizing impulse. Sumarizing Empson's famous account of Marvell's *The Garden*, in which the mind, having first discovered a delightful unity with Nature, then moves to transcend and annihilate it, de Man informs us with enviable authority that 'the pastoral theme is, in fact, the only poetic theme, that it is poetry itself'.[8] What he means is that pastoral enacts just that ironic dissociation of consciousness from its objects which is for him the properly demystified condition of all literature. Pastoral assuages de Man's early-Sartrean horror of 'inauthenticity' and 'bad faith', that dismal state in which the *être-pour-soi* cravenly congeals into the *être-en-soi*. 'What is the pastoral convention, then,' he asks, 'if not the eternal separation between the mind that distinguishes, negates, legislates, and the originary simplicity of the natural?'

To which the only answer, even on de Man's own account, is: a good deal more. For a few lines earlier he has noted that in Marvell's poem the thought which annihilates Nature is *'green'*; in the very act of dissociation, an equable correspondence between consciousness and the world is ironically reintroduced by this softly intrusive modifier, along with the sense, in Empson's words, of a 'humble, permanent, undeveloped nature which sustains everything, and to which everything must return'. De Man actually quotes this sentence of Empson's, but he does not allow it to qualify his own Sartrean dogma of eternal alienation; he seizes the moment of pastoral which best fits his own denial of all productive interchange between consciousness and its surroundings, and then redefines the whole genre – and, for good measure, poetry itself – solely in these terms. It is amusingly typical of de Man that he should find even pastoral depressing, and for reasons quite other than Williams's. Marvell himself, as Empson sees, has no such puritanical inhibitions: the wit and courage of his poem here lie in its refusal to absolutize even the moment of the mind's annihilating transcendence, confident and humorous enough in its own fictions to be able to reinvoke and indulge the notion of harmonious liaison between Nature and mind even at this point of mystical fading and dissolution of the real. De Man's attempt to appropriate both Marvell and Empson, in short, presses him into self-contradiction: he acknowledges the greenness of the thought, but then instantly erases its significance. For pastoral is not *only* a demonstration of the division between mind and Nature but also, across that acknowledged rift, a continuous sportive interplay in which each puts the other into question. Fulfilling correspondences between both terms can be delightedly pursued once the myth of any *full* identity between them has been dismantled; de Man's doctrine of eternal separation, for him the absolute truth of the human condition, is for the pastoralist no more than one truth among several, an ironic reminder not to take one's own fictions too seriously which then therapeutically clears the way for a fruitful alliance with the sensuous world. It is Empson, or Marvell, who is the deconstructionist here, and de Man the full-blown metaphysician.

De Man's puritanical fear of entanglement in the world of material process, so different from Marvell's deliciously masochistic yearning to be chained by brambles and nailed through by briars, finds a paradoxical echo in the very Marxism which de Man (as we shall see in a moment) is here out to worst. Few words have rung more ominously in Marxist ears than *natural*, and we have all long since learnt to rehearse the proper objections to it with Pavlovian precision. Having learnt that lesson, however, it is surely time to move on, rather than remaining like de Man fixated in the moment of bleak recognition that aardvarks are not people, and then repeating that traumatic moment compulsively. Since the consolations of identity have been unmasked as mythical (and pastoral, wrenched by a certain reading, can contribute to that end), we are liberated to inquire what fertile pacts and allegiances between Nature and humanity might in fact be generated, as the ecology movement has for some time been inquiring. The work of Sebastiano Timpanaro, Raymond Williams and Norman Geras, not to speak of the drama and prefaces of Edward Bond,[9] does not cancel the important *caveats* of historicist Marxism on this score, but at its best takes us through and beyond them, to the point where the concepts of Nature, and human nature, are not merely to be dismissed as ideological fictions but to be theoretically reconstructed. Pastoral asserts that some conditions and styles of feeling are more natural than others, and provided we do not absolutize the term there is no reason why it should not remain, as it has for long traditionally been, an integral part of radical social criticism. There seems something strangely self-thwarting about a culturalist or historicist Marxism which sternly forbids itself to describe as 'unnatural' a wholly reclusive life, or a society which found sunshine disgusting.

The political implications of de Man's misreading of Empson are ominous. For if the ironies of pastoral are allegorical of the critic's relation to society, or indeed of the relation of all intellectual to manual labour, then it is the uncrossable gulf between them which de Man wishes to reaffirm. This is one reason why his reflections on Empson culminate abruptly, though not wholly unpredictably, in an assault on Marxism, which is of course for de Man (if not for 90 per cent of Marxists) an impossible poetic dream of utter reconciliation between world and mind. In so far as Empson himself criticizes this drive as 'premature' in his chapter on proletarian literature, he has laid himself wide open to such enlistment; but one cannot imagine that he would support the tragic philosophy which is de Man's only alternative to the loss of the impossible. 'The problem of separation', de Man writes, 'inheres in Being, which means that social forms of separation derive from ontological and metaphysical attitudes. For poetry, the divide exists forever.'[10] It is very hard to see why, if the idea of some total identity between Nature and society is plainly absurd, the absence of it should be considered somehow tragic. Many human beings would quite like to live forever, but not all of them find it tragic that they will not. Some people feel repulsed and alienated by staring at the roots of trees, while others just sit down and have a picnic. The non-identity of consciousness and being is a fact, which may be construed tragically or not depending on how far you are still secretly in thrall to a vision of unity. The sharpest difference between de Man and Empson on this point is that for Empson the non-coincidence of mind and world, the sophisticated and simple, is not in itself tragic at all, though it may from time to time involve tragedy. It is true that in his remark that the poet is never at one with his or her public he suggests a transhistorical estrangement upon which de Man can then pounce, turning the point for good measure against the early Marxian Barthes; but for Empson the writer's lack of identity with an audience is simply a fact, not the basis of some melancholic ontology. For de Man it is an unquestioned good that consciousness should keep free of its objects, that the critic refuse all definitive identification; for Empson the typically pastoral attitude is a more ambiguous one: 'I (the artist/critic/intellectual) am in one way better (than the worker/peasant), in another way not as good.' Or, as he puts it more accurately elsewhere: 'Some people are more delicate and complex than others, and . . . if such people can keep this distinction from doing harm it is a good thing, though a small thing by comparison with our common humanity.'[11] The fact that in a given society some individuals have the means and opportunity to be more cultured than others is not to be guiltily repressed; this indeed would be the Sartrean bad faith or false identification whereby the intellectual seeks to empty himself into the *être-en-soi* of the masses. Part of the implicit courage of *Some Versions*, one feels, is exactly its ironic resistance to the Romantic versions of this most thirties of theses, which was powerfully in the political air, and from which the opening chapter on proletarian literature immediately takes its distance. But this is not to leave oneself with no option but Romantic alienation, endorsing the eternal isolation of the refined critic and the unchangeable lowliness of the common people. *Some Versions* begins with a brilliant critique of Gray's

'Elegy' which demonstrates just how the poem's imagery tries to trick us into accepting the obscurity of the rural poor as somehow inevitable. Though distinctions of sophistication and simplicity exist, Empson's crucial, most undeManian point is that they are a poor thing in contrast with our 'common humanity'. Pastoral, in manifesting such distinctions, is more than a ruling-class conspiracy because it also reveals them as continually ironized and encompassed by a wider ambience, a general sustaining Nature as it were, which transcends them in its importance. What makes us uniquely different individuals, as Derek Parfit argues in his *Reasons and Persons*, is just not important enough a basis on which to build an ethics – or, one might add, a politics.[12] Pastoral knows a moment of (potentially tragic) separation of mind from world, the cultivated from the simple, self-reflexivity from spontaneity; but it includes this moment within a richer, more complex relationship in which it is recognized that the intellectual must be taught by the masses, that the mind is after all a *part* of Nature and not just its other, that the rich are poorer as well as richer than the common people, and that even the intellectual – hard though it sometimes is to credit it – shares a common humanity with others, which ultimately overrides whatever demarcates him or her from them. The critic who recognizes all this is the critic as clown, and one of his several names in our time is William Empson. Paul de Man, for his part, inherits from Nietzsche a notion of action as *mindless* spontaneity (practice as 'pure forgetting') which however qualified (de Man goes on to deconstruct that 'pure') puts it eternally at odds with the complexities of theory.[13] It is a nineteenth-century irrationalist current which emerges at its most disreputable in such writers as Conrad, and which leaves its mark on the work of Louis Althusser.

De Man's epistemology of dissociated spirit most certainly entails a politics of intellectual elitism. For among the objects of consciousness are, of course, mass movements and political commitments, and the modern bourgeois-liberal critic can attain some negative authenticity only in that ironic gesture by which, in separating himself from such empirical engagements, he names them all as ineradicably inauthentic. 'The ironic language splits the subject into an empirical self that exists in a state of inauthenticity and a self that exists only in the form of a language that asserts the knowledge of this inauthenticity.'[14] In one sense, the intellectual has been discredited: he or she can no longer speak an authentic discourse to a society which has no particular desire to know about Hölderlin. In another sense, such an intellectual retains much of his traditional authority – retains, indeed, much of the classical *form* of relationship between liberal intelligentsia and society as a whole, and so is able to deliver an authoritative message. That message, however, is now wholly empty and negative: it consists in the ceaseless act of naming the inauthenticity of all empirical engagements. In a way, the form of the intellectual's relation to modern society – the act of rigorous self-separation – has become the content of the enunciation. That the intellectual should still be honoured but should really have nothing to say is the material basis of de Man's metaphysical dislocation of mind and being. It is not difficult to see how this doctrine grew up in the United States of America. The intellectual's own discourse is inevitably contaminated by inauthenticity (even Yale is situated in New Haven), constantly threatening to congeal into the reified beliefs of the unreflexive masses, and constantly recovering itself only in the blank space it keeps establishing between itself and such entanglements. Thus when it speaks it is untrue, and when it is true it must be silent; meaning and being are ceaselessly at odds, and it is easy to see why this Lacanian doctrine has an appeal when one is trying to teach Kleist in Reagan's America. But if the intellectual's discourse is inauthentic it is also because his ideological interests are indeed on the whole at one with the very society which his ironic self-distancing seeks to shut out. Only by the *form* of his or her statements can such interests be momentarily transcended; 'irony' is the device whereby the modern bourgeois critic can at once collude with and privately disown the ideological imperatives of the modern state.

This is not the case with Empson's mode of irony. For whereas de Man is the patrician who ironizes the ideological *doxa* of the peasant, Empson views the matter in a kind of Bakhtinian reversal: it is the canny sense of the peasant which must keep the ideologizing clerk in check. In a deeply Wittgensteinian gesture, the intellectual's fatal penchant to ride hobbyhorses (a saddening feature, it must be confessed, of the later Empson himself) must be prised open to the therapeutic influence of how language is practically used, exposed to the resources of that collective social wisdom crystallized in its key terms ('complex words'). It is, as it were, the common people, or at least common readers, who live ambiguously, innately suspicious of ideological

formalism which would prematurely synthesize such inconclu-
siveness; and Empson as critic is spokesperson of this 'good
sense'. Pastoral is a form of the people not because it is written or
read by them, or because it figures them other than in absurdly
or offensively stylized ways, but because it has about it a kind of
'productive looseness' (Christopher Norris) which is the structural mark of this state of ideological conflict and division. The
phrase 'productive looseness' has a Brechtian ring to it, and the
connection seems less surprising once we remember the two
men's fascination with John Gay's *Beggar's Opera*. 'Putting the
complex into the simple' is, after all, a snap enough definition of
Brecht's *plumpes Denken*. Looked at in one light, Empson's liberal
humanism, his constant striving to give what credit he can to
beliefs (such as Milton's) deeply repugnant to him, involves an
ironic provisionality of attitude not far from de Man's. Both
critics can in this sense plausibly be construed as baffled, somewhat self-agonizing bourgeois liberals. But there is also a sense
in which Empson's ironies carry him to a point closer to the
sensibility of a Brecht, for whom irony denotes the necessarily
unfinished, processual, contradictory nature of historical affairs,
a fact usually more obvious to the ruled than the rulers. There is
even a possible link through to Brecht in what Empson learned
from his Far Eastern experience: what he reads as the tolerant,
ironic magnanimity of the Buddha is very close to the 'Chinese'
Brecht's sense of the need to maintain a kind of cheerful
impassive equipoise in the difficult business of negotiating
contradictions.

Contradictions for Brecht were not only sometimes intolerable but also, as he once said with reference to Hegel, a 'joke'.
The jokiness of both Brecht and Empson – the one self-
consciously plebeian, the other iconoclastically English – strikes
a quite different social tone from the high European humour-
lessness of a de Man. Empson writes in *Some Versions* of a Soviet
performance of *Hamlet* (that most deManian of dramas) which
the audience spontaneously decided was farce. Such people,
Empson reflects, 'may well hold out against the melancholy of
old Russia, and for them there may be dangerous implications in
any tragedy, which other people do not see'.[15] I think Christopher Norris is right to suggest that Empson may well have
approved of such a response to the play. Tragedy for Empson is
an heroic mode associated with aristocratic absolutism and
ascetic self-renunciation, deeply at odds with his own ironic

humanism; and in this humanistic suspicion of tragedy he is again very close to Brecht. Like Brecht, the alternative form he offers is not some crass comic triumphalism but, as Norris argues of the quality of his 'complex words' ('fool', 'dog', 'honest' and so on), 'a down-to-earth quality of healthy scepticism which . . . permits their users to build up a trust in human nature on a shared knowledge of its needs and attendant weaknesses'.[16] This too is a pastoral mode of feeling: you must love and admire the 'high' human qualities of truth, beauty, virtue and courage, but you must not be too downcast if people fail to live up to them, or terrorize them with these ideals to a point which makes their weaknesses painful to them. Tragedy moves within the high-minded terrorism of such ideals; however 'deep', it is arguably narrower, more violent in its implacable expectations, than that large-minded plebeian wisdom which, without a breath of cynicism (the mere flip-side of such idealism) knows when not to ask too much of others. Empson's own companionable literary style is anti-heroic in this sense, designed not to intimidate a reader; *Milton's God* pushes raciness and iconoclasm to the very brink of academic indecorousness. Brecht's anti-tragic awareness that there are always other possibilities parallels Empson's reading of the 'Metaphysical' poets as constantly entertaining further possible levels of meaning, ironically including within a poem its acts of exclusion. Brecht's belief that an effective play ought always to convey a sense of the (potentially contradictory) meanings it excludes, the pressure of a further possible productivity, is classically Empsonian.

The fact that there is always more productivity where that came from should not be confused with the infinite regress of a certain mode of deconstruction. For Empson, interpretation is certainly in principle inexhaustible, and the limitation of the various types of ambiguity to a mere seven is more a joke at the expense of magical numbers than a serious taxonomy. That there is some continuity between Empson the liberal humanist and the anti-humanist deconstructionist is signalled in Norris's summary of his critical 'method': 'He seems constantly on the verge of defining the complex implications, verbal or generic, which might satisfy, by somehow pinning down, his sense of the poem's richness. Yet he constantly relegates this purpose, detecting behind these provisional structures a series of ironies and "placing" attitudes which prevent their treatment as an integrating function of form.'[17] This could clearly be said of Derrida or de Man; indeed the affinity is well enough mapped in Christopher Norris's own evolution from a sympathetic critic of Empson to an exponent of deconstruction. Yet such a trajectory tends also to impoverish Empson's work, isolating him as the author of *Seven Types* and pruning away (or conveniently repressing) the more 'sociable', proto-political later writing. The shift from *Seven Types* to *The Structure of Complex Words*, from 'Metaphysical' to 'Augustan', 'wit' to 'sense', reflects a growing recognition on Empson's part that wit and ambiguity, however idiosyncratically 'brilliant', are nurtured by collective contexts of tacit significances, as in that Popeian 'good sense' which marks the inscription of social logics within individual 'wit'. All discourse for Empson is inscribed by such social rationalities however much it may disrupt and transgress them; and this is why he turns in *Complex Words* to a period (the eighteenth century) in which the inherent sociableness of language, for all its normative violence, is more clearly apparent than in the seventeenth century of New Criticism. His appeal here, that is to say, is to 'common sense'; but though his work is shot through with the limitations of this most English of vices (it lacks, for example, almost any concept of ideology), it also goes some way towards refurbishing the concept. 'Common sense' in Empson is often enough his airy impatience with theory, a brisk plain-minded reliance on 'what the author probably meant'; if he is one of the few English critics to have taken the pressure of Freud, he does so with notable unease and discomfort. Yet at its best his writing demonstrates just how thin a line there can be between such anaemic commonsensicality and the richer Gramscian idea of proletarian 'good sense', the routine practical wisdom of those who, more intimate with the material world than their rulers, are less likely to be mystified by high-sounding rhetoric. When Empson declares his pastoral faith that 'the most refined desires are inherent in the plainest, and would be false if they weren't',[18] he is very close to a kind of Bakhtinian populism; indeed the remark is made in the context of discussing one of Shakespeare's clowns. It is Swift who for Empson presses this deconstruction of body and spirit, savagery and sophistication, to an extreme limit, and it is, significantly enough, a limit to which Empson cannot quite follow him. Empson the rationalistic humanist really does feel that Swift is 'blasphemous', rattled as he is by this virulent insistence that every generous human motivation can be rewritten in terms of a degrading vulgarity.

For 'Swift', here, one might well read 'Freud'.

To contrast Empson with a later middle-class critic like de Man is, most crucially, to contrast a pre-fascist liberal intellectual with a post-fascist one. Two of Empson's most substantial works were written before the full fury of European fascism was unleashed; and we might well wonder whether his belief in the essential sanity and generosity of the human mind is not in part dependent on that chronology. Empson's brisk untheoretical commonsensicality, his relatively sanguine trust in routine rationality, are serious limitations to any Marxist appropriation of his work. De Man, as I have argued elsewhere, is most interestingly viewed in the light of a bitter 'post-ideological' scepticism which belongs to the post-fascist epoch;[19] and Empson's buoyant Enlightenment rationality is just what he is out to embarrass. If neither position can be unequivocally adopted by Marxism, it remains true that Empson poses for us the more serious challenge, at least in this sense: that he reminds us forcibly, with what he himself would call a 'pastoral flatness', of just what complexity and ambiguity any programme of social transformation must encompass, without regarding that transformative end as in any sense unworthy. At the same time it is part of Empson's courage, and evidence of the seeds of socialism which can be detected in his work, that he finally refuses that liberal fetishizing of difference and ambivalence which still serves the cause of political oppression. To paraphrase his own version of pastoral, with a vigilant eye on the mystificatory dangers of any appeal to 'common humanity': some people are more delicate and complex than others, and this need not matter, indeed is a positive enrichment, provided such distinctions do not do social harm. But the most seductive subtleties, the most dazzling displays of heroism, virtue and intelligence, are a poor thing compared to our shared humanity, and whenever we are forced to choose it is always better to choose the latter.

11.

Brecht and Rhetoric

In a notorious comment, J. L. Austin once wrote that 'a performative utterance will, for example, be *in a peculiar way* hollow or void if said by an actor on a stage'.[1] Perhaps Austin only ever attended amateur theatricals. Bertolt Brecht approved of amateur acting, since the occasional flatness and hollowness of its utterances seemed to him an unwitting form of alienation effect. For Brecht, the whole point of acting was that it should be in a peculiar sense hollow or void. Alienated acting hollows out the imaginary plenitude of everyday actions, deconstructing them into their social determinants and inscribing within them the conditions of their making. The 'void' of alienated acting is a kind of Derridean 'spacing', rendering a piece of stage business exterior to itself, sliding a hiatus between actor and action and thus, it is hoped, dismantling the ideological self-identity of our routine social behaviour. The actor, Walter Benjamin remarked in 'What Is Epic Theatre?', 'must be able to space his gestures as the compositor produces spaced type'.[2] The dramatic gesture, by miming routine behaviour in contrivedly hollow ways, represents it in all its lack, in its suppression of material conditions and historical possibilities, and thus represents an absence which it at the same time produces. What the stage action represents is the routine action as differenced through the former's non-self-identity, which nevertheless remains self-identical – recognizable – enough to do all this representing rather than merely to 'reflect' a 'given' non-identity in the world. A certain structure of presence must, in other words, be preserved: 'verisimilitude' between stage and society can be disrupted only if it is posited. Brecht was particularly keen on encouraging his actors to observe and reproduce actions precisely, for without such an element of presence and recognition the absencing of the A-effect would be non-productively rather than productively empty. The internal structure of the effect is one of presence and absence together, or rather a problematic contention of the two in which the distinction between 'representation' and 'non-representation' is itself thrown into question. The stage action must be self-identical enough to represent as non-self-identical an apparently self-identical world, but in that very act puts its own self-identity into question. This self-cancelling or self-transcending of the theatrical signifier becomes a political metaphor: if political society were to know itself in its difference, there would be no need for this kind of representational theatre. It is because political society does not recognize itself as a *production* that it must be *represented* as such, which (since the concept of production itself overturns classical notions of rep-resentation) is bound to result in a self-contradictory aesthetic. It is not surprising that Brecht never seems able to make up his mind about the political value of representation. The A-effect, however, turns this contradiction to fruitful use, positing and subverting simultaneously; as a 'supplement' to social reality it posits its solid anterior existence *and* unmasks it as crippledly incomplete.

Another way of putting this is to claim that Brechtian theatre deconstructs social processes into rhetoric, which is to say reveals them as social *practices*. 'Rhetoric' here means grasping language and action in the context of the politico-discursive conditions inscribed within them, and Brecht's term for this is *Gest*. To view things gestically is to catch the gist in terms of the gesture, or rather to position oneself at the point where the one German word hovers indeterminately between the two English ones. *Gest* denotes the curve of intentionality, the class of socially typical performative utterances, to which in a piece of *plumpes Denken* the complexities of action or discourse may be reduced. An unpublished fragment by Brecht headed 'representation of sen-tences in a new encyclopaedia' would suggest that he thought all sentences, not just obviously performative ones like theatrical speech, could and should be treated in this way:

1. Who is the sentence of use to?
2. Who does it claim to be of use to?
3. What does it call for?

4. What practical action corresponds to it?
5. What sort of sentences result from it? What sort of sentences support it?
6. In what situation is it spoken? By whom?[3]

All discourse is gestic or rhetorical, but some – dramatic discourse – is more rhetorical than the rest. It *needs* to be, since its task is to reveal the repressed rhetoricity of non-theatrical utterances, a revelation which is for Brecht ineluctably materialist because it involves contextualizing what is said or done in terms of its institutional conditions. The function of theatre is to show that all the world's a stage.

But if all language is performative, what becomes of representation? Brecht's answer to this, briefly, is that what representations represent are performatives. The theatre simply lays bare the process by which we come to grasp 'constative' utterances in the first place only by an act of 'theatrical' miming. In a piece significantly entitled 'Two Essays on Unprofessional Acting', Brecht writes:

> One easily forgets that human education proceeds along highly theatrical lines. In a quite theatrical manner the child is taught how to behave; logical arguments only come later. When such-and-such occurs, it is told (or sees), one must laugh. It joins in when there is laughter, without knowing why; if asked why it is laughing it is wholly confused. In the same way it joins in shedding tears, not only weeping because the grown-ups do so but also feeling genuine sorrow. This can be seen at funerals, whose meaning escapes children entirely. These are theatrical events which form the character. The human being copies gestures, miming, tones of voice. And weeping arises from sorrow, but sorrow also arises from weeping.[4]

Rhetoric, in other words, precedes logic: grasping propositions is only possible by participating in specific forms of social life. As children we get the gist by miming the gesture, grow into 'appropriate' feelings by performing the behaviours criterial of them. Only later will logic bury rhetoric, the gesture be surreptitiously slid beneath the gist. What utterances 'represent' is not referents but practices, including other utterances: 'gestures, miming, tones of voice'. As with the A-effect, then, Brecht's focus is at once representational and anti-representational, mimetic and performative together. The child grows towards representational meaning by redoubling rhetoric, miming a miming, performing a performative; indeed when Brecht writes (perhaps by a slide of the signifier) of the child *copying miming*, he suggests the possibility of performing the performing of a performance.

The child, one might say, begins as an amateur or Brechtian actor, performing what he does not yet truly feel, and by dint of doing so ends up as a professional or Aristotelian one, fully at one with his forms of life. The aim of Brechtian theory, then, must be to reverse this unhappy process and regress us to a childlike condition once more, make us all amateurs again. The child and the Marxist move in opposite directions but meet in the middle: the child's understanding is at first purely practical, the effect of a spontaneous involvement with forms of life, and only later crystallizes out into a logical or representational system.[5] The Marxist is confronted by that (ideo)logical system and has to work his or her way back to the practical conditions it now suppresses, rewriting it as a piece of rhetoric or mode of social performance. We forget that we have to learn our emotions through sharing in forms of social behaviour, that feelings are social institutions; in the theatre we can re-enact our childhood at a conscious level, observe new forms of behaviour and so develop the forms of subjectivity appropriate to them. In both theatre and childhood, meaning is not 'representational' but the effect of representation, the consequence of a certain practical miming. Mimesis is what precedes and encircles meaning, the material conditions for the emergence of logical thought. In the end, child and materialist will come out at the same point: 'I now see thinking just as a way of behaving,' says the Actor in the *Messingkauf Dialogues*, 'and behaving socially at that. It's something that the whole body takes part in, with all its senses.'

To 'act' is to go through the motions of behaviour without really feeling it, lacking the appropriate experiences. Acting is a kind of fraud; and flagrantly 'fraudulent' acting, of an amateur or alienated kind, returns us self-consciously to the fictive formation of the self, re-opens that gap or lag between our action and its appropriate inwardness which was there in the first place as a consequence of our desiring the desire of the Other. Children are allegorists, confusedly hunting the elusive meaning of behaviour; adults are symbolists, unable to dissociate action and significance. Amateur actors, like political revolutionaries, are those who find the conventions hard to grasp and perform them badly, having never recovered from their childhood puzzlement.

Such puzzlement is perhaps what we call 'theory'. The child is an incorrigible theoretician, forever urging the most impossibly fundamental questions. The form of a philosophical question, Wittgenstein remarks, is 'I don't know my way around'; and since this is literally true of the child, it is driven to pose questions which are not answerable simply in rhetorical terms ('The meaning of this action is this') but which press perversely on to interrogate the whole form of social life which might generate such particular meanings in the first place. Theory is in this sense the logical refuge of those puzzled or naive enough not to find simply rhetorical answers adequate, or who want to widen the boundaries of what mature minds take to be adequate rhetorical explanations. The revolutionary questioner sees the world with the astonishment of a child ('Where does capitalism come from, Mummy?'), and refuses to be fobbed off by the adults' customary Wittgensteinian justifications of their practices: 'This is just what we *do, dear.*' He or she accepts that all justification is in this sense rhetorical, an appeal to existing practices and conventions, but does not see why one should not do something else for a change. The theoretical question is as utterly estranged as the metaphysician's traditional wonderment about why there is anything at all, rather than just nothing. Why do we have all *these* practices, utterances and institutions, rather than some others?

Since such a question is not of course simply requesting historical information, it is rhetorical in its turn – both in the sense that it implies its own answer (we *shouldn't* rest happy with such practices), and in the sense that like the discourses it addresses it is therefore animated by malice, scorn, insecurity, hostility, the will to reject. If the child's questions are naive, the revolutionary's are *faux naif.* 'I don't know my way around' implies, 'What the hell is all this?' The theoretical question, then, is as much a performative as the languages it challenges; it is just that it tries to view those other languages in a new way, as Brecht reported that it was only by reading Marx that he was able to understand his own plays. Theory begins to take hold once one realizes that the adults don't know their way around either, even if they *act* as though they do. They act as well as they do precisely because they can no longer see, and so question, the conventions by which they behave. The task of theory is to breed bad actors, of which Brecht's remarks about the A-effect is one small model.

Just as Marxism can be seen as a morality in the properly classical rather than narrowly fashionable sense, concerned with as many as possible of the factors (and not just interpersonal ones) which condition the quality of human behaviour, so 'theory' can be seen as rhetorical study in its broadest and richest sense, reckoning in modes of production as well as conventions of promising. Where theory is most importantly performative, however, is in the practical difference it makes to our routine rhetorics. 'Lamenting by means of sounds, or better still words', says the Philosopher in the *Messingkauf Dialogues*, 'is a vast liberation, because it means that the sufferer is beginning to produce something. He's already mixing his sorrow with an account of the blows he has received; he's already making something out of the utterly devastating. Observation has set in.' If the child's trek from rhetoric to logic is part of the problem, the sufferer's transition from screaming to explaining is part of the solution. When lamenting becomes propositional it is transformed: it becomes, like theory, a way of encompassing a situation rather than being its victim. To give an account of one's sorrow even as one grieves; to act and, in alienated style, to observe oneself acting: this is the dialectical feat which, for quite different reasons, neither child nor logician can achieve, and which is central at once to Brecht's dramaturgy and to his politics.

12.

Poetry, Pleasure and Politics

A terrible beauty is born.

(W. B. Yeats, Easter 1916)

Most people seem to feel that this last line of Yeats's poem is a
'good' one: a little shopsoiled and clichéd by now, perhaps, but
still enjoyable. I want to ask why it is that people like this line, as
a modest contribution to a theory of pleasure. To answer this
question will involve taking the line and blowing it up on some
screen of the unconscious – or, to change the metaphor, slowing
down the frames of its reading almost to a standstill so as to catch
the complex effects it has on us as they happen. This in turn will
involve a kind of crazed microscopic pedantry, which has not
even the saving virtue of originality, and which I am not recom-
mending as a paradigm of cultural analysis, partly because life is
too short. All I am claiming is that we shall not understand the
mechanisms of pleasure in art until we have been through this
form of inquiry, if only to leave it behind; and that, though I
have taken this line deliberately at random, simply as one that
most people seem to like, what I do with it could in principle be
done with any discourse whatsoever. To abstract a single line
from a poem is in any case to beg all sorts of questions relevant
to pleasure; it is just that the complexity of analysis involved
forbids the inspection of a larger discursive unit here and now.

The first reason why the line is pleasurable is because it is the
last one. After this we can relax, happily freed from further
investments of energy. But this of course also has its ungrati-
fying aspect, presuming that we liked reading the poem, because
it is now about to be removed from us. We approach the line
ambivalently, then, relief mingled with regret, as a presence
already hollowed by an impending absence. Like all human
beings we enjoy certain kinds of work, delight in our psychical

investments, yet of course we don't, and would rather be deliciously inert. Our anxiety at the impending loss of the object, however, is mitigated by the fact that the line is so nice and short. We can master those five words almost at a glance, and none of them is worryingly obscure. The eye incorporates the line at a stroke, delighting in its own dominance.

As the eye starts to crawl through the line, this pleasure is certainly not qualified, even if it isn't signally intensified, by the first word *A*. No problem there; an empty signifier taken easily in our stride, offering a bare minimum of frustrating resistance to our possession. Yet a flicker of anxiety instantly unfurls. *A* – *what*? *A*s have whats and this one doesn't, yet. The pleasure of mastery is accordingly modulated by a mild panic, which will not be put to rest even when we have laboured our way over *terrible*, for that is not a noun, and we must still wait, deferred over the work of three whole terrible syllables, to uncover the temporarily lost object. No need to give up, however, for there is an immediate pleasure in store for us to offset this unsettling suspense: the gratifying dental activity of *t*, an aggressively stressed phoneme. Gratifying and unpleasurable, of course, for who enjoys being roused from the happy untongued inertia of *A* to the difficult expenditure of that sound? Who, moreover, would not feel a mild mounting of anxiety at the very typographical sight of that *terrible*, bristling as it is with as yet unresolved problems, a cluster of curls and strokes, a positive mountain range of phonemes to be negotiated?

Yet all is temporarily well. The stressed consonant *t* carries us over to the unstressed vowels and soft consonants which follow, until the plosive of *ble* holds aggression and relaxation in balance, stabbing yet unstressed as it is, the downbeat of the small graph of desire inscribed in the whole word. *Terrible* binds together three different syllables, and we momentarily enjoy the paradox of that, to be immediately offered a new kind of pleasurable binding or repetition in the alliterative *b* of *beauty* – a pleasure which, in its smooth equivalencing, modulates the otherwise stressed, aggressive movement of the syllable. *Ty*, which is unstressed, then permits us to relax a little, as well as narcissistically binding us back to the alliterating and assonantal *ter* and *i*; in fact *ty* incorporates two phonemes from *terrible*, thus granting us the momentary delights of equivalence and identity within a stimulating play of difference. Having finished with *ty*, we now know what *A* belongs to, which yields some epistemophilic pleasure. Yet we don't quite know, for what we have is an oxymoron (*terrible beauty*) which gratifies us with its bold equivalence as it disturbs us with its dissonance. The oxymoron generates a pleasurable but anxiety-laden ambivalence, the sense of a knowledge at once in and out of place; it offers a resistance to our incorporation at once frustrating and – since it sets us thinking – enjoyable. It isn't a difficult oxymoron to grasp in the context of the poem, however, so the excitation of ambivalence is fairly quickly released into the pleasurable security of cognition: we 'get' it and like the fact that we do, enjoy surmounting the frustrating object and subduing it to our desire. *Is* binds assonantally with *ty*, its soft consonant and unstressedness providing an indolent moment before the gratifying lip-working labour of *born*. This pleasurably repeats and binds the previous *bs*, an easy-to-master word which signals the end of labour. Yet it is puzzling too, for how exactly can *beauty* be born? And since birth is a prelude, what is coming next? The pleasure of closure is overshadowed, then, by a mild excitation of deferral, since birth at once ends and opens. Anyway, we have closed our teeth around that final *n*, and that is surely satisfying.

As this excessively crude and fanciful analysis ought to have shown, psychoanalysis always has it both ways and is thus apparently unbeatable. We derive pleasure from both binding[1] and releasing, dominating and being dominated, expending and economizing, knowing and not knowing, equivalencing and differencing, articulating and identifying. What matters is that these various activities are rhythmically modulated or orchestrated in an acceptable way, as the rhythm of the line itself, with its distribution of symmetrical unstressed within stressed syllables, manages a certain economy. What I have tried to show here, perhaps arbitrarily, is a certain way of extracting the graph of desire from the little drama or narrative of a line, tracking the play of unconscious drives in language. This, so far, has largely involved bracketing off the semantic level of the line, attending mainly to what Kristeva would call the 'semiotic',[2] but not entirely so: you can't feel ambivalent about an oxymoron unless you can identify it. Meaning, in other words, is already caught up in the play of pleasure/displeasure from the outset, the semiotic and semantic already mutually imbricated. But what I have aimed for so far is a chiefly 'economic' rather than 'representational' account of pleasure, which is in itself primitive and insufficient; and I want now to develop a little the semantic field of pleasure which the line marks out. To do this will entail that we stop pretending that we haven't read the rest of the poem, or anything else by Yeats.

The Semantic Field

We might begin by looking back at that *terrible beauty*. This refers of course to the Easter rebellion itself, but I think that it also means Maud Gonne. Rose of Ireland and rancorous demagogue, Maud Gonne is the terrible beauty with whom the poem must come to terms; the question posed by that oxymoron is, among other things, the question: What is woman? Two conflicting drives – the drive to idealize and the sadistic impulse to destroy or deface – are condensed in that single *Darstellung* or representation, a condensation which, like punning or metaphor, affords its own economic yield of pleasure; but that economic pleasure is itself overdetermined by the triply condensed gratifications of sadism, idealization and defence. The entire trope operates as a defence against the threatening phallic woman, whose beauty it must at once tear at, deform, make terrible and yet, in a guilty reparative gesture, reinstate in that very act. (It is beauty, after all, however terrible it is.) The trope is a mechanism by which the line may ward off, disarm, the phallic woman, at once destroy and restore her, dismember the object yet leave it miraculously untouched. The woman still *is* whole, beautiful, somehow, even though she has been unmasked, sadistically, as a whore. If there is Kleinian ambivalence in this,[3] so too is there in the line's response to the political uprising: the oxymoron's function, there again, is to idealize, deface, defend and restore at a stroke. The trope, as it were, is a compromise formation: it releases its aggressivity on the uprising but in the same gesture seals the event in the inviolable realm of myth. Or, to express the ambivalence another way, it lets the pleasure principle rip – this bloody event is a beauty to be celebrated – in the very moment that the reality principle prudently covers its losses, with a canny eye on the event's possible future outcome.[4] The trope rationalizes guilt, and this is potentially part of its pleasurable effect.

The problem is to articulate the economic and representational levels of pleasure: to interrelate somehow the play of drives in language (binding, deferring, mastering, expending, releasing and so on) with the play of drives in the representations, the complex business of fantasy and defence, covering and unmasking, repression and uplifting. There is, presumably, no invariable set of relations here, no master-code which might translate the one into the other. What is obvious in any case, once we have 'risen' from the semiotic to the semantic without leaving the former behind, is that the concept of pleasure now has to engage the concept of ideology, and indeed, methodological distinctions apart, did so from the outset. It would clearly be disastrously crude to argue that economies of pleasure/displeasure belong to the id, whereas ideological responses belong to the ego, or superego. Activities thought proper to the ego such as cognition and perception certainly involve pleasure; the sadism of the super-ego is equally a libidinal matter; and, as Freud's later work makes clear, both ego and superego are themselves deeply rooted in the id. My pleasure or displeasure at the sexism and political vacillation of *terrible beauty* certainly is a matter of ego and superego, but both those formations are of course also a matter of the id. One could imagine the economic gratifications of the line as a kind of 'forepleasure', which tries to seduce me into admiring its fantasies and defences too, preparing the ground for that particular psychodrama, and this indeed may well happen. Presumably something like this is what happens with people who like the line *a lot*. If I am a woman or an Irish nationalist or both, however, the line is going to have to work harder, more deviously, to secure my gratification. It is perhaps unlikely to achieve this simply by its pulsional economy; it will have to persuade me to participate in the *general* mechanisms of its defence, fantasy, compromise formation and the rest, in a way which might surmount my resistance to its *particular* figuration. Whether it can cajole me into laying down my ideology, so to speak, is by no means merely a question of the pleasure principle seeking to subvert the reality principle, but a matter of whether it can successfully corner for its own ends some of the unconscious energy I invest in my 'beliefs', while reassuring me that I have no need to feel guilty or anxious about this. Or, more exactly, that it is worth trading that quantity of guilt or anxiety for the libidinal gratifications it will afford me. The unconscious will try to placate and accommodate the ego and superego, not just brutally unmask them as hollow.

I know plenty of people, mainly Irish people, who dislike this line intensely, finding in it nothing more than an evasive, posturing rhetoric, a climax of Yeats's shabby political beliefs. This, presumably, doesn't mean that they are immune to its play of drives and masks – simply that, given the unconscious infrastructure of their own ideological formation, such gratifications are in the end not worth the trade-off. Lest this be thought to reduce the 'relative autonomy' of ideology to the immediate traffic of the id, it is worth reminding ourselves that one reason we sometimes dislike lines of poetry, or artefacts in general, is because they are *not true*. Knowing the truth, understanding, is certainly a major source of pleasure, if I may leave aside for a moment the increasingly tedious arguments about whether truth exists. Like any other activity, this doubtless has its roots in the unconscious – Freud relates it to the greed of the eye, the primal scene and the castration anxiety – but it centrally involves the ego. One thing I dislike about the line is that it is extremely vague: it at once rhetorically flourishes and cavalierly withdraws an object of knowledge. (One can show, by a rhetorical and ideological analysis of the whole poem, just how precisely vague it has to be, just how determinate its indeterminacy is.) My dislike may therefore be to do with the demand for an imaginary object, which I fear has not been quite restored to me; but it is equally an 'ideological' demand for political clarity. Enamoured as I no doubt am by compromise formations and defence mechanisms in general, this particular one frustrates me. In this sense, then, my investments in a 'regressive' psychoanalytic structure may be politically 'progressive'; there is certainly no mere homology between the two.

There would seem, then, to be at least three 'levels' of pleasure/displeasure involved in a line of writing, which are only methodologically distinguishable. The first is, roughly speaking, economic, or semiotic in the Kristevan sense. To grasp this is to grasp the play of drives in a mainly somatic way, touched upon, but not yet fully stablized by semantic representation. The second is the level of *general* psychical mechanisms and strategies, always themselves with ideological content, but engaging our investments at this point primarily by their *forms*. The third level is that of concrete ideological meaning, itself a course always deeply cathected or decathected by any specific historical reader. From the viewpoint of libidinal pleasure, these three 'levels' may be seen as engaged in constant intricate trade-offs. When the loosely articulated drives achieve representation, for example, this will reorganize the pulsional economy itself. For a specific historical reader, these 'levels' may conspire, conflict, or one or two may gang up on the other(s). The mutual articulations of the 'levels', however, depend not only upon the specific historical reader, but upon history itself; it is itself a matter of ideology. For Samuel Johnson, there was absolutely no problem about 'aesthetically' enjoying a work which morally disgusted you. It simply couldn't be done. Johnson would have been incapable of reaping pleasure from a text with the moral ideology of which he was fundamentally at odds. The very concept would have been ideologically offensive to him, and indeed quite impermissible. If we interpret this merely as 'repression', not to say 'puritanism', we are simply ignoring the power with which certain deeply unconscious ideologies of pleasure help to produce certain historical subjects. In a fine, perhaps hopeless utopian gesture, Herbert Marcuse looks forward to an historical epoch in which we shall produce human subjects biologically incapable of violence. Presumably such people would not need to engage in complex libidinal exchanges in order to enjoy in Yeats's poetry a violence of which they also disapproved, but would just feel sick instead. We, meanwhile, in a certain transitional epoch where, for historical and ideological reasons, an ideology of the 'aesthetic' has been able to flourish, are confronted with a *political* problem about pleasure. I mean by that the problem of knowing how to harness pleasure to political ends, and formulate those ends in terms of pleasure, in a situation where, because of the psychic fragmentation of which the ideology of the 'aesthetic' is a part, the relation between the kind of pleasure people take in art, and the pleasure they derive from striving to realize their political needs, has become extremely obscure. If 'aesthetics' is a symptom of that fragmentation, so is psychoanalysis, one of whose historical conditions of possibility was just such a depoliticization. The very analytic instruments we deploy are in this sense ideologically guilty.

I have argued, to summarize drastically, that the answer to the question, 'Why do people like/dislike certain lines of poetry?', lies in an analysis of the mechanisms whereby different 'levels' of potential enjoyment are articulated or disarticulated. To a great extent, this will of course vary from reader to reader, not least when we take into account psychologically random connotations: I derive a certain narcissistic pleasure from the word *terrible* because a fragment of my name inheres in it, although I also feel uneasy at seeing my name incorporated into such a negative term. But some of these mechanisms are general ones, even if there is no reason to believe that they are universal. (The most apparently so – the somatic-semiotic − is surely deeply conditioned by the particular social practices of child-rearing.) One reason why it is worth studying these mechanisms, then, is to be able to produce a more politically effective culture. Another reason is that such study may also tell us something useful about political society itself. We need to know under what circumstances people will exchange the gratifications of relative inertia, imaginary investment, masochistic submission, repetition and the rest for the ambivalent pleasures/displeasures of political excitation. We need to know at what point narcissistic identifications become so paralytic and unpleasurable that they may be traded for the pleasurable anxieties of difference; or what the relations are between the deferments of gratification imposed by capitalism and the deferments involved in political engagement. The compromise formations whose inner instability need more analysis are less those of literary oxymoron than of social ideologies. It would be valuable to know more about how far lack of social mastery can in the end be traded for social fantasy, as well as about the mechanisms of ambivalence which govern collective attitudes of aggressivity/idealization. And so on. 'Culture', need one say, is not the main or only place of such mechanisms. But finding out what people like, and why, always helps, and art is one good place to do it.

13.

The Revolt of the Reader

The growth of the Readers' Liberation Movement (RLM) over the past few decades has struck a decisive blow for oppressed readers everywhere, brutally proletarianized as they have been by the authorial class. Readers are less and less seen as mere non-writers, the subhuman 'other' or flawed derivative of the author; the lack of a pen is no longer a shameful mark of secondary status but a positively enabling space, just as within every writer can be seen to lurk, as a repressed but contaminating antithesis, a reader. Reading is no longer a furtive, murmuring discourse confined to a few special meeting places, a reserve of the ambivalent and effete, but has taken to the streets and begun to affirm its power. What has been unleashed is nothing less than the *central contradiction* of the dominant textual economy – the fact that the reader must be ascribed certain quasi-autonomous capacities at the very moment that he or she is rigorously subdued to a mere function of the text. So rapid indeed has been the RLM's development that a genuinely revolutionary slogan, beyond mere textual reformism or reading-group consciousness, is now beginning to emerge: 'The authors need us; we don't need the authors!'

There were, inevitably enough, one or two false starts. As the long history of Romantic conservatism suggests, it is always possible for any protest movement to mistake as radical what is in fact a regression to pre-capitalist social relations, in which one form of oppression is nostalgically exchanged for another, *Gesellschaft* abandoned for an equally crippling *Gemeinschaft*. Such has been the thrust of the Black Forest school of criticism, which aims to oust capitalist textual relations by a full-blooded reversion to the feudalist mode of production. The reader as compliant serf, caught up in the commanding play of a discourse which is at once intimately sustaining and always elsewhere, a mystified peasant enthralled to a reverent and interminable listening – if the Black Forest school reproduces such feudalist reading relations, it is also surely clear how its resolute decentring of the individual textual entrepreneur for an organic collectivity of discourse, to which the reading class remains strictly subordinated, catches up certain rather more historically recent themes of German ideology.

Pressing beyond such reactionary solutions, which in a spurious radicalism would dislodge the classical-individualist author only the more thoroughly to enfetter the reader, the RLM has received no more striking reminder of the urgency of its tasks than in the blatant class collaborationism of the Geneva school. That readers should be forcibly subjected to textual authority is disturbing enough; that they should be insultingly invited to hug their chains, merge into empathetic harmony with their oppressors to the point where they befuddledly cease to recognize whether they are subject or object, worker, boss, or product is surely the ultimate opiate. Nor is it accidental that such work should engage the motifs of late capitalist consumerism: the text as auratic commodity, the radiant space or great ideological solvent in which not only conflicting social interests but distinct social identities may be lovingly resolved.

It would be disingenuous, on the other hand, to deny the existence of certain diverse, even sectarian tendencies within the RLM as a whole which seriously threaten its political efficacy. On the far right of the movement, the work of Roman Ingarden and his acolytes can plausibly be read as little more than a shabby authorial plot to permit readers the fantasy of participation while reserving power squarely in the hands of the authorial class. The text comes to the reader ready-equipped with certain localized indeterminacies, which the reader is then dutifully to fill in. Such transparent paternalism, equivalent in its way to allowing a medieval craftsman to doodle the odd gargoyle or mass marketing a child's painting to be completed with the help of numbers, scornfully underrates the seriousness of the RLM's demands. The centrist positions of the school of Constance advance some way beyond such meagre reformism toward genuine industrial partnership or limited textual democracy on the West German social democratic model. For the school of

Constance there can, of course, be no question of co-ownership or readers' power – ultimate hegemony remains firmly invested in the text – but the worker/reader[1] is assigned a more active role in the production process, and the necessity of his or her investments in the industry frankly conceded. The bourgeois-liberal character of this tendency is at one with Wolfgang Iser's view that the function of literature is to allow us to contemplate our own distasteful prejudices, free ourselves from ideological blinkers in a moment of self-recuperation and return to where we were, only more radically and clear-sightedly so.

Another centrist tendency of the RLM has adopted a somewhat different political strategy, equivalent to the Trotskyist Transitional Programme's demand to 'open the books'. This current, exemplified by the structuralism of Jonathan Culler, attends less to problems of alienation and creativity in the work place than to demands that reader/workers should be allowed access to the closely protected secrets of the boardroom – to the codes, blueprints, paradigms, and technical know-how which govern the manufacture of commodities. Such a trend, which disputes the political monopoly of knowledge rather than the nature and uses of the products themselves, is bound to remain idealist, helpful though it perhaps is as a kind of consumer information service which may prevent people from mistaking after-shave lotion for Scotch or using ballroom-dancing techniques to catch a bus. How valuable such consumer guidance really is, however, is now surely questionable. Recent consumer research at Yale has suggested that *all* of the products of the textual industry, without exception, are irredeemably faulty, flawed by some cunningly concealed crack or rattling with some broken part. The point of criticism, which used to be to fashion small-scale replicas of commodities as visual aids for consumer use, is now simply to write mildly unprotesting consumer reports indicating that, curiously enough, all the products are faulty in essentially the same way and (as with built-in obsolescence) are indeed intended to be so. The radicalism of this gesture is a matter of dispute.

It has in any case long been obvious that the liberal and centrist wings of the RLM were likely to be outflanked by the libertarian left. The shift from nakedly dominative textual relations to later incorporative, participatory, or social democratic forms clearly still leaves much to be desired; and a dominant strategy of the movement has accordingly become an all-out *putsch* to topple the text altogether and install the victorious reading class in its place. Revolutionary logic outstrips reformism as inexorably as Lenin overtook Kerensky, and 'all power to the readership' is its final demand. Revolutionaries, however, can rarely be too paranoid in their suspicion of conspiracies. Stanley Fish's bland confession that his 'readers' power' theory cannot answer the question of what it is one is having power over has an ominous ring of the old Keynesian ploy, whereby ruling classes in crisis consider letting workers bury money in the ground and dig it up again. The risk, in short, is of a partial regression to an artisanal or cottage industry mode of production, to which the textual manufacturers put out products or slabs of raw material so that readers may be kept harmlessly preoccupied with working them up into pleasing, exotic shapes, transforming melted-down balloons into little rubber men. Within such creative enclaves, equivalent in some sense to workers' co-operatives within capitalism, readers may hallucinate that they are actually writers, reshaping government handouts on the legitimacy of limited nuclear war into symbolist poems. Many of the products of the big manufacturers – so-called modernist commodities – are indeed now specifically deconstructed for such recycling. Yet it is not easy to persuade readers that they are writers. The internecine war of interpretations within market society, the deep Oedipal *ressentiment* of some small entrepreneurs against the patriarchal monopolists of textual production, the struggle to oust the ruling authorial lineages and pirate bits of their property, reveal well enough that you can only hallucinate some of the people some of the time.

A socialist criticism is not primarily concerned with the consumers' revolution. Its task is to take over the means of production.

14.

The Ballad of English Literature

(to the tune of 'Land of Hope and Glory')

Chaucer was a class traitor
Shakespeare hated the mob
Donne sold out a bit later
Sidney was a nob

Marlowe was an elitist
Ben Jonson was much the same
Bunyan was a defeatist
Dryden played the game

There's a sniff of reaction
About Alexander Pope
Sam Johnson was a Tory
And Walter Scott a dope

Coleridge was a right winger
Keats was lower middle class
Wordsworth was a cringer
But William Blake was a gas

Dickens was a reformist
Tennyson was a blue
Disraeli was mostly pissed
And nothing that Trollope said was true

Willy Yeats was a fascist
So were Eliot and Pound
Lawrence was a sexist
Virginia Woolf was unsound

There are only three names
To be plucked from this dismal set
Milton Blake and Shelley
Will smash the ruling class yet

Milton Blake and Shelley
Will smash the ruling class yet.

Notes

Notes to Chapter 1

[1] Pierre Macherey, *Pour une théorie de la production littéraire*, Paris 1966; translated by Geoffrey Wall as *A Theory of Literary Production*, London 1978.

[2] Strictly speaking, there cannot for Macherey be 'internal ideological contradictions', since the function of ideology is to create an imaginary unity from real historical contradictions. There can only be contradiction between an ideology and what lies beyond its repressive limits – history itself. The text '*puts* the ideology into contradiction' by illuminating its gaps and limits, revealing ideology as a structure of absences. In doing so, the text puts itself into question too, manifesting a lack or dissonance within itself.

[3] There are other, fruitful comparisons to be drawn between Macherey and Freud. In *The Interpretation of Dreams*, Freud is clear that the task of the analyst of dreams is not simply to lay bare the meaning of a distorted text, but to explain the *meaning of the text-distortion itself* – a distortion which produces a radically mutilated discourse characterized by gaps, obscurities and ambiguities, by 'breaks in the text'.

[4] The first article, written with Etienne Balibar and reprinted from the journal *Littérature* (No. 13), can be found in the *Oxford Literary Review*, vol. 3, no. 1, 1978; the second has appeared in the American journal *Sub-stance*, no. 15, 1976.

Notes to Chapter 3

[1] *The Romantic Survival*, London 1957; *The Characters of Love*, London 1960; *Tolstoy and the Novel*, London 1966; *Pushkin: A Comparative Commentary*, London 1971; *The Uses of Division*, London 1976; *An Essay on Hardy*, Cambridge 1978. I am grateful to George Wotton, of Hatfield Polytechnic, on whose specialist knowledge of Thomas Hardy I have drawn in this article.

[2] John Bayley, *In Another Country*, London 1954.

[3] An aesthetic irrationalism perhaps most powerfully countered by Galvano Della Volpe in his *Critique of Taste*, London 1978.

⁴ See Pierre Macherey, *Pour une théorie de la production littéraire*, Paris 1966.

⁵ Ian Gregor, *Essays in Criticism*, vol. 1, 1966.

⁶ See, for example, Helen Garwood, *Thomas Hardy: An Illustration of the Philosophy of Schopenhauer*, London 1911; E. Brennecke, *Thomas Hardy's Universe*, London 1924; A. P. Elliott, *Fatalism in the Works of Thomas Hardy*, London 1935.

⁷ *The Southern Review*, 6, Summer 1940.

⁸ Douglas Brown, *Thomas Hardy*, London 1954.

⁹ *The Chartered Mirror*, London 1960.

¹⁰ See, for example, David Lodge, *The Language of Fiction*, London 1966; Tony Tanner, 'Colour and Movement in Hardy's *Tess of the d'Urbervilles*', *Critical Quarterly*, 19, 1968; Ian Gregor, *The Great Web: The Form of Hardy's Major Fiction*, London 1974.

¹¹ See J. Hillis Miller, *Thomas Hardy: Distance and Desire*, Cambridge, Mass. 1970.

¹² See Perry Meisel, *Thomas Hardy: The Return of the Repressed*, London 1972.

¹³ See R. Gittings, *Young Thomas Hardy*, London 1975.

¹⁴ See Donald Davie, *Thomas Hardy and British Poetry*, London 1973.

¹⁵ See R. Balibar, G. Merlin and G. Tret, *Les français fictifs: le rapport des styles littéraires au français national*, Paris 1974; and R. Balibar and D. Laporte, *Le français national: constitution de la langue nationale commune à l'époque de la révolution démocratique bourgeoise*, Paris 1974.

¹⁶ Raymond Williams, *The English Novel from Dickens to Lawrence*, London 1970, pp. 106 ff.

¹⁷ Roy Morrell, *Thomas Hardy: The Will and the Way*, Oxford 1965.

¹⁸ Thomas Hardy, *Far from the Madding Crowd*, London 1975, p. 19.

¹⁹ This is a recognizably 'Oxford' tactic. It is remarkably similar to John Carey's insistence, in *The Violent Effigy*, London 1973, that Dickens criticism should cease its tight-lipped, tediously zealous search for moral, symbolic and historical meanings in Dickens and acknowledge instead that he is really just rather funny.

²⁰ Hardy, *Far from the Madding Crowd*, p. 13.

²¹ Bayley, *An Essay on Hardy*, p. 212.

²² '"Character" and Henry James', *New Left Review* 40, November–December 1966. Relevant works, besides Bayley's, include Iris Murdoch's 'Against Dryness', *Encounter*, January 1961, and W. J. Harvey's *Character and the Novel*, London 1965.

²³ The year of publication of Bayley's *The Romantic Survival*, 1957, also saw the appearance of the Canadian Northrop Frye's mighty 'totalization' of all literature, *Anatomy of Criticism*. Despite Frye's egregious defects, the implied comment on the state of English criticism is telling.

²⁴ *New Statesman*, 21 April 1978.

Notes to Chapter 4

¹ The leading New Critics were John Crowe Ransom, Allen Tate, Robert Penn Warren, Cleanth Brooks, W. K. Wimsatt, R. P. Blackmur, Austin Warren and Monroe Beardsley. For an excellent Marxist account of the movement, see John Fekete, *The Critical Twilight*, London 1977.

[2] The title of a work by John Crowe Ransom, published in 1938.

[3] See Richard Ohmann, *English in America*, New York 1976.

[4] Frank Lentricchia, *After the New Criticism*, Chicago 1980.

[5] Poulet in a letter to J. Hillis Miller (1961), quoted by Lentricchia, pp. 65–66.

[6] See the interview with Derrida in *The Literary Review*, no. 14, April–May 1980, one likely to prove somewhat embarrassing to his more incautious acolytes.

[7] Paul de Man, 'Action and Identity in Nietzsche', *Yale French Studies*, no. 52, Fall 1975, quoted by Lentricchia, p. 317.

[8] See E. D. Hirsch, *Validity in Interpretation*, New Haven 1967. See also Robert Magliola, *Phenomenology and Literature*, Indiana 1977, who argues that Hirsch commits some elementary blunders in his interpretation of Husserl.

[9] Lentricchia, pp. 189–90.

[10] There is much in this rich study beyond the critics I have referred to. There are also, for example, excellent accounts of Heidegger, Gadamer, Murray Krieger, Frank Kermode, Wolfgang Iser and Jacques Derrida.

[11] Fredric Jameson, *Sartre: The Origins of a Style*, New Haven 1961.

[12] Fredric Jameson, *The Political Unconscious: Narrative as a Socially Symbolic Act*, London 1981.

[13] Ibid., p. 82.

[14] Ibid., p. 182.

[15] Ibid., p. 62.

[16] Ibid., p. 10.

[17] Ibid., p. 102.

Notes to Chapter 5

[1] Terry Eagleton, 'The Idealism of American Criticism', *New Left Review* 127, 1981, p. 60.

[2] Fredric Jameson, *Marxism and Form*, Princeton, New Jersey 1971, p. xii.

[3] Ibid., p. xiii.

[4] Fredric Jameson, *The Prison-House of Language*, Princeton, New Jersey 1972, p. 154.

[5] Fredric Jameson, *Fables of Aggression: Wyndham Lewis, the Modernist as Fascist*, Berkeley, California 1979, p. 35.

[6] Ibid., p. 37.

[7] Fredric Jameson, 'Imaginary and Symbolic in Lacan', *Yale French Studies* 55/6, 1977, pp. 354–5.

[8] Fredric Jameson, 'Towards a Libidinal Economy of Three Modern Painters', *Social Text* 1, 1979, p. 190.

[9] Jameson, *The Prison-House of Language*, p. x.

[10] Ibid., p. viii.

[11] Ibid., p. 216.

[12] Ibid., p. xi.

[13] Jameson, *Marxism and Form*, p. xvi.

[14] Perry Anderson, *Considerations on Western Marxism*, London 1976, p. 70.

[15] Jameson, *Marxism and Form*, p. xviii.

¹⁶ Ibid., p. xix.
¹⁷ Ibid., p. 415.

Notes to Chapter 6

¹ Michael Ryan, *Marxism and Deconstruction*, Baltimore and London 1982.
² Interview with Jacques Derrida, *The Literary Review*, no. 14, April–May 1980.

Notes to Chapter 7

¹ Perry Anderson, *In the Tracks of Historical Materialism*, London 1983.
² See the interview with Jacques Derrida in *The Literary Review*, 14, April–May 10.
³ 'Le parergon', in *La vérité en peinture*, Paris 1978, pp. 23–4.
⁴ See Phillippe Lacoue-Labarthe and Jean-Luc Nancy, eds., *Les fins de l'homme*, Paris 1981, pp. 526–9.
⁵ See Etienne Balibar and Pierre Macherey: Interview, *Diacritics*, Spring 1982, p. 51.

Notes to Chapter 8

¹ Quoted in Rush Rhees, ed., *Ludwig Wittgenstein: Personal Recollections*, Oxford 1981, p. 171.
² Ibid., p. 231.
³ The comparison has been noted before. See Karl Otto Apel, 'Wittgenstein and Heidegger', *Philosophisches Jahrbuch* 75 (1967), pp. 56–94; and Hans-Georg Gadamer, 'The Phenomenological Movement', in *Essays in Philosophical Hermeneutics*, Berkeley 1976, pp. 130–181. See also Fergus Kerr, 'Language as Hermeneutic in the later Wittgenstein', *Tijdschrift voor Filosofie* 27, 1965, pp. 491–520.
⁴ See Rhees, pp. 63–81.
⁵ Ibid., p. 35.
⁶ Ibid., p. 101.
⁷ Ludwig Wittgenstein, *Philosophical Investigations*, translated by G. E. M. Anscombe, Oxford 1963. References to the numbered sections of this text are given in brackets after quotations; where a section is not numbered, the page reference is given instead.
⁸ Rhees, p. 120.
⁹ A recent comparison of Wittgenstein and Derrida can be found in Anthony Giddens, *Central Problems in Social Theory*, London 1979, pp. 33–48; though Giddens's attitude to Derrida is considerably more negative than my own. See also Charles Altieri's interesting article, 'Wittgenstein on Consciousness and Language: A Challenge to Derridean Literary Theory', *Modern Language Notes*, vol. 91, 1976, which like Giddens adopts a more negative attitude towards Derrida's work than myself.

¹⁰ A. J. Ayer, 'Can There Be a Private Language?', reprinted in George Pitcher, ed., *Wittgenstein: The Philosophical Investigations*, London 1968, pp. 251–66.

¹¹ A. M. Quinton, 'Contemporary British Philosophy', excerpted in ibid., p. 12.

¹² See Jacques Derrida, 'Limited Inc.', *Glyph* 2, 1977, p. 190.

¹³ Ludwig Wittgenstein, *Remarks on the Foundations of Mathematics*, Oxford 1956, 1, 115.

¹⁴ And, one might add, of simplicity and complexity: one of Wittgenstein's important insights is that these terms too are relative to contexts of discourse, that there is no 'absolute' or 'fundamental' simplicity.

¹⁵ '. . . ask yourself whether our language is complete; – whether it was so before the symbolism of chemistry and the notation of the infinitesimal calculus were incorporated into it, for these are, so to speak, suburbs of our language. (And how many houses or streets does it take before a town begins to be a town?)' (18).

¹⁶ See Wittgenstein, *On Certainty*, ed. G. E. Anscombe and G.H. von Wright, Oxford 1963, passim.

¹⁷ 'Wittgenstein's *Philosophical Investigations*', reprinted in Pitcher, pp. 91–2.

¹⁸ See Wittgenstein, 'La pharmacie de Platon', in *La dissémination*, Paris 1972, pp. 71–197.

¹⁹ See Feyerabend, 'Wittgenstein's *Philosophical Investigations*', reprinted in Pitcher, pp. 146–150. I have elaborated a little on Feyerabend's point here.

²⁰ Ibid., p. 145.

²¹ Wittgenstein, *Tractatus Logico-Philosophicus*, translated by D. F. Pears and B. F. McGuinness, London 1961, 6.54.

²² For an interesting 'deconstructive' reading of the *Tractatus*, see Sylviane Agacinski, 'Découpage du *Tractatus*', in Sylviane Agacinski, Jacques Derrida and Sarah Kofman, eds., *Mimesis: Desarticulations*, Paris 1975, pp. 19–53.

²³ See A. Duncan-Jones, ed., *Nikolai Bakhtin: Lectures and Essays*, Birmingham 1963. I owe much of my information about Bakhtin to Michael Holquist, co-biographer of Mikhail Bakhtin, in personal communication, but write, unfortunately, before the publication of Holquist's work.

²⁴ See Rhees, p. 28.

²⁵ Duncan-Jones, *Lectures and Essays*, p. 61.

²⁶ See Rhees, p. 28.

²⁷ Ibid.

²⁸ See Fergus Kerr OP, 'The use of Heidegger', *New Blackfriars* (February 1982), p. 54.

²⁹ Duncan-Jones, *Lectures and Essays*, p. 98.

³⁰ Ibid., p. 38.

³¹ Ibid., p. 140. Wittgenstein also comments that 'what confuses us is the uniform appearance of words when we hear them spoken or meet them in script and print' (11). It is interesting that in contrast with the usual Derridean gesture he here equates rather than opposes 'voice' and 'writing', detecting the possibility of a misleading homogenizing in both. One need not perhaps be guilty of McLuhanite banality to think that there may be something in this.

³² See Duncan-Jones's introduction to Bakhtin's *Lectures and Essays*, p. 2.

[33] I am endebted for this point to Michael Holquist, in personal communication.

[34] Now reprinted in Michael Holquist, ed., *The Dialogic Imagination*, Austin and London 1981, pp. 259–422.

[35] Ibid., p. 30. Subsequent page references to this text are indicated in brackets after quotations.

[36] Ibid., p. xxxi. This is surely an unworkably broad definition: it is difficult to see its relevance to, say, *Mansfield Park*. Bakhtin's claim that poetry and drama are inherently 'monologic' seems equally dubious: counter-examples, signally Brecht, could be adduced.

[37] It is not only post-structuralism that Bakhtin prefigures: contemporary hermeneutics and reception theory are equally anticipated. As for psychoanalytical criticism, the relevant text here would seem to be less his rather predictably 'orthodox' Marxist critique of Freud (*Freudianism: A Marxist Critique*, New York 1976) than his great study of Rabelais. The relevance of Bakhtin's work for feminist criticism remains to be explored.

[38] See his essay 'Representation of the End(s) of History: Dialectics and Fiction', in *Rethinking History: Time, Myth and Writing, Yale French Studies* 59, 1980, pp. 203–4.

[39] Bakhtin complains in his unsurpassed study of Russian Formalism that the Formalists suppress the fullness of the human utterance in a work of art by attending only to the materiality of its language. Paradoxically, however, he sees this suppression of a meaning which is always *elsewhere*, in the work's relation to its context, as a kind of 'logocentric' cult of the work's full, undivided presence: 'The fear of meaning, which, with its "not here" and "not now" is able to destroy the material nature of the work and the fullness of its presence in the here and now, is the fear which determines the poetic phonetics of the formalists' (P. N. Medvedev and M. M. Bakhtin, *The Formal Method in Literary Scholarship*, Baltimore and London 1978, p. 105.) It should also be remarked that Bakhtin's undeconstructive stress upon the living voice is complicated by the continual traversal of that voice by 'alien' elements.

[40] Though see Julia Kristeva, 'Word, Dialogue and Novel', in *Desire in Language*, London 1980, pp. 64–91, for a much more positive evaluation.

[41] Translated by Alan Bass, London, 1981, p. 62. Derrida has recently provided a rather fuller statement of his relation to Marxism, arguing that his own past silence on the subject should be seen not as 'neutral' but as itself a political gesture – a refusal to participate in an anti-Marxist front, despite his belief that the concept of revolution is naively metaphysical. He adds, however, that such a belief should not be taken to devalue the force which the concept may have in practical political situations, and declares that there is no question any longer either of a simple rejection of Marxism or of a simple taking up of position. In the same passage he acknowledges that certain American literary critical uses of his work contribute to an institutional closure which serves the dominant political and economic interests, but relegates responsibility for the use of his work to the reader. See *Les fins de l'homme*, Paris 1981, pp. 526–9.

[42] See Jacques Derrida, *Of Grammatology*, Baltimore and London 1976, p. 318, 19n.

[43] Mikhail Bakhtin, *Rabelais and His World*, Cambridge, Mass. 1968, p. 10.

[44] For a fuller account of Bakhtinian carnival, see my *Walter Benjamin, or*

Towards a Revolutionary Criticism, London 1981, pp. 144–46.

⁴⁵ Stanley Cavell comments on the dialogic style of the *Investigations* in his 'The Availability of Wittgenstein's Later Philosophy', reprinted in Pitcher, pp. 182–4.

⁴⁶ Saussure actually uses money as metaphorical for language at one point in his *Cours de linguistique générale*. Simon Clarke has recently recalled the centrality of the principle of exchange or reciprocity in the structural anthropology of Lévi-Strauss, and observes that 'for Lévi-Strauss it was the principle of reciprocity that was the key to the liberal democracy of the United States' (*The Foundations of Structuralism*, London 1981, p. 46). Clarke demonstrates how, in articles written in the United States and published in France in the 1940s, Lévi-Strauss advocated the principle of reciprocity, supposedly embodied in US society, as relevant to the political reform of his own society.

⁴⁷ *History and Class Consciousness*, Cambridge, Mass. 1971, p. 170.

⁴⁸ *Negative Dialectics*, London 1973, p. 146 (translation amended).

⁴⁹ Ibid.

⁵⁰ Eagleton, *Walter Benjamin, or Towards a Revolutionary Criticism*, p. 141n.

⁵¹ Adorno, *Negative Dialectics*, p. 111.

⁵² Ibid.

⁵³ Ibid.

⁵⁴ Ibid.

⁵⁵ Karl Marx, *Capital*, vol. 1, London 1971, p. 108.

⁵⁶ Russell Keat, in a critique of Jürgen Habermas, has indicated the political limitations of the psychoanalytic model, in a way relevant to Wittgenstein's notion of philosophy as a 'reminding': 'The victims of ideology may in some sense be said to be "unconscious" of certain things, but surely not of things that they had at one time been conscious of, and then repressed. To free oneself from ideology is not to recover a lost element of one's past' (*The Politics of Social Theory*, London 1981, p. 179).

⁵⁷ Since this was written, Mr Thomson has informed me that he did not discuss philosophy with Wittgenstein. But see note 70.

⁵⁸ In a celebrated epiphany, Wittgenstein was once much illuminated about the nature of language by a sudden Neapolitan gesture of Piero Sraffa's. Walter Benjamin also found evidence for his 'mimetic' theory of language in the gestural discourse of Naples. See 'Naples', *One-Way Street*, London 1979, p. 176.

⁵⁹ *The First Philosophers*, p. 341.

⁶⁰ Ibid., pp. 263, 315.

⁶¹ Ibid., p. 342.

⁶² *Intellectual and Manual Labour*, London 1978, p. 65.

⁶³ Marx, *Capital*, p. 41. Early post-structuralism by no means ignored this question: see in particular Jean-Joseph Goux, *Économie et symbolique*, Paris 1973. A more recent contribution is Gayatri Spivak's intervention in the Derrida colloquium now published as *Les fins de l'homme* (pp. 505–14).

⁶⁴ *Marx and Engels: Selected Works*, London 1968, p. 99.

⁶⁵ Rhees, p. 158.

⁶⁶ Ibid., p. 226.

⁶⁷ Ibid., p. 231n.

⁶⁸ *New Left Review* 73, May–June, 1971, pp. 83–4.

⁶⁹ 'Francis called himself and his companions "God's jugglers" (*ioculatores Domini*) Francis's peculiar world outlook, his "spiritual joy" (*laetitia spiritualis*), his blessing of the material bodily principle, and its typically Franciscan degradations and profanation can be defined, with some exaggeration, as a carnivalized Catholicism' (Bakhtin, *Rabelais and His World*, p. 57n.).

⁷⁰ Quintin Hoare and Geoffrey Nowell Smith, eds., *Selections from the Prison Notebooks*, London 1971, p. 323. Though we do not know whether Gramsci was a topic of conversation between Wittgenstein and Sraffa, we do know that the two men engaged in many philosophical and political discussions. See George Thomson, 'Wittgenstein: Some Personal Recollections', *The Revolutionary World*, vols. 37–39, Amsterdam 1979. In the same text, Thomson records that Wittgenstein read Christopher Caudwell's *Illusion and Reality* with enthusiasm, though his enthusiasm seems to have been directed more towards Caudwell's personality than his politics. Thomson also notes that Wittgenstein 'was opposed to [Marxism] in theory, but supported it to a large extent in practice'.

⁷¹ Ibid., p. 347.

⁷² Ibid., p. 199.

⁷³ Ibid., p. 201.

⁷⁴ 'Gramsci's Observations on Folklore', in *Approaches to Gramsci*, Anne Showstack Sassoon, ed., London 1982, pp. 221–47.

⁷⁵ *Letteratura e vita nazionale*, quoted ibid., p. 226.

⁷⁶ See *Prison Notebooks*, p. 333.

⁷⁷ Ibid., p. 330n.

⁷⁸ Ibid., p. 331.

⁷⁹ Rhees, p. 162.

⁸⁰ Alberto Cirese, *Approaches to Gramsci*, p. 219.

⁸¹ Ibid., p. 226.

Notes to Chapter 9

¹ Peter Bürger, *Theory of the Avant-Garde*, Minneapolis 1984.

² Jean-François Lyotard, *The Postmodern Condition: A Report on Knowledge*, Manchester 1984, p. 45.

³ Paul de Man, 'Literary History and Literary Modernity', in *Blindness and Insight*, Minneapolis 1983, p. 162.

⁴ For a vigorous critique of the political implications of de Man's arguments, see Frank Lentricchia, *Criticism and Social Change*, Chicago and London 1983, pp. 43–52.

⁵ See Fredric Jameson, 'Reification and Utopia in Mass Culture', *Social Text*, Winter 1979.

⁶ Gilles Deleuze and Félix Guattari, *Anti-Oedipus: Capitalism and Schizophrenia*, Minneapolis 1983.

⁷ Jean-François Lyotard, *Economie libidinale*, Paris 1974, p. 311.

⁸ Lyotard, *The Postmodern Condition*, p. 76.

Notes to Chapter 10

¹ Raymond Williams, *The Country and the City*, London 1973, p. 21.

[2] William Empson, *Seven Types of Ambiguity*, London 1961, p. 1.

[3] Raymond Williams, *Politics and Letters*, London 1979, p. 335.

[4] See Terry Eagleton, *The Function of Criticism*, London 1984.

[5] Christopher Norris, *William Empson and the Philosophy of Literary Criticism*, London 1978, p. 64.

[6] Ludwig Wittgenstein, *The Blue and Brown Books*, Oxford 1969, p. 25.

[7] *Seven Types of Ambiguity*, p. 197.

[8] Paul de Man, *Blindness and Insight*, Minneapolis 1983, p. 239.

[9] See in particular Sebastiano Timpanaro, *On Materialism*, London 1975, chapter 1, and Norman Geras, *Marx and Human Nature*, London 1983. See also Terry Eagleton, 'Nature and Violence: The Prefaces of Edward Bond', *Critical Quarterly*, vol. 26, nos. 1 and 2, Spring and Summer 1984. Perry Anderson has remarked that the question of Nature is one which Marxism must confront in the future (see his *In the Tracks of Historical Materialism*, London 1983, pp. 56–84).

[10] De Man, p. 240.

[11] William Empson, *Some Versions of Pastoral*, London 1966, p. 23.

[12] See Derek Parfit, *Reasons and Persons*, Oxford 1984.

[13] See 'Literary History and Literary Modernity', in Paul de Man.

[14] De Man, p. 214.

[15] Empson, *Some Versions of Pastoral*, p. 13.

[16] Christopher Norris, p. 86.

[17] Christopher Norris, pp. 46–7.

[18] Empson, *Some Versions of Pastoral*, p. 114.

[19] Eagleton, *The Function of Criticism*, London 1984, pp. 101–2.

Notes to Chapter 11

[1] J. L. Austin, *How to Do Things with Words*, Cambridge, Mass. 1975, p. 21.

[2] Walter Benjamin, *Understanding Brecht*, London 1973, p. 19.

[3] *Brecht on Theatre: The Development of an Aesthetic*, translated by John Willett, London 1964, p. 106.

[4] Ibid., p. 152.

[5] Walter Benjamin admired the way in which, in children, cognition was tied to action, and found in their behaviour a 'language of gestures' more basic than conceptual discourse. For Benjamin as for Brecht, children's behaviour was essentially mimetic, a matter of forging bizarre correspondences of the kind that the revolutionary theorist must also generate. See, for this neglected aspect of Benjamin's thought, Susan Buck-Morss, 'Walter Benjamin: Revolutionary Writer (11)', *New Left Review* 129, September–October 1981.

Notes to Chapter 12

[1] Freud speaks of the need for psychic energy, which he considers as loose or 'unbounded' in its unconscious state, to be controlled and channelled preparatory to its release in gratification. The 'binding' effects of narrative are interesting in this respect.

[2] By the 'semiotic' Kristeva means, in a sense special to her own work, the play of

bodily drives in such phenomena as rhythm, sound, movement and so on, before the point at which they receive articulation in language.

³ The psychoanalyst Melanie Klein is noted for her work on the ambivalent responses of the pre-Oedipal child towards its mother, its tendency to take her as an object of both love and aggression, to destroy the breast in fantasy and then make guilty reparation for this destruction.

⁴ For a fuller analysis of Yeats's evasions and ambiguities here, see my 'History and Myth in Yeats's *Easter 1916*' in *Essays in Criticism*, vol. 21, no. 3, July 1971.

Notes to Chapter 13

¹ I avoid the usual conflation 'wrecker', whose connotations I find politically distasteful, although perhaps appropriate in relation to the 'ultra-left' of the RLM.

Index

Adorno, Theodor, 6, 61–2, 66, 69, 75, 119–21, 124
Aglietta, Michel, 89
Althusser, Louis, 1–4, 18–20, 60–1, 73, 76, 80, 86, 138, 160
Anaximines, 123
Anderson, Perry, 5, 89–98, 138
Aquinas, Thomas, 105
Arnold, Matthew, 45, 51, 154
Auden, Wystan Hugh, 34–5
Austin, John Langshaw, 61, 134, 167

Bahro, Rudolf, 89
Bakhtin, Constance, 112
Bakhtin, Mikhail Mikhailovich, 6–7, 96, 111, 113–18, 122, 125, 129
Bakhtin, Nikolai, 111–14, 123
Balibar, Etienne, 95
Balibar, Renée, 20, 74
Balzac, Honoré de, 36, 38, 60, 61, 64
Barthes, Roland, 53, 66, 70, 159
Baudrillard, Jean, 57
Bayley, John, 2, 7, 33–9, 56
Beddoes, Thomas Lovell, 23
Benjamin, Walter, 5–6, 9–10, 62, 69, 73, 114, 117, 130, 135–6, 142–3, 146, 167
Bergonzi, Bernard, 56
Blackmur, Richard Palmer, 41
Blake, William, 50, 55, 185
Bloch, Ernst, 61, 66
Bloom, Harold, 50, 53, 55–6, 61
Bradbury, Malcolm, 56
Braverman, Harry, 89

Brecht, Bertolt, 6–7, 9, 69, 117, 140–1, 146, 162–3, 167–72
Brooks, Cleanth, 56
Brown, Douglas, 41–2
Bürger, Peter, 131
Burke, Kenneth, 61, 74

Carroll, David, 116
Carroll, Lewis, 150
Cervantes, Miguel de, 75
Chaucer, Geoffrey, 185
Chesterton, Gilbert Keith, 41
Cirese, Alberto Maria, 127, 129
Cohen, Gerry, 89
Coleridge, Samuel Taylor, 185
Colletti, Lucio, 90
Compton-Burnett, Ivy, 150
Conrad, Joseph, 23, 27, 30–1, 61, 63, 75, 160
Culler, Jonathan, 52

Dante Alighieri, 23
Defoe, Daniel, 9
De Kooning, Willem, 70
Deleuze, Gilles, 57, 70, 90, 142
De Man, Paul, 51, 53–6, 61, 136–8, 156–62, 164, 165
Derrida, Jacques, 53–6, 62, 79–81, 83, 85–7, 90–91, 94–5, 98–103, 109–10, 115–7, 119–20, 123, 146, 163
Dickens, Charles, 37–8, 185
Disraeli, Benjamin, 185
Donne, John, 185

Donoghue, Denis, 56
Dostoevsky, Fyodor Mikhailovich, 113
Dryden, John, 185
Duncan-Jones, Austin, 112

Eliot, Thomas Stearns, 35, 185
Empson, William, 7, 150–65

Feuerbach, Ludwig, 77, 100, 119
Feyerabend, Paul, 109–10
Fielding, Henry, 9
Fish, Stanley, 53, 184
Foucault, Michel, 4, 55–6, 58, 70, 79, 90, 95, 116
Frege, Friedrich Ludwig Gottlob, 104
Freud, Sigmund, 17, 61, 70, 122, 142, 154, 165, 177–8
Frye, Northrop, 50–2, 55–6, 64, 77

Gadamer, Hans-Georg, 61
Gay, John, 162
Geach, C., 99
Gellner, Ernest, 127
Genovese, Eugene, 58
Geras, Norman, 158
Goldmann, Lucien, 13
Gonne, Maud, 176
Goode, John, 47
Gramsci, Antonio, 4, 47, 54, 75, 118, 125–30
Gray, Thomas, 159
Greimas, A. J., 58, 61
Guattari, Félix, 142

Habermas, Jürgen, 57, 91
Hardy, Thomas, 34, 39–45
Hartman, Geoffrey, 53
Heidegger, Martin, 99, 121
Hegel, Georg Wilhelm Friedrich, 21, 62, 70, 72, 74–5, 77, 81, 99, 162
Hillis Miller, J., 52–53
Hirsch, E. D., 55–6
Hitler, Adolf, 130
Hjelmslev, Louis, 58, 70
Hofmannsthal, Hugo von, 60
Hoggart, Richard, 56
Hölderlin, Friedrich, 161

Holquist, Michael, 115
Holloway, John, 41
Hopkins, Gerard Manley, 23
Hulme, Thomas Ernest, 35
Hume, David, 133
Husserl, Edmund, 53

Ingarden, Roman, 182
Iser, Wolfgang, 183

James, Henry, 9, 37, 40–1, 46
Jameson, Fredric, 57–64, 65–78, 80, 86, 131–2, 135, 139
Johnson, Lionel, 40
Johnson, Samuel, 179, 185
Jonson, Ben, 185
Joyce, James, 23

Kafka, Franz, 143
Keats, John, 34, 37, 185
Kerensky, Aleksandr, 184
Kermode, Frank, 56
Kettle, Arnold, 56
Kipling, Rudyard, 34, 37
Kleist, Heinrich, 161
Knights, Lionel Charles, 56
Korsch, Karl, 4
Krieger, Murray, 51, 56
Kristeva, Julia, 94, 175

Lacan, Jacques, 69, 90, 96, 115
Lawrence, David Herbert, 34, 37, 185
Leavis, Frank Raymond, 41, 44, 46–7, 49, 51, 100, 118, 154
Lenin, Vladimir Ilyich, 18, 21, 74, 75, 84, 184
Lentricchia, Frank, 50–7, 62–4
Lewis, Wyndham, 67
Locke, John, 134
Lodge, David, 42, 56
Lukács, Georg, 4, 10, 60–1, 63, 71, 75–6, 114, 119, 124, 134
Lyotard, Jean-François, 93, 134–6, 138–9, 142, 145–6

Macherey, Pierre, 2, 9, 10, 13–21, 40, 44, 61, 95
Malcolm, Norman, 106

Mandel, Ernest, 89
Marcuse, Herbert, 66, 179
Marlowe, Christopher, 185
Marvell, Andrew, 156–7
Marx, Karl, 1, 27, 56, 62, 68, 72, 77, 80, 85, 100, 119, 122, 124, 142, 171
Mayakovsky, Vladimir Vladimirovich, 112–3, 131–2
Miliband, Ralph, 89
Milton, John, 154–5, 162–3, 185
Moran, John, 125
Morris, William, 133
Morrell, Roy, 44
Mulhern, Francis, 6, 7
Murdoch, Iris, 35
Mussolini, Benito, 130

Nietzsche, Friedrich Wilhelm, 110–1, 137–8, 141, 160
Norris, Christopher, 155, 162–4

Ohmann, Richard, 50

Parmenides, 123–4
Parfit, Derek, 160
Pascal, Fanya, 112
Pater, Walter, 142
Plato, 109, 112–3
Pope, Alexander, 185
Poulantzas, Nicos, 89
Poulet, Georges, 52, 56
Pound, Ezra, 35, 146
Proust, Marcel, 36, 146
Pushkin, Alexander Sergeevich, 38, 112
Pythagoras, 123

Rabelais, François, 116–7
Ransom, John Crowe, 50, 56
Rhees, Rush, 125
Richards, Ivor Armstrong, 49, 51
Richardson, Samuel, 6
Ricks, Christopher, 56
Russell, Bertrand, 100, 118, 130
Ryan, Michael, 5, 79–87

Said, Edward, 63
Sartre, Jean-Paul, 37, 51, 57
Saussure, Henri de, 53, 91, 96

Schelling, Friedrich Wilhelm Joseph von, 70
Scott, Walter, 185
Shakespeare, William, 34–8, 46, 166, 185
Shelley, Percy Bysshe, 185
Sidney, Philip, 185
Smith, Adam, 27
Sohn-Rethel, Alfred, 124
Spinoza, Benedict de, 21
Spivak, Gayatri, 79, 117
Sraffa, Piero, 126
Steiner, George, 56
Stevens, Wallace, 51
Strawson, P. F., 99
Swift, Jonathan, 164–5

Tennyson, Alfred, 185
Thackeray, William Makepeace, 9
Thatcher, Margaret, 93, 135
Therborn, Goran, 89
Thomas, Dylan, 35
Thomson, George, 123–4
Timpanaro, Sebastiano, 158
Tolstoy, Lev Nikolaevich, 18, 21, 34, 36–8, 112
Trilling, Lionel, 44
Trollope, Anthony, 185
Trotsky, Leon, 75, 83
Troyes, Chrétien de, 60

Verne, Jules, 15, 18
Voloshinov, V. N., 96, 114

Warhol, Andy, 132
Watt, Ian, 56
Weber, Max, 63, 76
Weber, Samuel, 79
Williams, Raymond, 43, 56–7, 64, 152, 154–5, 157–8
Wittgenstein, Ludwig, 5, 27–8, 99–114, 117–23, 125–30, 143, 156
Wodehouse, Pelham Grenville, 37
Woolf, Virginia, 185
Wordsworth, William, 185
Wright, Olin, 89

Yeats, William Butler, 34–5, 173, 176–7, 185